Onto the Final ᒪᒪᒪ

by

Swasie Turner

In loving memory of my Pillar of Strength,
My life's supporting rock,
My inspiration.......
       My beloved late wife, Marje, xxx

ONTO THE FINAL LEG

ISBN 0-9532991-3-9

First Published in 1999 by
Classfern Limited,
720 Borough Road, Prenton, Wirral, CH42 9JE.
Copyright © Classfern Ltd 1999

Printed & Bound by MFP, Stretford, Manchester.

I dedicate this book to all of my Police colleagues, past and serving, and also to those dedicated and tireless nurses, doctors, physiotherapists, and all the staff at our hospitals and limb centres who continually fight to repair, mend, and counsel injured and maimed police officers and their families when subject to such traumas of the Police service.

I personally thank all those above who have treated and assisted my family and I, and I send my sincere best wishes to those officers and their families who are sick, or are recovering from injury. God bless you all.

Swasie Turner P.L.S.M.

Foreword

by Derek Fowlds
(ex-Sergeant Oscar Blaketon of Yorkshire TV's 'Heartbeat')

About eighteen months ago a colleague of ex-Merseyside Police Sergeant, Swasie Turner, wrote to me asking if I would send a signed photograph to him as he had been forced to retire from the force due to being badly injured on duty. He explained that the character I played in Yorkshire TV's Heartbeat, Sergeant Oscar Blaketon, was Swasie's hero. He enclosed a copy of Swasie's autobiography. I was extremely flattered and sent off a photograph.

It was then that I began to read the 'Biography' entitled 'Off the Cuff' and I was totally unprepared for the experience! The 'tables were turned'; Swasie Turner became MY hero! What a career he has had, what a life he has had, and what a courageous man he is. With only half a right hand, minus a right leg and confined to a wheelchair (a legacy of the job he loved so much), he works tirelessly not only at his writing, but for many charities involving cancer research. Swasie and I had not met so I phoned him to tell him how impressed I was with his autobiography.

He talked non-stop with amazing energy and enthusiasm about his taking part in the Great North Run and his climbing of the three North West coastal lighthouses, Leasowe, New Brighton and Talacre, all with his ordinary, standard issue DHS wheelchair! "*By the way*", he said, "*would you like to read my other two novels?*" I knew I had to meet this man.

iv

We did finally meet in November 1997, only six weeks after Swasie lost his wife Marje to the scourge of cancer. He came with his lovely daughter Jo to visit the set of Heartbeat. It was a great thrill for me to meet him at last. All of the crew were amazed by his energy, his determination and obvious love of life.

With this new novel (again partly based on fact), 'Onto The Final Leg'; Swasie is bang on form again. His writing is exciting and controversial, and at times very funny. You won't fail to enjoy this book and if you haven't read his other two, 'Off the Cuff' and 'If the Cap Fits' I strongly recommend that you go out and buy them now.

Sergeant Swasie Turner is a one-off, an original! After they made him they threw away the mould. From actors like us who only play at being coppers, he has all our admiration. We just pretend, but he's been there, done it and got the T-Shirt. We salute you Swasie.

Derek Fowlds

INDEX

Other books published by Classfern Ltd;

"Wheelchair Pilot"   £9.95

A4 - 100pp - Full gloss colour chronicle of the extraordinary exploits, writings and cartoons of Swasie Turner. Written by John M Birtwistle, Editor/Publisher of Wirral Champion Magazine.

"Wirral Memories"   £6.95

A4 - 100pp - Full gloss colour compilation of nostalgic articles about Wirral, its people and its places, written by the editor of, and contributors to, Wirral Champion Magazine.

"Cheshire Girl"   £6.95

A5 - 196pp - The heartwarming and moving story of a girl's life from teens to eighties, through joy and adversity, set against the backdrop of the Cheshire countryside.

These books available in bookshops and by mail-order from publisher, tel; 0151 608 6333.

Other books by Swasie Turner;

"Off the Cuff"   £9.95

348pp - Autobiography of Swasie's colourful life.

"If the Cap Fits"   £9.95

240pp - A fictionalised account of police characters.

Both published by Avid Publications

Friends in high places !

The plump figure of Dolly Keffer the traffic warden, the scourge of Angel Street division, known by the town's motorists as 'Keffer the Heifer', finished adhering a fixed penalty ticket on the windscreen of Mal Foster's bakery van as the vehicle was standing on double yellow lines. Dolly was about to move away when the irate driver came rushing out of a nearby cake shop protesting vehemently. *"Can't yer see I'm deliverin' bread to the shop?"*, he said angrily. Dolly would not be moved however, *"You're on double yellow lines and you're outside permitted delivery time. You're only allowed...."*, *"It's about bloody time they transferred you back to Gestapo Headquarters so we can earn a bloody livin',"* spat out the angry baker. Dolly resumed her patrol apparently oblivious of the small gathering muttering their total agreement with the baker's irate sentiments. Dolly had heard it all before, she had been spat on, assaulted, on one occasion an angry motorist drove over her foot and cursed her mercilessly as he attempted to drive away, but to no avail, he had still received a ticket!

As she made her way along Dolly spotted another candidate. This time the offender was none other than Councillor Dominic Price. Price had parked his van outside his fruit and veg' shop but, unfortunately, the vehicle was standing on the 'zig zag' lines of a pedestrian crossing. Once again, out came Dolly's dreaded black book. As she prepared a ticket for the vehicle's hapless driver, out of the shop strode the arrogant figure of Dominic Price. Playing to his customers and passers-by, Price shouted for all to hear, *"Hey you! I'm loading up outside my own shop, so bugger off"*. *"You are illegally parked within the precincts*

1

of a pedestrian crossing, which is an endorsable offence....." started Dolly. "BUGGER OFF! before I stuff that bloody book up yer arse", snapped Price as his face started to change colour from red to purple. Price's outburst brought much amusement to those nearby witnessing the spectacle of the traffic warden receiving her 'come uppance'! Just then the big frame of Sergeant John Royle, the 'no-nonsense' officer from Angel Street appeared on the scene. "What's goin' on Warden?", he asked formally, his lisp very apparent as he spoke. His lisp tended to make the big, tough sergeant sound a little effeminate. Nothing, however, could be further from the truth.

Sergeant Royle was six foot and powerfully built. He had once been a Royal Marine Commando and was a very hard man. Due to his lisp, he had been affectionately christened by his colleagues, and was universally known as, 'The Gay Marine'! Sergeant Royle had had many altercations with this particularly arrogant and obnoxious councillor, Dominic Price. Price was a close friend of Chief Superintendent Bernard Gilmore, (the sergeant's boss), as well as being a member of Gilmore's Masonic Lodge. Many was the time that the Gay Marine had been summoned to Gilmore's office for a roasting due to the Sergeant having invoked Price's wrath over something or other. Price considered himself immune from his regular contraventions of various legislation, however, Sergeant Royle certainly did not. The Sergeant had even been threatened with being posted elsewhere if he did not cease his harassment of Mr Price. No way, however, would the Gay Marine be intimidated into turning a 'blind eye' to Price's constant misdemeanours. Unfortunately, this did not enhance the sergeant's future prospects as he was definitely NOT one of the Chief Super's favourites!

"What's the problem Doll?", he asked again as Price continued to rant on to all and sundry about his continual harassment and the injustice of not being able to park outside his own shop. "He knows the score Sarje, he's parked on zig-zags and he won't move his van", replied the Traffic Warden. The Gay Marine then instructed, "Start makin' a ticket out and I'll go an' whisper in 'is ear!". The sergeant moved menacingly towards Price and said, "'Ere, lets 'ave a look at this vehicle of yours Mr Price".

The Sergeant decided to give the vehicle his 'full attention'! The vehicle underwent a very close scrutiny to check its roadworthiness. The Gay Marine intended to see what he could find. The first thing that the sergeant noticed was the acute lack of tread on the front offside tyre and thought 'Oh dear, more endorsements'! It was seen also by the pedantic sergeant that the vehicle had only one mirror, and being a goods vehicle, Mr Price should have invested in two! The sergeant pointed out these offences to Price but Price was again busy playing to the gallery by writing down the sergeant's number and informing him of his intention to report him to his Chief Superintendent, Mr Gilmore. The sergeant thought to himself, 'Oh no, not the eleven o' clock walk again'! The Gay Marine continued his meticulous inspection of Price's van, taking hold of Price's sleeve and pulling him along and round to the rear of the vehicle. As he did so the councillor's brown smock caught on a protruding piece of jagged metal from one of the rear doors. Price tried to free his smock and in doing so he made a large tear in the garment. "*Jesus Christ, this is all your bloody fault*", ranted Price, "*I'll 'ave those bloody stripes off your arm by the time I'm finished with you*". Sergeant Royle ignored Price's threat and said slowly, "*Good heavens, I didn't notice that!*", and went on to point out the offence of having a vehicle in a dangerous condition. Sergeant Royle cautioned Price and told him he would be reported for summons for the offences disclosed. The sergeant then invited Traffic Warden Keffer to hand Mr Price the fixed penalty ticket for the parking violation. Price looked as though he was about to become a candidate for the cardiac unit of Warbreckside Infirmary.

As the Traffic Warden and her Sergeant left the scene, Price was ordered by the Gay Marine to move his van off the road forthwith or he would be arrested for 'wilful obstruction' of the highway. Realising the futility of arguing further Price, reluctantly, did as he was told. The crashing of gears and squealing of tyres as the vehicle moved off in a cloud of smoke from the burning rubber, indicated that Mr Price was cross! There was no doubt in the sergeant's mind that he would be hearing more about this from 'the boss'. "*What a nasty piece of work that man is*", said Dolly. "*That's putting it mildly*", replied the Sergeant and added, "*You *don't know half Doll, he's right up the boss's arse and believe me, he's capable of anything*".

The Gay Marine went on to elaborate as to how, in the not too distant past he had received many a dressing down accompanied with threats of dire consequences if anyone was found picking on the proverbial Mr Price. "*How come he's got the Chief Super's ear all the time Sarje?*", asked Dolly naively. "*He's got the boss's ear because they're 'palsie bloody walsies' and socialise together, go away on holiday together and are both in the same Masonic Lodge, plus their wives are never apart either!*", explained the Gay Marine. "*There's no doubt that we 'aven't 'eard the last of this little saga either*", said the sergeant and warned the traffic warden, "*'E'll 'ave you and I in separately and he'll tell you what a bastard I am and he'll suggest that I put you up to giving Price that ticket. He'll 'ave a bloody good go at trying to get me for harassment through you Doll, so beware!*". Dolly shook her head in disbelief and said, "*Don't worry sarje, I'll stick tickets on that bloody van like confetti after this, the Chief Super doesn't frighten me, I've always got the union haven't I?*". "*Good girl Doll, that's what I like to hear*", replied the Gay Marine, fully aware that the warden meant what she said and would not be intimidated by Price, or his friend the Chief Super.

Just then a patrol car drew up alongside them. The driver, Constable Ged 'Mule' Train leaned over and opened his passenger door. "*Jer wanna lift anywhere Sarje?*", asked Ged. The Gay Marine replied, "*Yes, I'll 'ave a bit of a run round with yer Mule,*" and bade farewell to the Traffic Warden as he climbed into the front seat. Dolly then made her way along the busy main street in keen pursuit of the town's traffic violators. As they parted, the Gay Marine said, "*Don't let the bastards grind yer down!*" and was left with Dolly's reply, "*Don't worry Sarje, they won't*".

Half a mile away the keen eyes of Norah Hazlehurst, one of the area's most successful (and notorious) store detectives spotted an equally well-known and immensely disliked petty thief, Kathleen Briscoe. Norah saw Kathy take a pair of jeans from a rack inside Henleys' Fashion Store where Norah had been keeping the errant female under observation for some time as she made her way around the store. Kathy secreted the jeans inside her coat then looking around her continually, she made her way furtively to the door, then out into the crowded Commerce Street and headed towards the railway station. Fortunately, Norah had a radio and quickly relayed what she had seen to her colleagues, informing them that she was pursuing Kathy with the intention of detaining her.

Eventually, Norah caught up with Kathy further along the crowded street. Norah drew level and touched Kathy's sleeve discreetly. *"Hang on a minute Kathy, what have you got under your coat?"* she asked. Kathy recognised the Detective instantly, *"Wha'?, there's fuck all under me coat"*, replied the eloquent young lady. Norah knew that she had not disposed of the item as she had not lost sight of her since she took the item from the rack, so she knew that she was on safe ground. *"C'mon Kathy, I saw you take a pair of cellophane wrapped jeans from Henley's a few minutes ago"*, said Norah confidently. As Norah was talking to Kathy a pair of jeans, wrapped in cellophane, dropped from under her coat which Kathy then kicked away from her. The item still had its price tag attached. Norah took a grip of the female thief's coat and recovered the pair of jeans. *"Well where did you get these from then?"*, asked Norah. *"Get what?, I've never fuckin' seen 'em before, so what yer on about?"*, replied the lady who had obviously either just left Swiss finishing school, or had recently come top of the charm school for air hostesses! Norah would not be thwarted by the emphatic denials from the epitome of regal low-life and maintained her tight grip on the offender's sleeve. *"Well you'll have to convince the Magistrates, 'cos I know bloody well where you got them from"*, said Norah. As usual, Kathy then started to play to all around her as to how she was being blamed for something that she hadn't done. Kathy had around twenty previous convictions for theft, as well as others for drunkenness and drugs - she was quite an asset to society. Her rantings drew the attention of the passing public, but, as is par for the course, everyone seemed to be on the 'nothing to do with me' section so Norah could expect no help as she tried to hang on to her prisoner who was now starting to fight. Norah was having difficulty contacting her colleagues via her radio and her requests for assistance from passers-by fell on stony ground.

The incident had not escaped the notice of a long haired,

dirty, pimply-faced yob clad in his filthy, torn jeans and equally dirty, holed and heavily stained tee-shirt. Twenty two year old Ronnie Starling, another drug addict with many convictions for theft and drugs, stood selling copies of 'Militant' to the few who sought the interest of its contents. Starling edged closer to the two women and pointed his heavily tattooed, puncture-scarred and dirt-ingrained arm towards Norah, who he also knew from previous experience, and said, knowing full well who she was, *"'Ey love, are you a fuckin' copper?"*. Norah maintained her grip of Kathy and the jeans, still trying to get through on her radio, and hissed at Starling, *"Bugger off Ronnie, you know damned well who I am"*, to which the ex-footman to the Monarchy replied, *"Yeah, well yer norra fuckin' copper so yer've got no power to touch 'er, leave 'er alone"*.

Just when things started to look really ugly, to Norah's grateful relief, the 'cavalry' arrived in the shape of her colleague, and fellow store detective, Denise Mackenzie, together with the young beat constable, Robert Clayton. Bob also knew the errant female Briscoe, he had dealt with her many times during the three years he had been in the force. Kathy was quickly taken back to the store where it was found that she was also in possession of other items which she had stolen from other stores in the area. Unfortunately, for Kathy, but to the sheer delight of all who knew, Kathy was on a 'bender', she was subject to a suspended prison sentence of six months! This had been imposed eight weeks earlier at Warbreckside Magistrates Court for similar offences. Therefore, now, all being well, the 'thorn in the side' of the main street stores would be put out of circulation for a while. Constable Clayton summoned transport and a short while later, he, together with the prisoner Kathy Briscoe, and Store Detective Norah Hazlehurst were conveyed to Angel Street Police Station.

After being documented and interviewed, all stood in front of the Station Sergeant, Mike Corson, known by his colleagues as 'the Balloon' due to his irritating, welfare orientated benevolence, which he always extended to all that were brought before him, irrespective of whatever foul deed they had perpetrated. When he bailed those miscreants he would always wish them well and say, *"Now don't let me down now will yer?"*. Kathy never failed, she

6

would always make allegations against officers involved in her apprehension. True to form, Kathy leaned on the charge office counter and looked at Sergeant Corson. *"I wanna make a complaint sergeant"*, said Kathy. The Balloon looked up and sighed, *"What is it Kathleen?"*, he asked. Kathy pulled open her coat and, thrusting her ample bosom towards the sergeant she said, *"See that dirty bastard there?"*, indicating young Constable Clayton, *"Well 'e felt me tits in the back of the van on our way 'ere"*. Constable Clayton countered, *"You lyin' bitch, I never bloody touched you"*, and looked to Norah for confirmation. Norah looked at the Balloon and said slowly, *"Sarje, I know this lying cow of old, as no doubt you do. That officer never laid a finger on her other than to put her in and take her out of the van. I was there all the time and she's lying"*. *"Okay, okay, we'll sort it out later"*, appeased the Balloon and continued to deal with the documentation relating to Kathy's apprehension and subsequent court appearance, as well as catering for the safe keeping of her personal property and the property subject to the charges.

Meanwhile, upstairs in the CID office, Detective Constable Richard 'Randy' Walker (whose nickname needs no explanation!) had just sat down at his desk after making a brew for those Angel Street officers present and taking one over to his sergeant, Frank Foster. The next thing there was a loud splutter followed by a curse from the Sergeant, *"Jeesus Christ Randy, you know bloody well I don't take sugar!"*. Randy returned to his sergeant's desk and apologising profusely, retrieved the cup and disposed of its offending contents before replenishing it with the correct beverage. Randy handed Frank the tea and said, *"I failed my initiative test there didn't I?"*. *"You were momentarily Superintendent material Randy, you'll 'ave to watch that!"*, bantered Frank to the amusement of the others present. It didn't matter what you did for Frank, he would always find something to moan about. He was always cynical or sarcastic to those he didn't like or who were not members of his 'clique'!

All present today were preparing to go and execute a search warrant hoping to retrieve a large consignment of cigarettes, cigars and tobacco which had been taken from an articulated lorry when violence was used by a gang on the driver and his mate, severely injuring both. The incident occurred two days earlier and information had been received from a reliable source that the property was now secreted at a large house belonging to a well known villain out in the 'sticks' in the neighbouring County force area. Frank sipped his tea and turned to address his 'troops', All sat with baited breath as they awaited enlightenment regarding their forthcoming engagement. The premises to be searched included a large house and its equally large, detached garage. The premises were at the end of a long, narrow and private lane, well away from prying eyes!

The owner of the house, set in acres of grounds, was well known to the Police, he was a 'Mr Big' of the area's crime fraternity and had contacts in many places, including some of those in high places, Franklyn Mayhew Esquire! Mayhew used to be the owner of the notorious den of iniquity, the infamous Vipers Club in Grundy Street, off the main Liverhead Road. After numerous stabbings, robberies, drug pushing and many other serious breaches of the indecency laws, all of which maintained a very high percentage of Angel Street's crime figures, the continual and determined efforts of Detective Sergeant Foster and all those working with him finally managed to bring about the demise of Vipers. After relentlessly pursuing lengthy enquiries regarding the seedy little club, Mayhew was successfully prosecuted and one of the many sources of his lucrative income was terminated when the club was closed down permanently. Mayhew was heavily fined (which Frank doubted had financially hurt him very much) but nevertheless it was a start against such an evil, non conforming member of society.

Frank spoke, "*As you know, Mayhew is one devious bastard and we anticipate trouble if any of his heavyweight cronies are about. It's possible that he may have one or two of his ex-doormen with 'im, as the 'snout' (informant) has told us that the gear (stolen property) is being divided up and moved on today. Of course you all know that the gear is from the lorry heist when two men were badly injured at Templeton's at the back of Commerce Street Station*". Frank went on to outline his plans and detailed who was to go where and do what. Although there had been no mention of firearms having been used at the original incident, nevertheless the lorry driver had been seriously injured and received a fractured skull and a broken leg when he had been badly beaten with a baseball bat, so Frank was leaving nothing to chance. Those of his officers qualified would be armed, as no doubt would be those of his opposite numbers from the County. There had been a whisper that Andy Pedder, a well known and widely feared armed robber, who was a friend of Mayhew's, had been seen at the large rambling house recently. Pedder was a vicious criminal who had only recently completed yet another lengthy term of imprisonment for armed robbery.

After a lengthy conference and numerous phone calls to the neighbouring County force to meticulously arrange meeting times and places of all taking part and going over all participants' tasks to ensure that those taking part were fully conversant with what was required of them, the firearms men were instructed to go and draw their weapons. The only female amongst the party, also a firearms officer, was W.D.C. Vicky 'Les' Bienne. 'Les' went and drew her favourite weapon, the Smith and Wesson, five shot 'snub nosed' revolver, which she would wear under her left arm in a shoulder holster.

Completely unaware of the high degree of Police activity concerning the impending raid on his lavish country home, Frank Mayhew Esquire sat comfortably in his large, deep easy chair on the deep-pile carpet in the sumptuous dwelling. On his lap lay a little white 'Westie' dog, 'Jock'. Mayhew gently stroked the animal's neck. At Mayhew's feet was sprawled a large black and tan, long haired German Shepherd dog, 'Major'. This dog was a very mean and vicious animal who was also well trained with regard to keeping strangers at bay and protecting his master, his family and their property. Uneasily sitting opposite Mayhew on a large settee were two of his ex-bouncers from Vipers Club, Brendan Balmer, universally known as 'Psycho', and his equally unpopular side-kick, Terry Oram, another well-known bully. All were discussing plans for the imminent removal and subsequent distribution of the 'hot' lorry load of cigarettes and tobacco from Templeton's, as well as the disposal of other stolen property here on the premises. Frank's wife had been discreetly sent to town shopping while some 'business' was conducted among some 'friends'!

Each time one of the two on the settee moved, Major's ears pricked up and he gave a low, menacing growl to make sure that each man knew exactly in whose domain they were being 'tolerated'. Oram looked at Frank and sat with a hand on each knee, clearly showing the bluebird tattoo on each hand between his thumb and index finger as well as the words 'love and hate' across the fingers of each hand. *"Jer know what Frank?"*, he muttered nervously, *"the times I've bin in your 'ouse an' I still don't trust that fuckin' dog o' yours"*. Mayhew grinned and replied, *"It's just as well 'cos e'd 'ave the bollocks off anyone who wasn't supposed to be 'ere, wouldn't yer lad?"*, and leant down to fondle the brute's massive head. The dog acknowledged by flattening its ears and lifting its head to look up at his master. Although Mayhew was considered a Mr Big in the crime world, he made sure that he never took an active part in any job. He would meticulously plan a job with military precision, but would always ensure that he remained strictly on the periphery of any enterprise, thus ensuring minimum risk to himself.

This 'job' had been no exception, Mayhew had a cast iron alibi as to where he was, miles away from the scene, as balaclava-clad and baseball-bat-wielding Balmer and Oram, sitting opposite him, together with Raymond Dempsey, physically carried out the crime. The latter was expected anytime now with a hired van to collect the incriminating property from the heist. Long before Dempsey's arrival, Major pricked his ears and lifted his head, again uttering the long, low, menacing growl. Mayhew looked towards the window and said, *"Aye, aye!, that'll be Ray with the van"*. Minutes later the sound of a vehicle could be heard approaching along the gravelled driveway. A subsequent check by Mayhew confirmed the arrival of Ray Dempsey with the van. *"Told yer!"*, said Mayhew, *"My dog never misses anything!"*. The three villains then made their way outside, after Mayhew first ensured that Major remained indoors, as the brute didn't know Dempsey so he wasn't taking any chances! Little 'Jock', the Westie filed out with the trio and made for the flowered border. *"Oi!, JOCK, stop pissin' on the flowers, Thelma will go bloody mad if she sees you doin' that!"*, shouted Mayhew as the little dog proceeded to relieve itself on the blooms.

Dempsey jumped down from the van and greeted the three. *"Hiya fellas, this is all I could get I'm afraid"*, he said, indicating the 30 hundredweight vehicle. *"Christ, we'll need to do at least 'arf a dozen trips to get rid of this lot"*, said Mayhew most concerned, as he had anticipated the removal and ultimate disposal in one trip. *"You're jokin' aren't yer?, I'd need to pinch another 'bender' (articulated lorry) to do it in one wouldn' I?"*, said Dempsey. *"Alright never mind, let's get ourselves moving then"*, instructed a worried Mayhew. The goods were loaded from the large garage and very soon the van was filled to capacity. The garage was again locked and the van made ready for its journey to down-town Warbreckside to deposit its cargo at a sweets and tobacconists shop belonging to another seedy character, Silas Temple.

Meanwhile, Major's frantic barking could be clearly heard from inside the house which made Mayhew think that all was not well, as it usually indicated the impending arrival of strangers. Mayhew's heart missed a beat as he started to panic. *"C'mon, get this bloody van to hell out of here"*, he snapped. Dempsey climbed aboard and started the engine, Mayhew instructed Balmer and Oram to join him to speed the unloading as he wanted rid of all incriminating property which was at present in his possession. *"'Urry up an' get back for the rest of it as soon as you can"*, he said feeling a little uneasy as the dog's barking had this time not revealed visitors. The van departed and sped down the drive before ultimately disappearing out into the lane.

Too late! .... Unknown to the four villains, Major, the alert dog was right! He had detected strangers approaching – the Police! Frank Foster and his merry men (and woman!) had secreted themselves and their vehicles behind hedges and amongst nearby trees ready to pounce. Dempsey and his disciples in crime, with their loaded van and its illicit cargo were intercepted and quickly taken, in custody, to Angel Street. Detective Sergeant Foster and Detective Constable Ronnie Wainwright then made their way on foot, discreetly 'shadowed' by colleagues, to the big rambling house. Again, the alert Alsatian announced the officers' presence long before they reached the house. Still uneasy and wondering what had set his dog growling and barking previously, as nobody had materialised, Mayhew, as yet unaware of what had befallen his accomplices, was about to go and look outside from the vantage point of an upstairs window.

As he was about to make his way upstairs, there was a loud 'DING! DONG!' as the bell chimes rang to assist the noise that the aggressive Alsatian was making together with the excited yapping from 'Jock' , the little Westie. As the bell rang Mayhew nearly jumped out of his skin! *"JEEESUS CHRIST!"*, he gasped, and, grabbing Major's chain collar he went to the large oak door in which was a frosted glass panel. He could just discern the two figures outside through the glass. *"Who is it?"*, he asked apprehensively. *"It's the Police, open up"*, replied Sergeant Foster. Mayhew's heart missed a beat, he was having difficulty keeping hold of the big dog's collar. *"What d'yer want?, I 've got the dog here so I can't open the door"*, shouted Mayhew to the blurred figures of the two officers outside. *"Open up Mayhew, this is Detective Sergeant Foster from Angel Street. The place is surrounded by armed officers an' if you let that dog loose we'll shoot it! Now open the bloody door"*, shouted the impatient Sergeant.

Mayhew knew Foster of old, it was he who had closed down Vipers Club which caused him to lose a lot of money. Mayhew knew the Sergeant's capabilities, fair means or foul. He knew it would be pointless to resist or try to kid the Sergeant. Mayhew went through to the kitchen and secured the dog inside a large broom cupboard, ensuring his long haired canine sentry was safely locked away, the last thing Mayhew wanted was a Police officer bitten.

Returning to the front door, Mayhew opened it and tried his best not to show any signs of concern at the Sergeant's presence. *"W-what is it Sergeant?, I was just having a doze!"*, he said, trying to appear as helpful as he could. Frank gestured for some of his colleagues to follow him as he entered the house and said to Mayhew, *"Mister Mayhew, there's an old saying, Never bullshit a bullshitter!"* *"I don't know what on earth you're on about"*, replied Mayhew and went on, *"Do you mind explaining the reason for your barging unceremoniously into my home without a warrant?"*, hoping by appearing to be so indignant, his ploy would impress. However, the unmoved Detective Sergeant produced a document from inside his jacket. *"Mister Franklyn Mayhew, sir"*, said Frank formally, "*I have in my possession a warrant, signed by a Magistrate, authorising me to enter premises at this address, by force if necessary, to search and recover stolen property which I have reasonable grounds to believe are secreted in, on or about these premises. I have reason to believe that there are stolen cigarettes, cigars and tobacco which were stolen from a lorry in Warbreckside two days ago*". Frank held out the warrant and asked Mayhew to read it. Mayhew went to take hold of the document but Frank said, "*No!, I'LL hold it, YOU read it!*".

Mayhew's face drained of colour. Only part of the incriminating haul had been removed, there was still a substantial amount behind the locked doors of his garage, as well as some previously 'obtained' tyres. Mayhew thought quickly, so long as the van didn't return while the Police were here, Mayhew would try and bluff things out, but he knew that those searching may not only recover the cigarettes, but what else would they find? If there was anything to be found, he knew that Foster would be sure to find it, however small or trivial it may appear to be!

Mayhew also hoped that his unsuspecting wife Thelma, the daughter of the ex-Mayor and Mayoress of Clintock-on-Dorlton, a small town in the Southern Shires, would not return from her shopping expedition yet. She was unaware of the depths of depravity Mayhew resorted to when he conducted his numerous 'business' transactions, although she did NOT approve of most of his unsavoury associates. The last thing Mayhew needed now was ear-ache from his wife or the possibility of her inadvertently saying something detrimental.

"*I'm going to ring my lawyer*", said Mayhew, it was his only hope. Sergeant Foster stood alongside Mayhew as he made his call to the notorious, unscrupulous (and devious) Barrister, Mr Brian Smethurst. Smethurst confirmed he would attend shortly. Frank stood there listening, making sure that Mayhew didn't contact any villains (apart from Smethurst!) and when the call was terminated Frank said, "*Right, let's get the show on the road!*" Turning to Mayhew the Sergeant asked, "*Mister Mayhew, Is there anything here that shouldn't be here?*". Mayhew answered with, "*Of course not, what d'yer think I am?*". Frank replied cynically, "*I won't answer that eh?*".

A meticulous search of the house was carried out from top to bottom. Every now and again the eagle eye of the Sergeant or one of his officers would spot something and Mayhew would be asked to account for its presence. Mayhew always had an answer but Frank knew that some items of expensive jewellery and other bric a brac were stolen but he could not prove it. Mayhew became angry at the sight of strangers rummaging through his and his wife's possessions and clothing. Secretly Sergeant Foster relished making a devious and sly criminal like Mayhew uncomfortable, frightened and angry. The likes of him, with his powerful friends who continually pulled strings on his behalf as he maintained his capability of buying himself out of trouble made Frank sick to the pit of his stomach.

Mayhew lived in the lap of luxury and wealth which he had stolen or extorted from others in society who had worked or saved long and hard for their property or money which they had then lost to parasites like him. Frank and his colleagues felt nothing but contempt for the likes of Mayhew, he could expect no sympathy whatsoever from any of those searching his property as each one was out to make sure they found something incriminating. Frank thought to himself as he eyed all the glitter around and about the opulently furnished room with its expensive antique furniture, 'what a bloody pity, some poor sod's most prized possessions were now almost certainly here, and some would be adorning Mayhew's wife when they graced various functions and occasions with their presence'.

Eventually the search of the house was concluded. The team then went to the large garage. The wide, double doors, each treble folding, were tightly secured. *"What's in 'ere Mister Mayhew?"*, asked Sergeant Foster. Just then a large Burgundy coloured Bentley glided to a standstill alongside those present. Out stepped the affluent and very obnoxious Mr Brian Smethurst, Mayhew's lawyer. He stood there in his navy blue, silver pinstripe suit, with a red carnation in his left lapel. The dust from the disturbed gravel was settling and laying a film on his highly polished patent leather shoes. Smethurst took the fat stump of his spent cigar from his lips and dropped it to the ground, treading it into the gravel, putting more dust on his toe caps!

14

"*Right, What's the trouble Mister Mayhew?*", he asked formally. Mayhew pointed to Sergeant Foster and wearing a hurt and pained expression said, "*It's this bloody man here, Sergeant Foster, now he's tryin' to get me for some lorry job!*". Detective Sergeant Foster, completely unimpressed by Smethurst's presence said, "*Will you open up the garage please Mister Mayhew?*", Smethurst cut in, "*May I see the warrant please sergeant?*". Frank replied, "*Mister Mayhew has seen the warrant, I don't have to show it to YOU, but I will however*", again he held out the document for inspection. Smethurst went to take hold of the document, Sergeant Foster snapped, "*Ah ah!, Lookie but no touchie!*". Smethurst grunted and the Sergeant returned the warrant to his inside pocket and turning to Mayhew said, "*Is there anything in the garage of an incriminating nature Mister Mayhew?*". Mayhew fumbled with his keys, seeking out the correct one. He may have thought that his face did not portray any form of emotion, but his hands said it all! They were trembling violently as he said, "*There's just a few fags an' that, I'm minding them for a business friend of mine*". The doors were eventually opened and..............all was revealed!.

"*Well, well well!*", said Sergeant Foster, "*Yer friend's a bloody 'eavy smoker by the look of things isn't he Mister Mayhew?*". From wall to wall and from floor to roof were cartons of cigarettes, cigars, tobacco and a number of new, heavy duty tyres, VERY expensive tyres!. "*Those tyres are for my Range Rover.........*", volunteered Mayhew. "*What? Two dozen tyres at a hundred quid each, what d'yer do, carry twenty spares at a time when you go out in it?*", snapped the Sergeant sarcastically and added, "*We'll come to the tyres later, what about these cigarettes Mister Mayhew?*" Before Mayhew had time to splutter any form of explanation he was instantly gagged by his lawyer who snapped, "*Say nothing! Don't say a word*". The cigarettes were thoroughly examined by the Sergeant and his officers, one of whom was instructed to arrange for a representative from the complainant firm to come and identify the consignment. Enquiries would have to be made with regard to the tyres as their owner would have to be traced before any steps could be taken. This wouldn't be too difficult as the manufacturers would trace the various garages via their suppliers. The Police photographic studio was summoned to photograph all of the property in situ. Most of the cigarettes would be returned to the complainants and a small amount (specimens) would be retained for evidential purposes.

Sergeant Foster said to Mayhew, *"Mister Mayhew, I am not satisfied with your explanation regarding the stolen goods we have recovered at your address and in your possession today. You don't have to say anything but if you don't mention when questioned something which you might rely on later in court, anything you say may be given in evidence. I'm arresting you.............",* Smethurst gleefully interrupted the Sergeant's verbal flow, *"NO, NO, NO, Sergeant! You really MUST learn the caution! It's - You do not have to say anything, but – it may harm your defence if you do not mention, when questioned, – very important Sergeant! - something which you later rely on in Court. Anything you DO say may be given in evidence".* Smethurst grinned and said, *"If you're going to caution my client Sergeant, set an example to your subordinates and do it properly!"*

Sergeant Foster seethed with anger at being so humiliated in front of all, however, nobody was impressed (although it pleased and amused Mayhew) and all felt sympathy for the Sergeant and complete and utter contempt for Smethurst. Probably all those officers present would not have got the new, ridiculous and totally offender-orientated caution word perfect had they had to administer it themselves. While the likes of Smethurst and his ivory-towered ilk sat in their plush, padded armchairs refreshing themselves with G & T's in their chambers, reciting the caution to perfection, yet another barrier to keep the Police at bay from their clients, those same officers were out among the angry men fighting crime! Frank Foster showed no sign of emotion and said firmly, *"Your client's been cautioned and I'm arresting him for Handling Stolen Property, knowing or believing it to be stolen property".* He then leaned over to Smethurst and said, *"Contrary to the theft act nineteen sixty eight, section twenty two –- Smartarse!"*

Mayhew was placed into a Police vehicle which conveniently appeared at Frank's signal and the supercilious grin disappeared from Smethurst's face as he turned to his client and said, *"I'll see you at Angel Street, don't worry, we'll sort things out!".* He then got into his Bentley and drove off to make his way to Angel Street Police Station.

Mayhew persisted in his story that he had agreed to look after the cigarettes for a friend while he went abroad on a business trip. He insisted that he had no idea that the goods were stolen. The 'friend', a Turkish Cypriot, Peter Contraliss, had been confirmed as having left the country and gone to Cyprus. Conveniently, he could not be contacted. As proof of Mayhew knowing or believing that the property was stolen was required beyond doubt, Smethurst maintained that his client had no idea that he was allowing his 'friend', a tobacconist, to leave property that was not legitimate in his custody. Likewise, the offenders caught in the van equally insisted that they were taking what they thought were 'legitimate' goods, tobacco and cigarettes, to a tobacconist's shop in Warbreckside and as they had not arrived at the shop, the shopkeeper, Silas Temple, could not be put in the frame!

Such was Smethurst's skill, he convinced the eventual Court hearing that there was certainly an 'element of doubt' regarding each and every defendant. The benefit of such doubt must not only be afforded to his client Mr Mayhew, but to all four as they were all working in concert taking part in what they all thought was a 'perfectly legitimate' enterprise. Although it was established that the person for whom Mayhew had 'done a favour' by looking after what he 'genuinely' thought were his friend's cigarettes, but who could not at present be contacted, that in no way was detrimental to his client's story, on the contrary, it assisted, as it proved his client was telling the truth. In actual fact Peter Contraliss had no intention of returning to England (although this was only known to Mayhew - and Smethurst!) so it was quite safe for Mayhew to have used Contraliss's name. It was to the address of Contraliss in the Turkish Cypriot quarter that Mayhew and his wife sometimes went for their holidays. Contraliss had been a 'partner in crime' with Mayhew on occasions in the past.

As the evidence was not considered in any way substantial against all four defendants, (not to mention the fact that his client Mr Mayhew had not been cautioned correctly) the case against all four was dismissed. Enquires proved negative with regard to the tyres, but everyone knew they were stolen!

Sergeant Foster however, would not forget. Frank knew that the likes of Mayhew would come again, they always did, and when the time came, Frank would be waiting! As they left the Court Frank turned to his colleague, Detective Constable Wainwright and said, "*I'll make sure the bastard doesn't slip the net next time Ron!*". Ronnie shrugged his shoulders and sighed, "*That's how it goes when you 'ave friends in high places Sarje!*"

Oh for a bit of decorum !

It was 10.45 pm on Saturday night. Sergeant Royle, the 'Gay Marine' brought the night shift parade to attention and checked the attendance of his men and women on the section.

"Constable Evans," he bellowed, his lisp very prominent as he did so. *"Here Sarje,"* replied the officer known to all as 'Old Arse' due to his lengthy service at Angel Street. *"Constable Smith"*, (known as 'Plums' due to God's generosity with regard a certain part of his anatomy!), *"All present and correct most esteemed and illustrious Sergeant"*, replied Barry sarcastically. *"Constable Train"*. *"Here Sergeant" "W.P. Perry"*, *"Sir!"*. *"Constable Garvey"*. *"Sar!"*. *"Constable Grundy"*. *"Sergeant"*. *"Constable Andrews"*. *"Yeo!"*. The section were all present. There was actually nobody off sick, 'that's a bloody change' thought the Gay Marine!

Inspector Platt, the shift Inspector (disliked by all, and known as Platt the Prat), entered the room and stood alongside Sergeant Royle at the desk bearing the small lectern. Next door to the parade room was the snooker room and this evening Angel Street had been hosting a snooker match between the Division and a team of bus drivers from Brecksville Passenger Transport Services Butler Street depot.

Every now and again there would be a crescendo of noise as those next door applauded the participants in the match. The loud noise would interrupt the parade's formal proceedings, as the officers would have to wait until the noise died down to continue with the business in hand.

The Gay Marine cursed as he moved along the line of officers, handing out various files or forms which required the

19

attention of those concerned. The Sergeant then returned to the desk and stood alongside the Inspector. Sergeant Royle picked up the 'Families from Home' book and proceeded to recite the addresses of those needing attention while the occupants were away on holiday or where premises were empty due to hospitalisation or the occupant's demise. At the conclusion of this task, Inspector Platt then commenced to read from the 'Reading Out File' and passed on the various items of Criminal Intelligence and other equally confidential information and instruction. Some of this had to be recorded in the books of the officers to assist them as they went about their patrols.

As the Inspector was briefing the section, the dividing door separating the snooker room from the parade room, opened, as it did so the noise from next door magnified ten fold! A bus driver, still in his uniform, entered the parade room carrying a tray of empty beer glasses. Even after seeing those lined up on parade, the unconcerned man back heeled the door which then slammed with a loud bang. Either the man just did not care, or he was completely oblivious to the gravity of the formal proceedings being conducted before him.

The Gay Marine was mortified! *"Oh bugger this!"*, he muttered angrily, then said loudly, *"S'cuse me for a moment sir!"*, before striding over and intercepting the blatant invader by grabbing hold of his shoulders, turning him about and not too gently propelling him back to the door. The indignant individual protested vehemently, *"I'm going up to the bar for more ale!"*. The Gay Marine opened the door and pushed the disrespectful individual back into the smoky atmosphere of the snooker room and snapped, *"OUT!, THAT'S the door from the snooker room over there"*, indicating a door which gave access to the same corridor as that outside the parade room.

The protesting driver tried to inform the Sergeant that Chief Inspector Franks (who was sitting at a table at the far end of the room) had told him to take a short cut through the parade room as the bar was about to close, but Sergeant Royle was having none of it. *"I don't care if the bloody Chief Constable wants a pint, you're not comin' through 'ere, NOBODY wanders through 'ere when there's a parade on!"*, he snapped. He then closed the door on the open-mouthed snooker fraternity and returned to the Inspector who was still standing there aghast at the Sergeant's latest little saga, which would no doubt spread throughout the force in no time, enhancing his already very wide reputation. The section were highly amused, they loved to see their sergeant sorting things out that they would like to but either couldn't, or didn't have the 'bottle' to do so.

The Sergeant looked to the Inspector and said, *"As you were saying Sir, before you were so rudely interrupted!"*. Inspector Platt, as usual minus courage, and in 'grovelling' mode, said, *"You shouldn't have done that Sergeant, after all, the Chief Inspector gave his permission for him to come through!"*. The Gay Marine replied, *"With respect sir!, while there's a parade goin' on, the Chief Inspector, who is off duty for the weekend, being a nine to five man, wouldn't have got through 'ere rattlin' a tray full of glasses while there's a parade goin' on, never mind a bloody civvy!"*. The Inspector shook his head and muttered, *"Well if the Chief Inspector said it was okay, it was okay by me. I'm having no part of it, it was your doing. If anything comes of it you'll have to sort it out, you're on your own Sergeant!"*.

The Gay Marine was not surprised at the Inspector's attitude. He was well aware of his 'lack of moral fibre' which seemed par for the course among those who aspired to high rank and greater things by making sure that they didn't make ripples or rock the boat.

The parade was duly dismissed and went to collect their radios and carry out their other pre-patrol tasks before making out onto the streets, but not before the eagle eye of the Gay Marine had spotted Constable Garvey's red socks! The Sergeant called him back and pointing to the offending attire asked, *"Constable Garvey, what in hell's name 'ave you got on your feet?"*. Garvey's face went as red as his socks and he stumbled to explain, *"I was late getting out for work an' they were the only ones I could find, I'm sorry boss, I didn't think it would matter seeing as I'm driving"*. The Gay Marine wasn't accepting this, *"Well it bloody well does matter, I don't care how you do it but get yourself sorted out and* correctly dressed or you can just go back home, yer not goin' out like that!".

The Sergeant and the Inspector made their way upstairs from the basement parade room. As they climbed the stairs to the front office to collect their own radios, Inspector Platt said, "There was no need for that with young Garvey John, after all he IS driving!". Sergeant Royle looked up and sighed before replying, "I don't give a monkeys sir, he's improperly dressed and that's all there is to it!". Miraculously, Constable Garvey either begged, borrowed or stole, a pair of black socks within ten minutes of the Gay Marine's rocket. The Sergeant guessed, "I bet he's borrowed them from one of the lads upstairs in the club bar who was now going home (sockless) from afternoon duty!".

Later, during the following week, Sergeant Royle was entering Angel Street station from the car park just as Chief Inspector Franks was leaving to go home (well before 5 o clock!) The Gay Marine looked at the Chief and thought, 'another early dart!'. "Afternoon sir", greeted the Sergeant. Chief Inspector Franks stood there as the Sergeant approached. "Ah, Sergeant Royle, the very man!". The Gay Marine knew what was coming! "Yes sir, what can I do for you?" he asked. "Sergeant Royle, I have spoken to Inspector Platt regarding the incident on Saturday night in the snooker room and he tells me that you refused to allow Mister Mottershead the bus driver through, even though he said he could!". The hair on the back of the Sergeant's head stiffened and he thought, 'what a lying prat the Inspector really is'. "Yes sir", said the Gay Marine, "it was entirely my decision to prevent Mister Mottershead as you call him, from walking through the parade room, Inspector Platt had absolutely nothing to do with it".

The Chief Inspector went on icily, "Mister Platt said he told you to let him through!". The Gay Marine was really fuming at his colleague's acute lack of backing in something he considered to be a cut and dried issue. He'd sort it out himself however as there was no way that he would become involved in the same game as Platt and tell tales to the 'teacher'. "Well, probably due to the noise, I didn't hear the Inspector's instruction sir", conceded the Gay Marine (for now!).

Sergeant Royle went on to receive a severe reprimand from the Chief Inspector, who didn't fail to remind his subordinate that if the Chief Super, Mr Gilmore, were to find out, there could be repercussions, as the Sergeant was certainly not one of his favourites. As there were some of his bobbies arriving, the Gay Marine decided to terminate proceedings to eliminate his being humiliated in front of them. Sergeant Royle said, *"Sir, there was a parade on and confidential information was being discussed with regard to criminal intelligence, plus the fact that there is no way I will allow unauthorised personnel to cavort through the ranks of my men in the guise of a barman, just to satisfy the thirst of a load of busmen, – and off duty senior officers!"*. The Gay Marine then left the Chief Inspector standing there looking after him, mesmerised, and made his way into the building to ready himself for yet another (hopefully incident free) pre-shift parade.

During another wet and windy tour of night duty, Sergeant Royle drove his supervision car through the streets of Warbreckside, a large, Northern, industrial town which also housed a number of docks and warehouses. Tonight, the Gay Marine was accompanied by the Inspector, Platt. The Inspector had asked the Sergeant if he could accompany him during his nocturnal run through the town while he pegged (visited) his 'troops' as they patrolled their beats and areas. After the decadence of the snooker episode and the subsequent portrayal of the Inspector's pedigree to Platt by the Gay Marine, following the Sergeant's chastisement by the Chief Inspector, Inspector Platt was eating out of the Sergeant's hand like a domesticated parrot. However, a leopard never changes its spots and Sergeant Royle would always be aware of how dangerous and untrustworthy the crawling little despot could be.

The Sergeant and the Inspector drove around the streets of the division in the early hours and as they proceeded along Railway Road towards Druids Hotel in Commerce Street the Gay Marine spotted Policewoman Vera Perry. It didn't matter how warm it was or what the season was, Vera always felt the cold and subsequently always wore numerous layers of clothing. Due to this, and the fact that she had flaming red hair, Vera was known to all and sundry as, the Red Onion! Sergeant Royle drew alongside his officer and the Inspector wound down his window.

The Policewoman leaned on the roof of the car and greeted her supervisory officers. "*Alright sir?, Hiya Sarje!*". The Gay Marine cringed and thought to himself, 'here we go again!. "*Hi Vee*", acknowledged the Inspector. Sergeant Royle leaned across the Inspector. "*Vera!*", he said sharply, "*When you were at the Police Training College at Beresford, didn't they teach you how to greet senior officers?*". The Policewoman stood and made no reply. The Gay Marine went on, "*Have you fell out with the Inspector and I or what?*". Vera bent down and looked into the car at her Sergeant, even though it was dark, she could see via the light from the street lighting that his face indicated 'all was not well!' "*What d'you mean Sarje?*" asked Vera. Sergeant Royle went on to enlighten her, "*When you were in training at Beresford, how were you taught to greet an Inspector?*". Vera stood with a silly grin on her face and said embarrassingly, "*Stand and salute!*". "*CORRECT!*", confirmed the Sergeant and went on, "*Assuming that you have nothing to report and all is well, what do you say?*".

Vera replied, "*All correct Sarje!*". "*Correct again!*" confirmed the Gay Marine and said, "*I'm not falling out with you Vee, but let's 'ave things right eh?*". "*Yes Sarje, I'm sorry*", replied Vera. The Sergeant accepted her apology and said, "*Good girl, give me your book an' I'll show you a visit.*" The policewoman handed her notebook to her Sergeant who endorsed the time and place of the visit. Handing back the endorsed book to her, Sergeant Royle said, "*Two thirty at Roderick's kiosk, Okay?*". Vera retrieved her book and replaced it into her breast pocket, somewhere down inside her numerous coats and jerseys and replied, "*Okay Sarje*". She then stood smartly erect and threw up a perfect salute. Platt said, "*Oh that's alright Vee!*".

The Gay Marine then drove off to find another officer and show him a visit. As they drove along the Gay Marine said, "*Boss, will you stop contradicting my instructions to the section, you an' I have had this out before!*". Platt countered, "*Personally John, I think you're bit over the top regarding discipline*". The Sergeant replied, "*As I've said a thousand times, discipline, punctuality, respect, smartness and turnout, ALL contribute to the end result, efficiency"*, and asked, *"How many times have you gone to an incident and attended at the scene minus your cap?"*. Platt stuttered and stammered, *"Ah yes, but it's always there in the car"*, whined Platt. *"But when you get out of the car to deal with an incident you don't go dressed like a third rate bloody security officer do you"*, snapped the Gay Marine and added, *"Take the officers in Traffic, you always see them with their caps on as they drive along and even at major incidents, no matter how serious, they're always correctly and smartly dressed. Even if they were as thick as two short planks, the main thing is, they LOOK efficient and consequently the public, and all concerned, have confidence in us and feel that the matter is being dealt with properly"*. The Sergeant knew that he was wasting his breath but he had to make a stand.

There were one or two on the section that would utilise the fact that there were differences of opinion regarding discipline between him and the Inspector. The Gay Marine drove in silence. It was obvious that he and the Inspector would never see eye to eye, there was more chance of Hell freezing over than the two becoming friends. The Gay Marine had pointed out that it was just as important to be acknowledged correctly at two thirty in the morning, as three o'clock on a busy Saturday afternoon in full view of the public, but again, his comments were wasted and fell on stony ground.

Sergeant Royle and Inspector Platt had been at daggers drawn ever since the Inspector's arrival on the section. The Inspector had soon revealed himself for what he was, a groveller to those senior to him, and a little tyrant to those below him. He was a man who was unable to make decisions or command the respect of his subordinates. He ran with the hares and hunted with the hounds. Very soon the Gay Marine found that if he made a correct and popular decision or took a course of action which produced satisfactory, good or excellent results, then Platt would endorse those actions with his blessing, in writing, specifically to ensure that he would (hopefully) share any forthcoming accolade from those in high places. However, if the opposite was the case, Platt would very soon distance himself from anything he considered those upstairs would not approve of, or which would invoke disdain among those senior officers with shiny trousers, or 'shiny arses' as they were known to those who resented them. Indeed, the Inspector was so concerned not to put a foot wrong, he would not only distance himself from the Gay Marine when he upset the powers that be, but would put his disapproval of whatever it was, on paper to let those concerned know his sentiments.

Sergeant Royle on the other hand, was a very able and competent leader. The welfare of those on his section was paramount. Sergeant Royle would fight tenaciously on their behalf, even at the risk of landing himself in hot water by upsetting the 'chairborne infantry' upstairs, or downtown at Headquarters. He could not, and would not, however, tolerate shirkers, cowards and those who were a burden to their colleagues, nor could he tolerate senior officers of a similar ilk, and there were many who fell into that category!

Sergeant Royle had worn the Chief Superintendent's carpet threadbare by his regular attendances before the proverbial Mr Gilmore for one thing or another, but the Gay Marine would not deviate from performing his duties in an honest and forthright (although he accepted, sometimes unorthodox!) manner, the job came first, full stop. The Gay Marine fought many battles for and on behalf of his 'troops' and even if he had occasion to chastise them severely for some misdemeanour or other, he held the undivided respect of them all.

One of the Panda drivers, Constable Ged 'Mule' Train, became the cause of Sergeant Royle's acute indignation during a morning shift when the sergeant, who was patrolling on foot, spotted Ged's patrol car as it travelled along Foxburn Road. Ged should have been alone in the vehicle, but against Sergeant Royle's specific instructions, the sergeant saw that there was a passenger in the car, the beat man from the other end of the division, Constable Grundy. To say that the Sergeant was annoyed was putting it mildly! He immediately called the officer on his personal radio and arranged a rendezvous outside Druids Hotel, opposite Commerce Street Station.

Constable Train duly arrived as instructed (solo) and greeted his Sergeant, "*All correct Sarje!*". The Gay Marine lisped, "*Is it?*". Ged looked his Sergeant and said, "*What d'yer mean Sarje?*". Ged wondered if he had been spotted with Grundy in the car or was the Gay Marine referring to something else? He was as yet undecided whether to 'cough' about the unauthorised passenger. Sergeant Royle would not tolerate beat officers riding in cars when they should be patrolling their beats on foot.

The Gay Marine pointed his long, heavy signalling stick at Ged, the steel ferrule was inches from his face as Ged looked up at his Sergeant through the open window of his panda car, the Sergeant looked a lot bigger than his six feet as he stood on the kerb towering over him. Sergeant Royle let go with both barrels, "*Don't try takin' the piss out of me Mule, you know bloody well what I'm on about. D'you think I'm going to walk my balls off while the bloody recruits are ridin' around in cars, miles away from their beats? Don't try and underestimate my intelligence for Christ sake*". Ged decided to be sensible and come clean as he knew Grundy would get a broadside as well, "*Okay Sarje, I just gave him a run round for half an hour*", he said apologetically.

The Gay Marine gave Mule an almighty rocket, leaving the Constable in no doubt whatsoever that he was somewhat cross! Young Grundy likewise received very stern 'advice' about the dangers (from irate sergeants!) of riding round in patrol cars when he should be walking. For the whole of the following week's tour of duties, Ged was made to walk a down-town beat during which time he was subjected to the Gay Marine's close scrutiny. After this Ged sulked for quite a while as he thought he had been badly done to over 'such trivia', but it would be a very, very long time before he would pick up a footman again. The words of the Gay Marine continually rang in his ears, – "*I'LL say who walks an' who rides!*"

Sergeant Royle found that his form of discipline always bore results whereas other supervisory officers who continually appeased wrong-doers among the ranks were more often than not treated with disdain and taken advantage of. The Gay Marine always believed that kindness, in such cases, was always interpreted as a sign of weakness!

It had just turned half past three on a blustery Wednesday afternoon. The Autumn leaves were being blown from the Copper Beech tree outside and propelled against the window of the Sergeants' office, sounding like the pitter patter of hundreds of tiny feet. The Gay Marine sat at his desk enjoying his mug of hot, sweet tea, after seeing his 'flock' off to patrol the streets at the conclusion of the afternoon parade. The Sergeant was catching up on some outstanding paperwork at his trusty, steaming typewriter. The Licensing Sergeant (another 'Day' man!), Andy Brown, was doing likewise, but his typing was regarding his wife's coffee morning to be held shortly in connection with her tennis club! Andy sat on the opposite side of the room but Sergeant Royle hadn't failed to notice that his colleague's endeavours were certainly not Police duty orientated! The staccato of both typewriters sounded like machine guns being discharged at an imaginary enemy.

B-R-R-R-R-R-R-N-G!! - Proceedings were interrupted by the telephone as it rang for attention. Both Sergeants cursed and pushed back their chairs. As each reached to pick up the instrument the Gay Marine lisped, *"S'okay Andy, I'll get it, I'm nearest"*, then added cynically in banter, *"Anyway it might be serious Police duty!"*. Andy didn't miss the sarcasm, *"Piss off John"*, he said and returned to the matter in hand, sorting out who was to collect the pies and fancy cakes on his wife's big day!

Sergeant Royle lifted the receiver, *"Hello, Angel Street Police Station, Sergeant Royle!"*, – *"Call for you!"*, said the crisp voice of the female switchboard operator at Headquarters. The Gay Marine repeated, *"Sergeants' Office, Angel Street, Sergeant Royle speaking"*. "Oh, hello Sergeant, I'm sorry to bother you, I'm Canon Devereux from Mallory Church in Corkhill Road", said a very articulate and cultured voice. *"Yes sir, what can I do for you?"*, asked the Sergeant politely.

The reverend gentleman went on to inform the Sergeant that a disco was to be held that evening at the church hall youth club starting at 7pm, to mark the club's second year in being. The Minister asked for attention during the evening, especially at ten o'clock when the disco ended. As the Canon and the Gay Marine conducted their telephone conversation, Sergeant Brown mistyped one of his words and spoiled his text, *"Oh FUCK!"*, he shouted angrily as he reached for the little bottle of correcting fluid. The quick-thinking Gay Marine turned and shouted, *"Keep that foul-mouthed prisoner quiet in there!"*, then resuming his telephone conversation he said loudly for his colleague's benefit, *"Sorry about that Vicar! One of our regular, foul-mouthed drunks has just been brought in!"*.

The Minister was assured of the utmost attention during the evening's festivities at the Church and he sincerely thanked the Gay Marine, informing him that there would be no alcohol allowed in or on the premises and that he and his Curate, Alasdair Tetley, would be present throughout the evening. The Canon concluded their 'chat' by informing the sergeant that he and his officers were always welcome to call at the vicarage for tea or coffee should the opportunity present itself. *"Thank you very much sir, I'll make sure the patrolling officers are aware of your kind invitation"*, said The Gay Marine.

Indeed he would inform his section, as not only was it a nice little tea speck, but it could also be a good source of intelligence as to what was going on, and who was up to what! Sergeant Royle replaced the receiver and returned to his files. *"Right!"*, he muttered to himself, *"Let's get these bloody files out of the way"*. Turning to his colleague he said, *"Yer could 'ave lost your bloody day job there, swearin' in front of the Vicar!"*. Andy just carried on typing and ignored his colleague's remark.

Among the shops at the corner of Casey Walk and Pender Vale was a launderette which was managed my Mrs Flood, mother of 14 year old Gary 'Gazza' Flood. Gazza had just entered the shop to see his mum, while his mate, Cedric 'Seddie' Whitehead waited outside. Whitehead leaned against the lamp post outside the shops and cleaned the dirt from under his nails with the blade of his lock knife. He considered himself somewhat of a hardcase amongst his cronies and was held in awe by some, including Gazza. Whitehead was also fourteen but big and mature for his age. He had acquired a 'skin head' hair cut to enhance his macho and intimidating image. He wore a tee shirt, no coat, jeans supported by broad red braces, and trainers, no socks, - another sign of hardness! Occasionally he blew a bubble with his pink bubble gum that would expand and burst with a 'plop', sticking to his nose and eyebrows. Passers-by looked, but didn't laugh!

Next to the launderette was Nilahl Dinhali's sweets and tobacconist's shop, known by the locals as the 'Pakki Baccy' shop. If all went well and Gazza's quest to his mother was successful, they would be able to call into the 'Baccy' shop and get themselves some cigarettes. Both teenagers were pupils of Gilbey Comprehensive School (when they attended!) but both did come from reasonable homes and their parents were good parents. However, both sets of parents did despair at the attitude and behaviour of their offsprings. Whitehead was certainly starting to show signs of becoming a problem.

Eventually Gazza emerged from the launderette, a wide grin on his face. In his hand he held a five pound note. "*I told me mam I wanted to go swimmin' with a gang from school an' the silly cow believed me an' give me this!*", he said holding the money out to show Whitehead, hoping it would improve his street cred with his dominant mate. Whitehead grunted, "*Right, let's go an' get some fags then!*". The two went into the shop and bought cigarettes, matches and more gum. As they made their way from the shop Flood threw his chest out and said, "*See, yer wouldn't 'ave 'ad this if I 'adn't 'ave got the money would yer Gaz?*". Gazza looked at his mate scornfully and informed him, "*Yer jokin' aren't yer? I'd 'ave just fuckin' robbed 'em!*"

Once they were well away from the shops and out of sight of Gazza's mother, the two stopped and lit up. Whitehead blew the expired smoke from his mouth and said, "*There's a disco on at 'Mallo's' church tonight, let's go an' see what's doin'*". "*Oor yeah!*" enthused Gazza, "*Let's go an see if there's any talent!*"

'Boom-Tiddy-Boom-Tiddy-BOOM.............BISH!!'. The din from the disco could be heard some distance away, as the energetic boys and girls enjoyed their 'hop' at the Mallory Church hall. All was going well, everyone was happy and there was no signs of trouble or discontent among the youngsters. Some of the sweating participants ventured outside to cool off and get some fresh air. Canon Devereux and his Curate busied themselves as they mingled with the youths, handing out sandwiches and soft drinks from trays. One or two were smoking, but a blind eye was turned as, otherwise, those present were behaving themselves.

Whitehead and Flood sauntered along to the church and stood by the gate. Although they could have gone to the club if they wished, (Canon Devereux would never turn anyone away!) Whitehead considered it was only for kids or whimps, but he didn't mind eyeing up some of the girls present. Gazza would have indulged, but was fearful of invoking his mate Whitehead's disapproval.

Whitehead, still chewing, and with the proverbial status symbol (a ciggie) dangling from the corner of his mouth, shouted over to Dougie Smith who was standing outside with a small group near the hall's doorway, *"Dogga, 'ere a minute!"*. Smith came over as instructed, as it would be a brave lad who ignored Cedric Whitehead! *"Hiya Seddie, alright?"*, he asked, a slight hint of apprehension in his voice. Not everyone liked Whitehead! Whitehead looked at Smith and asked, *"Is there any ale in there or wha'?"*. *"No, just pop an' orange juice an' that"*, answered Dougie. *"What the fuck are yer doin' 'ere if there's no fuckin' ale?"*, said Whitehead angrily. Whitehead looked over at the group near the door then asked, *"Is that Sylvia Gordon yer with Smithy?"*,

(Whitehead used to 'go out' with Sylvia when they were both twelve, two years ago). Dougie replied, *"Yeah, we're all together, me, Sylv, Brenda Turner, Tina Wardale and Teddy Sherlock"*. Whitehead grabbed Smith's shirt and pulled him to him, *"You're not shaggin' Sylvia are yer Dougie?"*, he asked menacingly. *"No honest, we're just friends"*, insisted the frightened youth. Whitehead, still gripping Dougie's shirt, growled, *"Well if I find out yer' are, or Sherlock is, I'll kick yer 'ead in, d'ya 'ear me, eh?"*. The by now terrified Smith, again reassured Whitehead that the friendships among their mixed party were nothing other than what they were, friendships.

Gazza then decided to play the big man by joining his mate

Whitehead's overbearing conduct and intimidating rhetoric by adding, (hoping it would impress Whitehead) *"Who are yer shaggin' then, if it's not Sylvia Gordon?"*.

Whitehead released his hold of Smith but not before asking, *"Yeah!, go on, who are yer shaggin' then?"*. As the three youths stood there, none of them noticed the slim, bearded figure of the young Curate Mr Tetley as he joined the trio, having been alerted by one of the girls at the door. *"What's all this about shagging I hear?"*, he asked in his cultured voice. Dougie Smith just stood there, he didn't know what to say. Whitehead however, stood there with his legs apart and folded his arms after discarding his cigarette. Leaning his head to one side and staring at the Curate, who was a couple of inches shorter than him, Whitehead said cockily, *"Why don't you fuck off before I tear yer frock!"*

The young churchman instructed Smith to return to his friends and make their way inside the hall. After they had done so, the Curate turned to Whitehead and said, *"Will you please go away, we don't want any trouble here"*. Again Whitehead said, *"Didn't yer 'ear what I said? I said fuck off"*. The Curate then advised Whitehead to go home and wash his mouth out. Whitehead became even more aggressive and, to the utter amazement of Flood who he was trying to impress, grabbed hold of the Curate's cassock. In doing so the minister's 'dog' collar was dislodged and fell to the floor.

Unfortunately for Whitehead, and unknown to all but a few, before his arrival in the parish, and before his ordination, Mr Alasdair Tetley was a Northern Counties judo champion and was the holder of a Martial Arts Black Belt! As Whitehead was about to utter more obscenities to the Curate, he suddenly found himself upside down in the large holly bush alongside the church gate, squealing like a scalded cat! *"Oh dear!, are you alright?"*, asked the Curate as he helped Whitehead to his feet, completely uninjured except for his severely damaged ego. Whitehead gripped and rubbed his elbow as the Curate released him. Then he made off and, ensuring that twenty yards or so separated him from the churchman, Whitehead shouted, *"Bastard, yer just caught me off guard that time, I'll 'ave yer next time though!"*, he then made a humiliated retreat homewards, leaving Flood standing there unable to believe what he had seen.

Meanwhile back at Angel Street 'Nick', the Gay Marine had just finished his meal break and was driving the station's Ford Transit personnel carrier out to meander through the streets of the division. Aboard the vehicle were three members of his section and two Special Constables. If there was any trouble at the church disco tonight, he was ensuring that it would be more than adequately dealt with! They drove past the church but all appeared to be well, the little 'incident' involving Whitehead and the Curate would not be the subject of a police report, although it may well be mentioned in conversation some time in the future. As yet, even the Canon was not aware of Whitehead's ministerial retribution!

The Gay Marine did a second circuit and as he returned along Parkfield Way, and up towards the church, he spotted young Flood emerging from the small front garden of a house opposite the church, fastening the front of his trousers. Sergeant Royle drew alongside Flood and lowered his window. *"What the bloody 'ell's goin on 'ere, what are you doin' in that front garden?"*, he asked. Flood shrugged his shoulders and said, *"I was just avin' a piss!"*. *"Oh I see, whenever yer wanna piss, yer just go in someone's garden do yer? 'Ave yer never 'eard of a bloody toilet?"*. Flood informed the Sergeant, *"There's no toilets, an' they won't let me into the disco"*, he said cockily. *"No, I wouldn't either, yer little scrote. What's yer name lad?"*, asked the Gay Marine. *"Why?, I 'aven't done nuthin"*, replied Flood, making his first mistake! Sergeant Royle alighted from the vehicle, *"I'll ask yer again, what's yer name?"*, he asked impatiently. Flood stood defiant and said, *"Why?"*. Sergeant Royle was joined by Constable Leitch.

Flood was ordered to empty his pockets. At first he refused but the Gay Marine managed to 'persuade' him to comply with his request! As he produced items from each of his pockets, Flood maintained as to how the Sergeant couldn't do anything as he (Flood) hadn't done anything wrong. The little exercise revealed a lock knife, a packet of condoms, a steel comb with a pointed handle, a packet containing fourteen cigarettes and some small change in copper and silver.

The Gay Marine took the lock knife and opened out the wicked looking blade. *"What's this for, sharpening pencils?"*, he asked. Flood stood there silent. *"What's it for I asked?"*, repeated the Sergeant. *"It's for when I go fishin'"*, said Flood. *"Why don't yer use a bloody 'ook like everybody else?"*, said the sarcastic Sergeant. Holding out the condoms the Sergeant asked, *"An' when you've caught the fish d'yer slip these on 'em to stop 'em gettin' wet if it rains?"*. *"No"*, replied Flood. *"Right! Well for the last time, what is your name?"*, sighed the Sergeant. *"Gary Flood"*, replied Flood knowing the futility of prolonging the proceedings. The articles removed from Flood's pockets were placed into an envelope from inside their vehicle, which was retained by Constable Leitch.

It was ascertained that Flood lived with his parents at 12 Lindfield Loop. The Sergeant decided that poetic justice was the order of the day! *"Get in, we're takin' you home"*, lisped the Sergeant. *"Wait 'til I get 'ome, I'm tellin' me dad of you!"*, threatened Flood, but he was too late, the Gay Marine already had his plan as to how Flood would be dealt with!

Before leaving Parkfield Way, the Gay Marine had thought of knocking at the front door of number 79 and informing the occupier as to how Flood had been doing them a favour by irrigating their floral assets, but decided on a better solution, plan B! As they drove along towards Flood's home the youth continued to protest vehemently as to how he had been picked on for nothing by the Police, he threatened all in the vehicle with dire consequences once his father found out!

"What's yer dad's name son?", asked Sergeant Royle. *"Fred Flood an' everyone knows 'im, he'll soon sort you out"*, said the cheeky youth. *"Yeah, but what do 'is mates call 'im, cos I've never 'eard of 'im"*, said the Gay Marine denting young Flood's pride. There was method in the Sergeant's madness. He wanted to speak intimately with Flood's father, so he wanted to know how best to address him! *"They call 'im Flash!"*, muttered Flood.

Eventually the large Police carrier drew up outside the home of Gary Flood. As Flood went to get up the Gay Marine instructed him to remain where he was until he was called. Sergeant Royle went up the path of the council semi and knocked on the recently painted front door. Looking round, he saw a number of curtains move in nearby houses as the neighbours peered out to see what was going on at number twelve. A dog barked from within and a woman's voice shouted, *"Sheeba!, c'mere, can you go Fred? I've got the dog"*. A man's voice shouted, *"Alright, I'm comin'!"*, an inner door slammed.

The front door was finally opened by a man dressed in a vest and navy blue trousers with braces hanging down their sides, he was in dire need of a shave. Hoping that the man was Flood's father the Gay Marine said, *"Hello Flash, bloody 'ell!, long time no see!"*. Mr Flood looked aghast at the Sergeant, and the large white personnel carrier at his gate. *"I don't remember yo---!"*, he started to say but was cut in by the Gay Marine, *"Christ you 'aven't altered Fred"*, who then went on to elaborate, *"I'll tell you why I've called Flash, it's only 'cos it's you that I'm doin' this. Your lad's been giving one of my Policewomen some stick, he spat at her and told her to fuck off and when I told him I'd tell you he said, 'my old fella will do fuck all! As I knew bloody well you'd sort him out we didn't arrest him"*

By now Mister Flood's chest had swelled enormously by the Sergeant's complimentary rhetoric. To make matters worse the Sergeant presented Mr Flood with the items from his lovely son's pockets, just as they were joined at the door by Mrs Flood, *"What's going on Fred?"*, she asked. *"Nothing love, you go in I'll sort it out"*, seeing the knife he said, *"This is my bloody fishin' knife, get the bugger in 'ere Sarje!"*. Sergeant Royle signalled for one of his men to bring young Flood to his father. By this time Mr, AND, Mrs Flood had spotted the condoms. The cocky young Gary sauntered up the path, shaking himself free from his escort. *"Hey Dad!, 'see 'im, (indicating the Sergeant) he --!"*, he was rudely interrupted, BANG! Mr Flood hit him across the back of his head with such force that Flood was catapulted into the hall of their house. Before he had gathered his faculties Mr Flood dragged him to his feet and hit him again. Gary was flung onto the stairs and told to get up to his room forthwith, and was hit yet again! *"I'll be up to sort you out good an' proper in a minute, I'll teach you to swear at a police lady! I'll show yer whether I'll do fuck all or not!"*.

35

Turning to Sergeant Royle Mr Flood said, "*Thanks Sarje, I'll sort 'im out don't you worry about that!*", and lied, "*I do remember yer now, thanks again*". Sergeant Royle replied, "*Thanks Flash, I knew bloody well I could rely on you to sort things out properly, I warned 'im but he wouldn't believe me!*". Taking his leave the Sergeant said, "*I'll leave it with yer Flash, okay?*".

The Gay Marine and his 'troops' then drove off to resume their patrol. Constable Leitch, who was sitting in the front alongside his sergeant, turned and said, "*I don't know how the bloody hell you think of these things Sarge!*". Sergeant Royle turned and grinned, "*Easy when yer know how, it's called poetic justice, that'll teach the young brat to 'ave a bit of decorum in future!*"

Overtime, for some !

Detective Constables Randy Walker and Ronnie Wainwright stood watching the crowds as they gathered before entering Warbreck Rovers' football ground to watch the first division match between the Rovers and Windsor Athletic, the visiting side from London. The two officers were on the lookout for a team of pickpockets believed to have travelled with the away team supporters. Information had been received that those being sought included females in the gang. There were a number of plain clothes officers strategically placed in and around the ground today as every effort would be made to apprehend those who sought to dwell on the misery of others.

Although the rivalry was intense between the two teams' supporters, generally most were well behaved and shared mutual, harmless banter. However, it was doubtful if this would be the case at the conclusion of the game should one of the teams lose, as no doubt the losing fans would invade the local drinking establishments to seek solace via alcohol!

The pickpocket patrols were allocated their own areas to patrol, but if necessary all could contact each other via personal radio should the need arise. The most opportune time for pickpockets is when crowds group together and surge. The best time for such activity is when the turnstile queues start to crush near kick-off time. Many of the supporters had already imbibed at the various hostelries and some were seen relieving themselves in the entries adjacent to the ground.

As the two Detectives wandered up Jason Street they saw

one of the away supporters, obviously worse the wear for drink, swaying to and fro as he urinated quite openly against the wall and front door of one of the terraced houses. He was even oblivious to the cheer that went up from his red and white clad fellow supporters as they passed him by, many of whom were females, and some children, most were highly amused at the man's antics as he sprayed the front of the house, exposing his manhood for all to see. Just then a uniformed bobby appeared on the scene. Some of the crowd tried to bundle the man away, one or two having been anointed with the balm of misguided loyalty, seeing that it wasn't their house! It was no good, however, the offender had been spotted. The officer pushed aside those trying to whiz the drunken urinator away, and grabbed him. One or two nearby shouted obscenities at the Constable, telling him to leave the man alone, but the Constable would not be deterred and radioed for transport for him and his unlucky prisoner. The man had been arrested for being drunk and disorderly and would be taken to Angel Street. He wouldn't be watching his beloved Windsor Athletic team play today!

Randy and his colleague stood discreetly nearby keeping an eye on the officer. They didn't want to blow their cover but would not hesitate to join him should anyone try to free his prisoner.

Both Ronnie and Randy had experienced similar incidents themselves when they were uniformed bobbies working the matches. The two weren't sure if the crafty officer had discreetly tapped on the door of the house or not, but suddenly the door opened and a big, swarthy man in his middle thirties appeared on the doorstep. The man must have enquired what was going on because whatever the Constable had said, the man became very angry. While the officer looked away 'to see if his transport was coming, the irate householder thumped the man responsible for peeing all over his door and polished red bricks, then returned inside, slamming the door behind him. "*Nice one mate!*", muttered Randy. "*I love it, serves the bastard right*", added Ronnie. The van arrived and the hapless (and sore!) drunk was bundled into the back followed by his uniformed escort. The van then drove off to place the inebriated Southerner into temporary incarceration.

38

The dynamic duo continued to wander about keeping an eye on the crowds. They saw one of the Constables from Central Headquarters, Dennis Hunter. Hunter normally worked in plain clothes between nine and five every day, with every weekend off. *"What exactly does he do in Headquarters?"*, asked Ronnie. *"I don't know Ron, nobody knows what the hell he does for sure, but it's supposed to be something to do with recruiting!"*, answered Randy. *"I'll tell yer what Randy, he's always led a bloody charmed life, mention street and he'll 'ave a bloody thrombo!"*, said Ronnie spitting venom.

Nearly all of Hunter's twenty seven years service had been spent in some hidey hole or other, he had hardly ever seen street duty and because he, and many others, were not bobbies at the 'sharp end', they tended to be resented by those who were. Ronnie hadn't finished and said, *"Dennis Hunter, just look at 'im! If anything happened now he wouldn't know what the bloody 'ell to do. Isn't it funny Randy? When a uniform bobby on shift work wants to work a match, they make bloody sure his normal duty is arranged to cover it, but when a 'day' man works a match, not only is he on overtime when he gets his uniform out of the cupboard, but they always get stuck somewhere out of harm's way, such as the Directors' box, the stand, the Press box, but never where there's someone likely to be 'naughty'!"*. Ronnie went on, and scoffed *"Sod it Randy, I'm gonna join the magic 'andshake brigade!"*.

By now Hunter was nearing the detectives and, not being the epitome of discretion he called out for all to hear, *"Alright Ron? Alright Randy? .....An''where are Angel Street's ace detectives off to now? Off to see the match, or are you both on duty?"*. Without dignifying proceedings with a reply the two angry detectives quickly distanced themselves from the unsuitable candidate for MI5! *"Stupid prick!"*, snapped Ronnie. *"What a bloody tosspot!"*, agreed Randy. *"Just as well we weren't tailing anyone"*, Ronnie retorted, *"the likes of 'im are to the Police force what lead is to lifebelt manufacture"*. *"Oh, I wouldn't say they were as good as that"*, quipped Randy.

They turned the corner and could see that by now the

crowds were really pushing, shoving and crushing at the turnstiles. Officers on horses were keeping the queues in reasonably straight lines. Detectives Wainwright and Walker observed proceedings and once three o'clock came they made their way into the packed ground via the Police entrance. Careful to avoid those officers who had come inside to 'unofficially' watch the game now that the pressure outside the ground had diminished, (they would resume their positions again, ten minutes before the end of the game). The two decided to split up but keep within sight of each other in the stand and on the terrace.

It wasn't long before Ronnie caught sight of a fat, blue and white clothed, home supporter. His blue and white plastic bowler hat at a jaunty angle on his head. He appeared to be jostling those about him. A closer scrutiny revealed that the man, obviously another of those who had earlier imbibed in the happy juice, was in fact urinating profusely into the jacket pocket of a fellow supporter who was standing in front of him completely oblivious to the fact that he was taking on unwelcome fluids belonging to another! Ronnie was only interested in catching pickpockets, although he was however, highly amused at the audacity of the man's actions!

There were no incidents during the first half of the game and once the half-time whistle blew, Ronnie and Randy both met and went for a quick cuppa and a pie from one of the little booths under the main stand.

As they both stood there chatting one or two of the bobbies who saw them discreetly gave them a wide berth and ignored them. It was at this time that the attention of the two detectives was drawn to a group of away supporters. All were in their late teens or early twenties and among them were a number of girls. It was seen that all of the group wore 'bum' bags and each also carried a plastic carrier bag. It was obvious to the officers that the gang were up to something. Randy and Ronnie decided to watch this little group very closely during the second half. They left the immediate area and made their way to a secluded spot to brief control as to what they were about to do and circulated the descriptions of the gang before returning to maintain their observations.

Earlier the same day Sergeant Royle was also preparing for duty at the same match. Being a P.S.U. (Police Support Unit) Commander, a unit specially trained for 'confrontational' roles, on match days he was always drawn with his unit to perform duty at the ground. He cleaned the personnel carrier and checked the vehicle's equipment then awaited the arrival of his 'troops'. He always asked them to attend early so as to enable them to arrive at the ground well before parade time, which was at one o'clock, two hours before kick off. Their duty today was 12.00 noon to 8.00 pm.

The Gay Marine would arrive at the ground, then after their vehicle was safely parked in the Police pound the section would utilise their early arrival by two of them being dispatched to the nearby fish and chip shop to purchase takeaway meals and cans of coke. After their meal they would then make for the parade.

When the lads arrived and boarded the vehicle their driver, Clive Thomas, 'Tommo', wandered round making a final check that all was well, then climbed in behind the wheel. The Gay Marine sat alongside him in the front. He looked round to ascertain if all had arrived. "*Are we all 'ere?*", he lisped. Les White replied, "*Jeevesy 's not 'ere yet Sarje*". 'Plums' remarked, "*He's gonna fuck things up if he doesn't 'urry up!*". The reason that the Gay Marine liked to leave early was to enable the lads to avail themselves with an 'early dart' on their return to Angel Street. The Sergeant would let them go as soon as they got back due to them (officially) not having had a refreshment period, (they would in fact had 'dined' in the back of the Carrier in the car park before the parade!).

Eventually Barry Jeeves rode into the yard on his bicycle. The troops in the back of the vehicle hissed and booed their colleague. "*C'mon yer gobshite, we're gonna miss our chips!*", shouted Micky Doyle. Barry dismounted from his bike, stood erect and extended his right arm. He then gesticulated at the Carrier with his two fingers! The Gay Marine fired a verbal broadside, "*Move yer arse Barry or there's no early dart!*". That did the trick. Barry immediately put his brain in gear and quickly readied himself before joining his hissing colleagues in the vehicle. "*Sorry I'm late*

Sarje, the baby's been playin' up", he offered lamely. *"Christ, Barry, try something original, that's an old one"*, said the Gay Marine then turned to the driver and instructed, *"Okay Tommo, let's get movin'!"*.

The section then made their way to the ground at Rayburn Road. As Tommo turned into Jason Street Plums spotted Randy Walker and Ronnie Wainwright and remarked, *"I see the two Rs are out sleuthing eh?"*. Sergeant Royle replied, *"They're two sound blokes those two"*. *"They're the best Jacks we've got at Angel Street, I'll tell yer that"*, added young Garvey. The Carrier passed the two Detectives and although they, and those in the vehicle, saw each other, neither gave any acknowledgement to the other.

The Carrier turned into the pound from the crowded street. Tommo neatly negotiated other parked vehicles before neatly parking his vehicle behind the large, Police horse van.

Turning in his seat, the Gay Marine said, *"Right!, who's goin' for the 'jockeys (jockeys' whips, - chips!) then ?"*. As usual there were no volunteers to join a queue full of half drunk pre-match supporters in a crowded chip shop! Sergeant Royle snapped, *"Well as sure as hell I'm not, so somebody better get their arse in gear!"*. Still no volunteers. The Gay Marine said, *"Right, I'm puttin' me delegatin' 'ead on, Jeevesy, you go!"*. Barry Jeeves protested, *"Are 'ay Sarje, I went last time"*. The Sergeant was quick to point out, *"Yeah, well seein' as you were late, you can go today an' all!"*. Barry left his seat and mumbled as he dismounted from the vehicle. There was a loud chorus and the lads started laughing at Jeeves. The Gay Marine turned to the giggling Mick Doyle and said, *"Seein' as you appreciate a good joke Mick, you can go with 'im!"*. The change of expression on Doyle's face brought peels of laughter from the rest of the section. *"C'mon, what d'yer want?"*, snapped Barry. Everybody started to order at once and Barry snapped, *"Piss off, one at a time will yer"*, as he fumbled with his pen and paper. After securing everybody's order, Constables Jeeves and Doyle made for Whitelocks' fish and chip shop in Jason Street.

Eventually the two returned and passed the gastronomic

parcels of fayre around, together with the cans of coke and lemonade. As they all settled down to eat, one or two expressed their disapproval at having received an incorrect order. *"Fuckin' 'ell Jeevesy, I said rice not chips"*, moaned Tommo the driver. *"There's no friggin' salt on me chips"*, added Plums. *"Where's my peas?"*, asked Paul Garvey. Barry realised that the lads were taking the micky and he countered, *"Oh, piss off! Yer can go an' get yer own next time"*. Finally the meals were consumed and washed down with the coke or lemonade followed by a long, loud –BRRRRRRRRRRPP! from the back of the vehicle, accompanied by –– PFFFFFT! Echoes of *"Yer dirty bastard"* and *"Jeeesus Christ, who's shit?"*. *"Yours if yer wannit!"*, answered some sarcastic soul.

The Gay Marine said, *"Pwar! let's get to hell out of 'ere"*, as he quickly vacated the vehicle. *"Papers an' cans in the bag an' over to the litter bin one of yer"*, he instructed. The last man out, Constable Cross, held his nose and muttered, *"It bloody reeks in there!"*. *"That was bloody Jeevesy"*, said Garvey. *"No it wasn't it was Mick Doyle, e's got form for that!"*, protested the affronted Constable Jeeves. *"Don't look at me"*, said an indignant Constable Doyle as they all made their to join the pre match parade.

"PARAADE, – P'RADE......SHON!", barked the dulcet tones of the Chief Inspector as he brought the large parade of bobbies to attention. He went on, *"Listen for your number and allocated position or patrol area"*. The parade was then informed as to what and where each officer would be performing his or her duties. As the Chief Inspector was speaking, someone in the ranks broke wind and the loud rasping sound could be clearly heard all over the parade. Someone was heard to say, *"Poooer, you dirty bastard!"*. The immediate area around the perpetrator fell about with hysterical laughter, policewomen were giggling uncontrollably! *"QUIET!"*, barked the Chief Inspector but the mirth continued with stifled giggling and tittering. Eventually normality returned to proceedings until finally the parade was dismissed, with stinging comments as to the maturity and dignity of those who considered themselves police officers. After being told to 'Fall Out' the parade made for their individual areas.

As the Gay Marine walked along to his 'beat' area in Hudson Lane, he saw two youths wearing the home team's colours as they walked behind a lone Policewoman. One of them was emulating the sex act and was obscenely gesticulating to his mate. The other youth then spat on the Policewoman's back and a large white globule ran down the back of her tunic. She was completely unaware of anything untoward until the Gay Marine reached the two, grabbed each by their necks and slammed them both together. The two youths' heads collided violently, drawing blood from the nose of one.

The two were too surprised to offer resistance and when all was revealed to the Policewoman, a recent transfer from the West Mids force, the two 'unfortunate' youths were arrested. *"What yer lockin' us up for, we were only messin'"*, protested Danny Gorman. His mate, Peter Parkhouse, wiped his bloody nose on the back of his hand and said, *"I'm gonna report you for Police brutality"*. The Gay Marine snapped, *"Good, yer'll get yer chance then, cos you're gonna end up in Angel Street before the day's out"*. *"Wha'for?"*, asked bloody nose. *"Well, seein' as you've both been drinkin', drunk an' disorderly and assault on the Police lady, 'ow's that for starters?"*, replied the Sergeant.

Sergeant Royle and the woman Constable then took the two youths to the detention room under the stand, from where they would later be conveyed to Angel Street. The Gay Marine had already administered 'summary justice' to them!

Later, the whistle blew to signify the start of the game. Sergeant Royle and his section patrolled the inside of the ground looking for any contraventions of the law, and at the same time, watching the first division clash!

By the time that the second half of the game had commenced, Detectives Walker and Wainwright had ensured that all Police personnel inside, and outside the ground, were aware of the gang from down South with their yellow plastic carrier bags with the red 'Shoportunity' logo of Warbreckside's biggest store, who were mingling with the crowds.

The second half was more exciting. Randy and his

colleague, Ronnie, were enjoying the game immensely, but not to the detriment of their observations. Although the whole of the gang could not be monitored at once, hopefully, other colleagues were watching the others wherever they were 'operating'. The two split up and kept those they considered to be most suspicious under close scrutiny. Randy was near a tall heavily tattooed youth wearing a red and white woollen 'bobble' hat, red and white scarf and red shirt. He wore a 'bum' bag and held a yellow, 'Shoportunity' bag (which appeared to be empty), down at his side.

Suddenly the crowd gave a deafening roar and surged forward when the away team attacked the home goal and scored. The away supporters cheered and chanted deliriously. They jumped up and down with ecstasy at their teams' sudden lead. As Randy watched the youth, he pretended to stumble and be carried forward by the crowds' momentum. He placed his hands on a man in front of him purporting to steady himself and then deftly slid his hand into the unsuspecting man's pocket. The youth's hand was in and out in a flash, but not before Randy saw a wallet being quickly transferred into the 'bum' bag of a female accomplice nearby. Randy watched as this procedure was repeated a number of times, all of the unsuspecting victims were the couples' fellow, London supporters. Finally Randy managed to attract Ronnie's attention and signalled for him to join him. Further assistance was summoned and the two detectives were joined by other colleagues, some of whom were uniformed officers The despicable couple were arrested and taken to the detention room where they were thoroughly searched.

Each search was very enlightening!

The Policewoman who searched the female recovered a number of wallets, purses, watches, cash and cash cards. Many of the wallets contained return tickets to London. Each was interviewed at length separately and the female, Caterina Sonya Daul, from Wandsworth, London, admitted having stolen some of the items, but most were stolen by her partner in crime, Malcolm Founds, also from Wandsworth, who then handed the stolen items to her.

Daul was on the run from Holloway Prison, having failed to

return from home leave four months ago. She was serving a term of three years imprisonment for an offence of 'Conspiracy to Rob'. Founds had a long record for theft, robbery and violence, and was presently on bail to Horseferry Magistrates' Court, London, for an offence of theft. Substantial enquiries would have to be made with regard to many other similar outstanding offences before the two could be returned southwards.

Quite by chance, two more of the gang were apprehended separately by two of the Gay Marine's officers. Constable Doyle popped into the Gents' toilet near the main stand to relieve himself and in doing so disturbed Ted Lacey from Streatham, as he was transferring wallets from his carrier bag into his 'bum' bag. Nearby Constable Garvey caught Doreen Tate, who hailed from Brixton, as she removed a purse from the coat pocket of a woman supporter in front of her.

Constable Doyle had to run the gauntlet of the crowd and asked a fellow Constable, (Dennis Hunter, no less!) to accompany him and his prisoner to the detention room, *"Just in case!"*. Constable Hunter refused, informing young Doyle, *"I can't, I'm not supposed to leave the players' entrance!"*, which puzzled Constable Doyle as they were among the crowds near the tea stall! Constable Doyle eventually managed to incarcerate his prisoner in the ground's detention room without incident.

While in the detention room, the Gay Marine visited his officers to congratulate them on their success in apprehending such low life. *"Well done lads, I'm proud of yer!"*, said Sergeant Royle with sincerity. Later, Constable Doyle casually mentioned to Detectives Walker and Wainwright, about a colleague refusing assistance when he asked for it. Once the two had realised that the bobby was Dennis Hunter from Headquarters, they nearly exploded. *"I'll make sure the Gay Marine gets to know about this"*, said Ronnie. *"He'll have a bloody fit when he finds out"*, confirmed Randy. The two then explained to their uniformed colleague the reason for their intense dislike for the Headquarters bobby.

Later, when Tommo had put the Carrier to bed and the lads were sorting themselves out, Micky Doyle asked Sergeant Royle, *"Can you leave my book please Sarje, it's not made up yet with me lockin' up at the match?".* The Gay Marine replied, *"'Course I can Mick, you did bloody well nailing that thievin' bastard, well done!".* Turning to the others he said, *"Right lads, it's just on seven. Yer not off officially 'til eight, but seein' as you've 'ad no scoff, you can 'ave yer scoff time now, off you pop!".* The section thanked the Sergeant in unison and left for a well earned pint. The Gay Marine would no doubt join them as soon as he completed the day's paperwork.

It wasn't until many days later that Sergeant Royle was made aware of Constable Dennis Hunter's acute 'neglect of duty'. The Gay Marine rang Hunter at his departmental 'hidey hole' at Headquarters. He made it very plain to Hunter that he was seriously considering having him put on paper for refusing a fellow officer assistance when so requested. Hunter was terrified, he envisaged his nine to five day job evaporating before him. Even worse was the thought of the possibility of having to walk the streets where angry men shout naughty words at you, or someone may ask you to make a decision, or sort out a problem.

All these nasty thoughts terrified Hunter. He bleated as to how he was told not to leave the players' entrance by one of the bosses. *"Which Boss?",* asked the angry Sergeant. *"I forget now",* whined Hunter. *"Well let me tell you this",* went on the Gay Marine, *"I've got a bloody good section of lads, and girls, and there isn't one that would refuse a colleague assistance. You lot down there in yer ivory towers aven't a clue what real policin's about."*

The Sergeant went on to lecture Hunter as to how it was wrong for people like him to be allowed to claim overtime for working matches when his men had to have match duties incorporated into their shifts, to eliminate them having to be paid overtime. The Gay Marine could tell, even over the telephone, that Hunter was very apprehensive as to what the Sergeant might do so the Sergeant finally bluffed with the threat, *"Well you forget to work overtime at the matches, an' I'll forget to pursue the 'neglect of duty' allegation!".*

The Gay Marine knew that Hunter would be too terrified of getting a stain on his sheet to chance calling his bluff, and he sure as hell didn't want to see Hunter posing around the ground as a useless ornament in his moth-eaten uniform. *"Okay Sarje, I'm sorry about the other day with your bobby"*. The Gay Marine just grunted, *"Right, that's it then"*, and replaced the receiver. At the other end was a very relieved Constable Hunter. Nobody knew what had taken place between Hunter and the Gay Marine, but Hunter didn't intend to work the matches again!

Preference, and Prejudice

The night had so far been quiet and uneventful as Constable Garvey patrolled his beat along Railway Road adjacent to the waste land which separated him from the nearby railway line and signal box which governed the Commerce Street Station approaches. The only sound to disturb the night's tranquillity was the occasional clanking and banging as a locomotive shunted a line of wagons from one place to another. The officer was making his way to Druids Hotel, the section's tea speck, for an early morning mug of tea with the hotel's night staff.

As Paul passed the waste land which was thick with dense undergrowth, brambles, bushes and trees, some of which stood like silhouetted sentinels against the sodium-lit orange coloured sky in the background. He shuddered at what those same bushes had hidden in the not too distant past. The officer remembered vividly how he and his colleagues had combed the area, sometimes on their hands and knees, in search of clues after the body of little Wendy Lowe had been dumped there after her life had so ruthlessly taken from her by a perverted sex fiend. Thankfully the person responsible was apprehended and brought to book before he could strike again.

Constable Garvey was rudely snapped out of his complacent lethargy when a cat suddenly burst out of the undergrowth, screeching loudly as it was pursued by another angry and hostile feline, the two cats shot across his path and vanished down a nearby entry on the opposite side of the road. *"Jeeesus Christ!"*, exclaimed Paul, glad that there was nobody about to witness his temporary humiliation as he nearly jumped out of his skin! Paul

49

didn't believe in ghosts but he was certainly glad to get past that bloody waste land!

Paul continued to make his way towards Druids and as he did so he thought about his recent (second) application to join his plain clothes colleagues in the CID. A recent item in Chief Constables orders had invited applications for a place on a CID course which would commence shortly. He had still not received any acknowledgement to his first application, so, on the advice of his sergeant, the Gay Marine, he had applied again. Constable Garvey had always held aspirations of becoming a detective since joining the force. He was also studying very hard for his sergeant's exam. Constable Garvey had been commended on two occasions for his bravery and initiative. He had also been seriously injured in a house fire after he had entered the burning building on being (wrongly) informed that children were trapped. Due to his horrific injuries, which almost cost him his life, and his career, he received a Chief Constable's commendation. Paul sincerely hoped that these facts, together with a strong recommendation from his Sergeant, would assist his application for the CID.

Also on the section was a fellow officer, a fairly recent addition who also wished to leave the ranks of her uniformed colleagues for those of the Criminal Investigation Department. Policewoman Malumba Adikki had less than a third of Constable Garvey's eight year service but already she seemed destined for greater things.

She had already served in the Community Relations Department, where she flew a desk, had been posted to Recruitment and was a member of the ladies' police hockey first team side, a very substantial accolade! The latter did not please the section Sergeant one bit! Sergeant Royle was constantly annoyed at having to grant her time off to play hockey when he could not allow other members of the section time off for more important reasons due to regular manpower shortages. Every time the Gay Marine went upstairs to complain about the policewoman being allowed time off for hockey, he was told curtly by the Chief Superintendent, "*Facilities will be granted for Policewoman Adikki to play hockey and that's final!*" Everyone sincerely hoped that the popular Constable Garvey's application for the CID would be successful as all considered that Paul had well and truly 'earned his spurs!'

Eventually Paul arrived at the large impressive hotel situate across the road from Commerce Street Station. He made his way round to the staff entrance and as he did so he noticed an immaculate split windscreen Morris Minor car parked among the other vehicles in the car park under the powerful security lights. The vehicle's green paint and shiny chrome were in showroom condition. The officer entered the gastronomic temple and followed the well-worn path to the kitchen.

There, to greet society's nocturnal protector was the hotel's ever present workaholic, Vic Dawson, the head Chef. "*Hiya Paul, come in*", greeted Vic, adding, "*D'yer take sugar? I can never remember*". He proceeded to pour a strong brew of tea from the big brown, metal teapot into a large mug bearing the British Rail logo. "*Two please Vic*", answered the grateful officer and went on, "*Whose is the Moggie Minor outside? Bloody 'ell it's mint!*" "*Dunno, it belongs to one of the guests I think*", replied the chef. Paul took a long, appreciative sip from his mug. Looking around he asked, "*Where's little Barry Murdoch?*", (Vic's second in command). Vic replied, "*He's tucked up in bed, bloody 'ell Paul some of us 'ave to sleep yer know!*" The two sat and chatted. "*D'yer do much during the night?*", asked Paul. "*Oh yes*", answered Vic and went on, "*Mind you, it depends on the trains and if there's a big match on. Whether there's a lot in or not, you'll always get someone ringin' down for somethin', whatever the hour*".

Vic went on to inform the Constable that his Sergeant had been in earlier with the coloured policewoman. "*I don't wanna be awful but she's a snobby bitch Paul, she looks at yer as if yer bloody muck*", said the chef. "*Why? What's she done?*", asked Constable Garvey. "*It's not what she's done, it's just her attitude, like she's too good for the likes of me 'cos I'm only a chef*", complained Vic. Paul knew exactly what Vic meant. Everyone on the section thought the same as Vic but nobody would say anything because the question of racial prejudice would raise its ugly head. The Gay Marine had already been warned about chastising her when he rebuked her for deserting an already

51

depleted section due to sickness, to play hockey. It mattered not that the question of colour did not come into it, the section was short and Sergeant Royle didn't agree with Adikki being granted time off for sport. Superintendent Gilmore dismissed the Sergeant, and his logic, out of hand.

The Chef, Vic Dawson, was a very decent chap who not only always looked after the bobby, no matter how busy he was. Even when off duty officers went to Druids for a meal with their wives or friends, he would always ensure that they were well looked after. Constable Garvey was annoyed that Vic should feel insulted, especially by someone who was a comparative newcomer. Surely, thought Paul, the Gay Marine would have noticed her behaviour and 'had a word' with her. Paul would not comment however, as the job must 'close ranks'. He would however, pass on the chef's sentiments to Sergeant Royle when the opportunity presented itself. *"Anyone else bin' in?"*, asked Paul. *"Yeah, Mule Train was in earlier, other than that it's bin' quiet"*, informed Vic as he rose to replenish the big brown pot with yet another brew.

"Chalky White the porter and 'Ronnie' (Veronica, the voluptuous waitress and 'intimate' friend of many Angel Street officers) Wade'll be in in a minute, they're both on early today", said Vic as he ensured a forthcoming brew for all. *"Oh right, I'll stay for another brew then"*, said Paul with enthusiasm. It wasn't so much the tea that was now the source of Constable Garvey's detention. It was the thought of seeing Veronica! One or two of the lads at Angel Street had had their wicked way with Ronnie! She was well known as being very 'sociable' and 'obliging' to members of the Constabulary!

Minutes later the little figure of Chalky White, the bald-headed porter, entered the kitchen. He rubbed his hands and after nodding a greeting to Constable Garvey he asked his colleague, *"Oooh, where's that bloody tea Vic?, I'm gasping"*. Vic duly obliged and replenished Paul's mug also, again asking, *"Yer take sugar don't yer Paul?"*. Paul grinned and replied, *"Bloody 'ell Vic, it's only two minutes since you asked me, two please!"* Vic grinned and said, *"Bloody 'ell Paul, it's the long hours, me 'ead's goin', I'm crackin' up!"*. The three sat and talked about this and that as they consumed their nectar.

Suddenly there was one almighty crash. The three jumped with fright, Vic spilled the contents of his mug down the front of his white jacket leaving a deep brown stain and burning his groin. Vic's mug fell to the tiled floor and smashed into a thousand pieces. "*I bloody near shit me'self then*", said Chalky who also emptied some of his tea down himself. The three turned to see Veronica, "*Friggin 'ell!*", exclaimed the equally startled woman as she bent down to retrieve a large saucepan and its lid which she had knocked from its stand as she entered the kitchen and caught the handle with her arm. The three men gawped lustfully as Ronnie bent down with her back to the trio, exposing her smoke blue panties and bare legs as her short skirt rode up her ample thighs. Constable Garvey crossed his legs as he felt things move in his 'embarrassment' area, he'd have to remain seated for now! He thought to himself 'no bloody wonder most of Angel Street are after her'.

Returning the pan to its original position, Ronnie turned and joined the trio. She wore a white blouse, the top four buttons of which were undone revealing the deep cleavage between her large breasts. Even though there were pockets in the garment and a flimsy bra underneath, these failed to conceal the thimble like protrusions of her nipples. Dangling down each side from her collar was the black 'dickie bow' tie which Ronnie would tie when she later donned her stockings prior to going on duty.

"*Sorry about that fellas, aren't I a silly cow? Didn't see the bloody thing!*", said Ronnie as she poured herself a cup of tea into one of the hotel's crested cups. She then sat on a large box of tinned beans next to Paul. As she did so up went her skirt again revealing those luscious thighs. Thoughts of Constable Garvey's CID application and forthcoming Sergeant's exam were temporarily relegated to the back boiler as the officer missed his mouth and spilled his tea down his tunic due to his ogling. "*How's things at Angel Street Paul?*", asked Ronnie. Paul shrugged his shoulders and replied, "*Nothin' much doin' Ron, nuthin' from the serious rumour squad either I'm afraid*". Veronica then asked Paul, "*Who's that coloured girl at your station? She's a snotty bitch!*". "*I've just bin tellin' 'im about 'er, she was in 'ere with Sergeant Royle earlier*", added Vic. "*Well she's certainly not very friendly that's for sure"*, continued Veronica. More idle chat and tea were consumed and eventually Constable Garvey informed all he would have to resume his beat. As he was leaving Veronica said, *"I've got to go an' get ready so I'll walk to the door with you"*. Paul bade farewell to Vic and Chalky and thanked Vic profusely for the tea. *"No problem Paul, any time!"*, replied Vic. Paul then made his way through to the car park accompanied by Veronica.

Paul and Veronica both stood in the doorway of the staff entrance and it was obvious to Paul that Ronnie wanted to say something. *"What do you do of an evening when you're off duty Paul?"*, asked Ronnie. Paul's mind ran riot! He wondered what was to follow such a leading question. He thought to himself, 'surely she's not 'sussin' me out. *"Well, I'm studyin' for exams at the moment"*, he answered. The conversation continued and Ronnie ascertained that Paul sometimes liked to go out into the country to do a spot of trout fishing from some secluded river bank. *"When are you going again?"*, asked Ronnie. *"Dunno, a couple of weeks I suppose"*, said Paul. *"Do you fancy some company next time you go if I get the day off as well?"*, asked Veronica, keen to share a day out in the remote reaches of an angler's Paradise with the handsome young bobby. *"Certainly Ron, I'll sort it out and let you know when"*, said a very enthusiastic Constable Garvey. Paul couldn't believe his luck, he would certainly keep his mouth shut back at the station!

Constable Garvey duly informed The Gay Marine of the dissenting comments made by 'members of the public' concerning Policewoman Adikki.

Days later Constable Barry 'Plums' Smith was out on mobile patrol in company with Policewoman Adikki when they were sent to a domestic dispute in Dalton Avenue. The two arrived at the run down council semi and were greeted by a pretty little ten year old coloured girl sporting neat pigtails each secured by a red ribbon. The girl was sobbing uncontrollably. *"What on earth's the matter Sweetheart?"*, asked Plums as he lifted the thumb sucking child up into his arms. *"Me dad's hittin' me mam in ther"*, sobbed the child pointing to the house with her other hand. *"Okay love, don't cry, let's go and sort things out eh?"*, consoled Plums. He put the child down and asked his colleague to look after her while he went to see what was going on. Plums walked round to the back door, following the sound of breaking crockery and a female's screams. The door was open and the officer entered. On doing so Plums saw a well-built, coloured man holding the long blonde hair of a white woman with one hand while he was striking her in the face with his other hand. Plums dived in and separated the two warring factions and ascertained that the lady was the little coloured child's mother, and wife of her assailant. The man turned on Plums and shouted with a venom, *"Who axed you here man?"*, then, turning to his wife he shouted, *"Did you call the man?"*, *"No, no, no I didn't"*, screamed the woman hysterically. The lady's nose was bleeding. Plums grabbed the man and snarled, *"I can smell ale on your breath, come outside, I want a word with you"*.

The man, Ignacious Mandella, cockily followed the officer outside. Once outside Plums took his arm and said, *"Let's talk in private!"* then escorted Mandella out to the police car. *"Just get in the back for a minute"*, directed Plums. Mandella in his ignorance climbed into the back of the vehicle for what he thought was 'a chat with the policeman'! Plums then got into the front of the vehicle. He was joined by Policewoman Adikki as she sat in the front passenger seat and closed the door. *"Where's the little girl I asked you to mind?"*, asked Plums. WPC Adikki snapped, *"The child is with her mother, and what d'you think you going to do with him?"*, indicating the back seat passenger. *"I'm gonna lock 'im up for D an' D (Drunk and Disorderly) an' assault on the lady"*, said Plums. On hearing this the rear seat passenger once again became aggressive and attempted to get out of the vehicle via the locked rear doors. *"What you am takin me in for man? You ain' gonna take me nowhere man"*, shouted Mandella and tried to kick the back of Plums' seat. Matters were not helped by WPC Adikki informing her colleague that she intended to report him as he only took the course of action he did because the man was black. Instead of calming the situation, her remarks made matters worse as Mandella, thinking he had an ally became more abusive and renewed his attempts to get out of the vehicle.

Inevitably, some neighbours started to gather and Plums envisaged the matter getting out of hand. Fortunately, the area was free of racial tension of any kind among the residents of differing cultures on the estate. A tearful Mrs Mandella appeared and tapped on Constable Smith's window. Plums lowered his window, *"You stay in the house love an' I'll call to see you later"*, he said to the still distressed woman, who by now had been joined by her still distraught little girl, Nadine. *"Don't take 'im away sir, I know he hit me but I'll only get more when 'e gets 'ome later!"*, pleaded Mrs Mandella. Before Plums could reply, WPC Adikki leaned across him and informed her, *"It's alright Mrs Mandella, your husband's not going anywhere, he'll be in in a minute!"* The relieved woman thanked the policewoman saying, *"Oh thank you miss, we won't bother you again"*, then made her way back into the house with young Nadine, who, still sucking her thumb, asked, *"Are they takin' me dad away mum?"*. *"No love, they're just talking to 'im, e'll be alright now"*.

The die was cast, Plums, now that he had been compromised by his interfering colleague who had stolen his thunder, had no alternative but to let the obnoxious and inebriated Mandela leave the vehicle and return to the house. Plums got out of the vehicle and opened the rear door. He leaned in and gave Mandella one last warning. *"If we're called back because you've beat your wife up, you'll be locked up an' kept in custody 'til you appear in court, d'yer understand Mandella?"*. *"Yes boss"*, replied the relieved bully. Mandella was released and made his way back to the house. The neighbours, realising that there was no drama to be witnessed, dispersed and returned to their own homes.

As Plums drove off he relayed the outcome of the visit to Dalton Avenue, *"Scene visited, advice given, over!"* and his call was duly acknowledged and logged by Control. As he returned the microphone to its clip on the dashboard Plums mumbled, *"I'd send the buggers back then we wouldn't 'ave 'alf this bloody trouble!"* Unfortunately his comments were heard by his colleague who turned to him and snapped, *"What are you inferring? That all black people should be deported because they're black? How dare you!"* Plums turned to the angry policewoman and retorted, *"D'yer know what Malumba? You're about as useful as a chocolate fireguard, every time there's an incident involving a coloured person, you suddenly become their bloody mentor. It doesn't matter what it is they have done, you immediately take up their cause and not only*

56

compromise your bloody colleagues in the process, but inflame the bloody incident". "What are you trying to say?", snapped Adikki. "What I'm trying to say", replied Plums, "is that you're a bloody pain in the arse to work with an' you've got an attitude problem. In other words, no bugger wants ter know yer or work with yer, you're a bloody liability!" "I'm going to report you when we get back", informed the policewoman. "Feel free!", replied Plums, still smarting from the humiliating debacle regarding his dealings at the Mandella house. The two officers then made their way back to Angel Street in stony silence.

On their return, Plums filled in the vehicle log book and checked the oil, water and fuel levels before leaving the vehicle for his colleagues on the forthcoming shift. Policewoman Adikki made straight for Inspector Platt's office where she related the circumstances of the Mandella incident and the subsequent conversation in the Police car on their return into the sympathetic ear of 'Platt the prat'. At the conclusion of the policewoman's tale of woe, the Inspector was mortified. Such allegations were of such gravity that the Inspector noted every crucial word, then, after a sympathetic pat on the woman's shoulder he promised her that her complaint would be pursued with the utmost vigour. Platt then contacted the Complaints and Discipline Department after consulting Chief Superintendent Gilmour, who was equally horrified at the (alleged) conduct of one of his men.

In the meantime, knowing how things could turn out should Adikki carry out her threat and report matters, Plums made for his Sergeant and informed the Gay Marine of the circumstances of his and WPC Adikki's outing to the Mandellas'. Sergeant Royle listened sympathetically. When Plums had finished the recital of his and Adikki's little verbal altercation the Gay Marine sat and pondered. "Hmmmm!, I understand how yer feel", lisped the Sergeant, "But, yer led with yer chin there Plums, she's one dangerous little bastard". "Yer can say that again Sarje!", agreed Plums. The Gay Marine made his decision! "Right, deny everythin' d'yer hear? DON'T even admit it's daylight at noon. It's your word against 'ers". "Surely I'll 'ave to say somethin' Sarje, they'll know she 'asn't made it all up!"

The Sergeant thought some more. He had no intention of

allowing one of his most competent men to be thrown to the wolves for the sake of some go-getting and well got prodigy who the officer had correctly described as bloody useless. "*There's no doubt about it, she'd cause fuckin' mayhem in an empty church*", uttered the Gay Marine adding, "*If yer asked, just say you told her off, inside the Police car, for standing and doing nothing at a domestic, when she should 'ave bin more 'elpful in a potentially volatile situation. Then it'll look as is she's reported you for spite, but, get yer tale right, an' stick to it!*" Constable Smith tendered his deep gratitude to his very understanding Sergeant and awaited possible developments with trepidation. If Adikki had reported the matter to Platt, thought Plums, then it would surely go somewhere.

Plums was interviewed on a later date at great length by Inspector Platt, and later again by an officer from the force Complaints and Discipline Department. However, Plums emphatically stuck to his story and would not be moved or swayed from his version, that he reprimanded his colleague for standing idle at an incident, as any officer would in similar circumstances. Attempts by those who interviewed Constable Smith to substantiate the WPC's allegations were unsuccessful and led nowhere. Finally it was decided that as there were no other witnesses to substantiate Adikki's claim, the matter would not be pursued further. However, there was an outcome! Constable Smith was suddenly transferred from mobile patrols and posted to a foot beat.

Not long after the dust had settled over this little incident, Inspector Platt received another complaint from WPC Adikki. She complained that while dining upstairs in the canteen, one of her colleagues had asked her, "*Malumba, pass me a spear, er, I mean fork, please!*". Again, the officer concerned was interviewed by Platt, but the officer insisted that he asked his colleague to pass him a 'chair'. The officer pretended to be most affronted at such a suggestion that he was being racial. Again the matter went nowhere, but WPC Adikki was now being treated as a fracture by most of her colleagues. Her reputation as a troublemaker spread and all who worked with her did so with reluctance and apprehension.

To add further fuel to the anti 'Politically Correct' lobby,

Policewoman Malumba Adikki was selected for the advertised CID post ahead of more eligible colleagues who had applied, including the luckless Constable Paul Garvey. The disappointed Paul would now have to wait and hope that sometime in the future his prospects might be brighter.

Bad feeling, and many adverse comments regarding appeasement by the powers that be to some members of the force were rife among the Angel Street Division. One night the Gay Marine drew Constable Garvey to one side as the section stood at the bar enjoying a post afternoon shift pint. The Sergeant whispered into Garvey's ear, "*Listen son, you know why yer didn't get into the Jacks, I know why yer didn't get into the Jacks, an' the whole fuckin' division knows why yer didn't get into the Jacks, don't despair, your turn will come. I'll keep pluggin' for yer don't worry. Take my advice Paul, get yerself a sun tan before you apply next time!*"

At four thirty, one morning some weeks later, Constable Garvey pulled onto the Druids Hotel car park in his Volvo estate. He was taking advantage of a few days off and today he had arranged to take the lovely Veronica out for a day's fishing into the wild countryside of Wales. No sooner had he brought his car to a standstill than the figure of Veronica Wade, who lived at the hotel, emerged from the staff doorway. She wore tight, black trousers, a white cotton blouse and carried a green, wax jacket over her arm. She looked absolutely stunning! As she climbed into the front passenger seat of Paul's sturdy Volvo he remarked, "*Christ Ronnie, you look fantastic*". Veronica flickered her eyelids and replied, "*What, at this time of the morning? Thanks Paul, flattery will get you everywhere!*" Bloody hell, I sincerely hope so thought Paul in lustful anticipation. "*I've brought my jacket in case I feel cold*", informed Veronica. "*I can assure you Ron*", said Paul, "*if you do feel cold, you definitely will not need that jacket to warm you up!*". "*Oooh, sounds promising!*", teased Veronica as she patted Paul's knee.

The red estate made its way through the deserted and dirty streets of Warbreckside then out into the open countryside. Two hours later they passed the sign bearing the words 'Croeso y Cymru' (Welcome to Wales) above a red dragon. and entered

59

another world, 'the land of song'! To enhance matters, there wasn't a cloud in the sky as the big red sun appeared and started to climb its way up into the heavens.

Paul and Veronica meandered through the beautiful Welsh countryside and admired the breathtaking panoramic views. Leaving civilization behind they ventured among the deserted hills and valleys. Paul stopped and consulted his road atlas to ensure they were heading in the right direction. They continued on and eventually a sign appeared at the roadside bearing the names that Paul was looking for. *"What the hell does that say?"*, asked Veronica. *"It says 'Llyn Goch, Ynpysgod Brithyll', which means Red Lake, Trout Fishing!"*, translated the informative Paul proudly. *"Can you actually speak Welsh?"*, asked Ronnie, clearly impressed. *"Yes"*, answered Paul, *"I went to night school, or I should say 'ysgol nos', for two years to learn it"*.

The two drove down a narrow lane until they came to an unmarked and unsigned junction. *"It should be around here somewhere"*, mused Paul, *"I've only bin 'ere once before an' that was about two years ago"*, he muttered as he debated which direction to take. Just then an old man appeared. He was carrying a stick and was accompanied by a black and white sheepdog. Paul lowered his window and greeted the old man, *"Bore da, Sydych chi?"*, he asked. *"Da iawn, diolch"*, replied the old man. Paul went on to ask, *"Ble mae'r Llyn Goch?, D'chi nabod?"* (where is the Red Lake? D'you know?). The old man asked Paul where he had learned to speak Welsh so well and on being told that Paul had given two years of his spare time to attend night school, the old man was very impressed at the Englishmen's ability to speak such a difficult language. The old man not only proceeded to direct the couple to the lake, but also informed them as to the best spot to catch the biggest fish!

Paul sincerely thanked the old man then resumed their journey. As they drove through the narrow, hedge lined lanes Paul turned to Veronica and said, *"D'yer know, since I learned the language, it has certainly opened a few doors for me when I come here?"*. *"I bet it took a lot of learning as well didn't it?"*, asked Ronnie. *"I must admit, it was a bit difficult"*, agreed Paul modestly.

Paul meticulously followed the old man's instructions as to the route he should take and in a short time they arrived at a little clearing at the lakeside. Paul stopped the car and switched off the engine then he and Ronnie got out of the vehicle and both had a good stretch. There was utter peace and tranquillity. The only sound was the distant bleating of sheep as they foraged on the mountain sides.

Paul retrieved his glass fibre rod from the car and set it up ready for the day's fishing, and after selecting an appropriate, tempting fly, he then proceeded to spread the ground sheet and set out the contents of the wicker picnic basket ready to 'dine' later. Also present was a freezer box with some cans of 'liquid refreshment'! The next important job, was to set up and light the little primus stove and furnish the first cuppa of the day. *"Bloody hell Paul, you're certainly well organised aren't you?"* said Ronnie. *"Too right! There's nuthin' better than bein' out 'ere, especially now, with the added bonus of such a lovely lady for company"*, buttered Paul. *"I told you before Paul, flattery will get you everywhere"*, replied the appreciative Veronica. Paul grinned and said, with a glint in his eye, *"Will it now? I'll hold you to that!"*. Paul wondered just how much fishing would take place today!

During the course of the morning Paul caught a small roach then three reasonably large trout. He threw the former back but kept the three trout in the keep net. *"I'll keep the trout in the net to keep 'em alive 'til we go, then you can give them to Vic to cook for you, him and Barry"*, said Paul, hoping to impress with his selfless generosity! *"Thank you, but what about yourself?"*, asked Ronnie. *"If I get another, I'll 'ave that, if not, I'll keep one next time we come"*, said the sincerely hopeful Constable. *"Oh!, there is going to be a next time then?"*, asked Ronnie as she moved closer to her generous angler. Paul looked into his companion's eyes and said, *"Ronnie, you can come fishing with me anytime, or anywhere else for that matter, there's nothing I'd like more"*. *"Mmmmm!, is that so?"*, said Ronnie, pouting her lips provocatively.

With Ronnie being so intimately close, Paul eventually lay down his fishing rod and pulled Veronica down alongside him. Instinct made him look around to check that they were completely alone and not being observed. He lay on his back and Ronnie

61

kissed him passionately on the lips. In a very short time things gathered momentum. Paul removed his shirt, then off came Ronnie's blouse, quickly followed by her bra!

Nearly an hour later, the two lay naked and sweating profusely after a marathon orgy of mad, passionate and noisy lovemaking. Each lay there and then again embroiled themselves in each others' arms before the sheer efforts of their sexual activity caused them to fall asleep in the sunshine. Eventually, Ronnie awoke then gave Paul a shake. Paul grunted and opened his eyes. *"We've been asleep for nearly two hours"*, informed Ronnie. Even after what he had already so lustfully sampled Veronica's beautiful, full body, Paul couldn't take his eyes of her large firm breasts and the enticing neat little 'black triangle' below the bikini line, and thought how things had turned out to be so wonderful.

Eventually the two recovered their garments which had been scattered in all directions during their period of sexual frenzy, and got dressed, each lustfully helping the other to do so. When this was complete, Paul again ignited the little primus to provide yet another refreshing cup of tea, cold drinks later! The sandwiches were then consumed and Paul had a final attempt at catching trout number four. *"You will bring me again won't you?"*, asked Ronnie. *"I'd like to see you as often as I can"*, said Paul sincerely. He wondered however, how long it would be before her roving eye would spot someone else and relegate him from her passionate desires. Anyway, Paul was prepared to take on any competition and take his chances. Veronica was certainly worth fighting for he thought. *"Right then, next time we have a day out, I'll make the sandwiches seeing as you did them this time"*, said Ronnie. *"It's a deal"*, conceded Paul.

At the conclusion of their very pleasant and enjoyable day, after indulging in the 'ways of sin' just once more, Paul managed to land the elusive number four for himself. The tired, but very happy couple then made their home, stopping en-route for a meal at a little pub, the Acorn, among the wilds of the moors.

Finally Paul delivered Ronnie, and the three trout for the staff, to Druids. After a nightcap, and yet again another 'session', the greedy Paul left the hotel and made his way home, getting in just after midnight, at the conclusion of a very tiring day! Paul most certainly intended to maintain his relationship with Veronica, but, for how long?

The final day's uniform duty for Policewoman Malumba Adikki was nearing completion. Her 3pm to 11pm shift was almost over, just over an hour to go. Eleven o'clock was but an hour away, then the WPC was to start her new career as a Detective Constable. As she patrolled her beat past the Broken Spear pub, a notorious watering hole for the town's riff raff, little Tommy Whitehouse, the bookies' runner, staggered out into the street. He went to the wall by the door and, supporting himself with one hand on the wall, he proceeded to urinate in full view of passers by, including WPC Adikki, hiccuping and burping loudly as he did so. The Policewoman went to him and told him to behave and go home. *"'Ang on! Lesh finish me piss firsh!"*, he slurred. The officer didn't know Tommy. She again told him to behave and go home. *"Fuck off will yer, yer can see I'm pissin' can't yer?"*, he replied angrily.

By sheer chance, and good luck, Constable Garvey spotted his colleague and Whitehouse as he drove past on mobile patrol. Paul pulled over to the opposite pavement, alongside the two, and got out of his vehicle. He opened the rear door then joined his colleague, *"Throw the dirty little tyke in the back Malumba"*, he instructed. Whitehouse was very abusive and his remarks to the Policewoman included some that were racially motivated. The obnoxious and abusive drunk was staggering about and trying to break free from the lady officer's grip, his manhood still protruding from his wet and soiled trousers, for all to see. *"No, just take him home Paul"*, said WPC Adikki to her colleague's astonishment. *"You can't allow this little drunken bum to humiliate you like this in front of 'alf the bloody town"*, said Constable Garvey angrily. His female colleague however, could not be persuaded to take more positive action against the offending reveller. Paul didn't want to hear any more, he grabbed the hapless drunk and propelled him into the back of the Police car and locked the door. *"I'm not a bloody taxi Malumba, I'm takin' 'im in for D and D (Drunk and Disorderly), for the sake of the cloth, yer can't 'ave anyone taking the piss out of bobbies in front of everyone like that!"*, he snapped.

"That's okay Paul, you have 'im. I start my new job on Monday so I don't want to get involved with a smelly drunk", said a cocky WPC Adikki.

The still very abusive Whitehouse was still sounding off as to how he was being arrested for nothing and he started kicking at the door of the car. Fearing for the window, Paul opened the rear door to move the drunk around so he could be handcuffed. As Paul leaned into the vehicle Whitehouse suddenly was violently sick and vomited into Paul's face and down the front of his tunic. WPC Adikki was unable to be of any assistance as she was already sitting comfortably in the front of the vehicle!

As they drove back to Angel Street, Paul nearly wretched himself at the foul, offensive smell, emanating from his soiled uniform. Malumba sat there and it was only with considerable difficulty that she managed to prevent herself bursting out into hysterical laughter at the sight of her drenched colleague.

Later, when fully cleaned and changed, and his prisoner was safely incarcerated in the cells, Paul imbibed in a well earned pint in the club bar upstairs before making his way home (via Druids!). He was joined by Malumba Adikki, who ran the gauntlet of silence from some and caustic comments from others, as she paid for Paul's pint. *"Thanks for tonight Paul, I appreciated your timely arrival at the Broken Spear. Sorry about the giggling, I just couldn't help it"*. Paul eventually saw the funny side of it but not before he again administered a strong lecture on maintaining the dignity of the cloth. *"The job's 'ard enough without lettin' toe rags like Whitehouse demean the uniform in public!"*, he emphasised. *"Point taken Paul"*, conceded Malumba. Paul appreciated Malumba's comments and her buying him a pint. He looked at her then raised his glass and clinked it against hers and said, *"Good luck in the 'jacks'. Christ, first yer get the job I wanted, then I get covered in sick from your prisoner, who finishes up mine! I just can't win"*. After another drink, during which a number of snide remarks were passed by some present, the two officers left the building. However, Paul wasn't going home just yet!

Hazards of the occupation

It was getting on for ten o'clock and the Royal British Legion Club in Duke Street was full of the usual Saturday night revellers, bingo players and snooker enthusiasts. Phil Smedley was enjoying his game of snooker and was about to attempt to pocket the black ball and hopefully increase his lead over his opponent, his mate Alan Grisedale. Next door in the large hall, which incorporated the bar, a small stage and the dance floor, the muffled sounds of the bingo session could be heard. All was quiet except for the occasional whisper as those in the snooker room watched Phil, in anticipation of him potting the black.

Suddenly the door burst open with a crash and in staggered Chris Beddoes, a local dock foreman. Chris was well known for his aggression and acute lack of sobriety! Tonight was to be no exception. Beddoes failed to notice the one small step down into the room as he entered. It was obvious to those present that he was drunk. He stumbled, then losing his balance, he staggered forwards and fell into Phil at the table. In doing so he emptied the contents of his pint glass as it slipped from his hand and smashed onto the table, the beer forming a large, staining pool before it was absorbed into the green beige rendering the table useless for playing on. Phil miscued and rounded angrily on Beddoes, "*Why don't you piss off somewhere else yer drunken bastard, yer neither use nor fuckin' ornament!*".

Beddoes staggered to the nearby cue rack. Taking one from the rack he held it menacingly. Adopting an attacking pose he faced Smedley and slurred, "*Why don't yer fuckin' make me?*". Phil had returned his own cue to the rack as it was now obvious by the state of the table, that further play was completely out of the question.

"*C'mon shit'ead*", provoked Beddoes, and made to strike Smedley with the cue he held. Beddoes hadn't noticed Phil's mate Alan Grisedale (who was still in possession of his cue), move around the table to assist his opponent. Beddoes raised the cue above his head ready to strike Smedley with the thick end. Before he could complete the manoeuvre however, Grisedale's cue whacked Beddoes square on his right temple, flooring him instantly into an unconscious heap at the side of the table. Even though Beddoes was not the most popular of persons in the area, he did have some cronies and drinking partners. Unfortunately, some of those were present this evening!

Suddenly pandemonium broke out, nobody could say how it started or who started it, but in an instant of Beddoes being felled, all hell broke loose. Chairs were broken, cues smashed, the large piano in the corner was overturned and windows were shattered. Everybody appeared to be fighting everybody else. Others from the bar next door dived in and tried to restore order but finished up fighting in the melee instead. Blood, beer, splintered wood and broken glass was everywhere. The steward, Terry Anderson, sent for the Police and Ambulance, as already it was obvious that a number of people would require hospital treatment.

Receiving the call in the control room at Angel Street, Andrew Salisbury, who was also one of Angel Street's keen 'Specials', noted the contents of the steward's call. Andrew could clearly hear the mayhem and the sound of breaking furniture, together with hysterical screams in the background.

Attempting to put Mr Anderson at ease Andrew informed the steward, "*Mobiles en-route sir, they'll be there in a couple of minutes*". At the same time Andrew was contacting Ambulance control. In a calm and controlled voice Andrew then relayed over the air to all mobiles, "*Will mobiles make the British Legion, Duke Street? Large scale disturbance. Early report please. I repeat.....*", Andrew went on to repeat his transmission again. A number of patrols replied at once as each officer, his adrenalin flowing, made for the scene with haste. "*There's a number of patrols on at once, one at a time please.....over!"*, commanded Andrew.

First to arrive at the Legion was 'Mule' Train and his observer Vera Perry, the Red Onion. The sound of klaxons and sirens could be heard approaching from all directions. An ambulance arrived and its crew went inside where fighting was still going on. The Gay Marine arrived just as Mule and the Red Onion were struggling with an extremely violent youth they were ejecting from the premises. The Sergeant joined his two officers and the youth was unceremoniously thrown out onto the street. The three then returned inside the building to assist other colleagues who had arrived.

Eventually, after a number of arrests had been made, including the drunk and semi conscious Beddoes, the instigator of the evening's hostilities! Order was finally restored and the premises were cleared. Arrests were made for offences of assault, criminal damage, drunk and disorderly and other related offences. As the last of the prisoners were being taken off to Angel Street and the premises were now empty except for the staff and a couple of officers, Inspector Platt arrived. *"Everything under control Sergeant?"*, he asked. The Gay Marine looked at him with contempt at his late arrival and replied sarcastically, *"I think my officers have managed to quell the riot sir, but thanks for managin' to get 'ere anyway!"*. The Gay Marine's cynicism went over Platt's head and he replied, *"I had to finish the crime figures ready for the boss tomorrow, he wants them up to date first thing in the morning"*. *"Well the lads will certainly rest easy when I tell 'em that the statistics are up to date an' done sir, that's fer sure"*, commented the Gay Marine.

Suddenly WPC Perry tugged at Sergeant Royle's sleeve, *"Hey Sarje! There's Phil Grundy, he's hurt!"*, she exclaimed with concern. Constable Grundy had just appeared from round the side of the building. He was minus his cap, radio microphone and one of his epaulettes had been torn from the shoulder of his tunic. A cut above his eye was bleeding, as was his nose, the front of his shirt and tunic were heavily bloodstained. Phil's left arm was hanging limp and appeared deformed. Vera and the Sergeant rushed forward and grabbed the officer just as he was about to sink to his knees. *"Okay, we've gotcha Phil, take it easy son"*, said the Gay Marine. He instructed Vera to help him place the young officer into his car. *"I'll take him straight to the hospital, it'll be quicker that sendin' for an ambulance"*, he said. Inspector Platt asked, *"Is he alright Sarje?"*. The Gay Marine replied, *"Yes, he's okay sir, just a touch of migrane!"*. Constable Grundy was placed into the Sergeant's car and then conveyed to Warbreckside Infirmary.

The Gay Marine drove through the streets like a bat out of hell! Klaxon blaring, blue light flashing he deposited his wounded colleague at the Warbreckside Casualty Unit. During Constable Grundy's painful journey, the young officer managed to name the three persons responsible for the vicious attack on him. Sergeant Royle assured his officer that all three would very, very soon, be apprehended, of that there was no doubt!

Constable Grundy was examined and three stitches were inserted to close a cut above his left eye. An X-ray revealed a badly broken left arm, his nose was also broken. Phil was taken to theatre as an operation was necessary to repair and set his arm. Finally, all patched up, the broken bobby was transferred up to the wards to recover.

Even before Phil had opened his eyes as he came round from the anaesthetic, those responsible for his horrific injuries had been found and arrested. The three yobs, Andy Fisher, Michael Flynn and Terry Dowd, all with previous convictions for dishonesty and assault and all only in their late teens, had been charged with a number of grave offences and would be kept in custody for their sins, until their appearance before the court. The Gay Marine had remained behind after his section had gone off duty and assisted his night duty colleagues until the three who injured his officer so badly were finally apprehended.

It was five days before the doctors would allow Constable Grundy to be discharged. It would be some considerable time before the officer could even think of resuming his duties. The day after his discharge from hospital, Constable Grundy was sitting at home with his feet up and propped up with pillows as he read the morning paper. Phil's wife Denise had just brought in a tray of tea and toast for them both while all was still quiet before their little toddler Samantha, the little 'horror', came down to play, when their solitude would be shattered.

DING DONG!!, the sudden sound of the door bell's loud chimes startled the two. Denise rose and answered the front door. Phil heard a man's voice, then Denise said, *"Please, do come in won't you?"*. Almost immediately she returned, accompanied by a middle aged gentleman dressed in a smart grey suit, his grey hair meticulously groomed. *"Phil, this is Mister Whittaker"*, announced Denise and asked if he preferred tea or coffee. *"I'd love a coffee, one sugar please, if I may"*, asked Mister Whittaker politely.

Denise then disappeared to cater for their visitor's refreshment. Whittaker went to Phil and gently squeezed his good, right arm, *"Nigel Whittaker's the name, I'm from headquarters, Welfare. The reason I've called"*, said Nigel, *"apart from seeing how you are and to check if you need anything, is to see if you'd like to go to the Police Convalescent home down at Dansford for two or three weeks"*. Denise entered the room with Nigel's coffee. She removed her handbag and a copy of the TV Times from an armchair. *"Please sit down Mister Whittaker"* she said. *"Nigel's the name, it's okay, I'll pinch one of these if you don't mind then I can sit next to Phil an' it'll be easier to write"*, replied Whittaker as he removed a dining chair from under the nearby table. Sitting crossed legged with a writing pad on his knee, his coffee having been strategically placed nearby by for him by Denise, Nigel asked Phil what he thought of the idea. *"That sounds great"*, enthused Phil. *"It'll do you the world of good love"*, encouraged Denise.

"Right, I'll just take a few details, then I'll give you a form to take to your doctor. Get him to complete the appropriate sections for you, then return the form to me at Force Welfare, it's as simple as that", instructed Nigel. He went on to describe in detail the therapeutic advantages of such a stay and informed Phil that he would commence arrangements for the forthcoming period of convalescence on his return to the office. *"Should your wife wish to visit and stay for a day or two, that can also be arranged"*, added Nigel. *"Sounds good"*, said Phil, *"we'll see 'ow things go with baby sitters"*.

Mr Whittaker left, and as promised, completed the formalities for Phil's period of convalescence. Within three weeks of Phil sending in the completed medical form from his doctor, he received notification that he would be accommodated at the home for a period of three weeks, the letter also included the commencement date which was just over a week away. He would travel down by train and be collected at the station by the home's minibus.

Phil still suffered considerable pain and discomfort and his arm was still splinted and in a sling as he travelled the three hundred miles down to Dansford. After the long and uneventful journey, during which Phil enjoyed the varied scenic views of the countryside, the train finally pulled into Overchurch Station which almost sat on the resort's bustling sea front. One of the train's passengers, a kind old lady, took Phil's case after she saw him struggling to get from the train and down onto the platform. This didn't escape the eagle eye of Donald, the minibus driver from the home, who was scrutinising those that were leaving the train. The dapper little figure made straight for the pair as they neared the ticket collector at the end of the platform.

Donald sported a plastic identification card at his lapel which bore his photograph. Intercepting the old lady and Phil, and hoping he had guessed correctly, Donald asked, *"Excuse me sir, are you Mister Clayton, Mister Phillip Clayton, from Warbreckside?"*. *"Yes, that's correct, but how did you know?"*, confirmed and asked Phil. *"Well with respect sir, there aren't a lot who look as though they've been knocked about like you have, and I am from the convalescent home to collect a patient"*, and touching the identity disc he went on, *"I'm Donald, the driver and general dogsbody"*. Turning to the lady he said, *"Here, let me take your cases"*. *"Oh, we're not together, I just helped the gentleman with his case"*, said the kind lady.

Donald informed the lady that he was making for the Police Convalescent home and would be travelling along the scenic sea front. The lady was asked where it was she was heading for and although her destination was slightly off Donald's route, he kindly offered to take her to Puffin Walk, her ultimate destination, and her home. The grateful lady was taken and deposited then Phil was treated to a slow ride along the sea front and given a conducted tour through the wonderful holiday town of Dansford.

Eventually they arrived at the Home and there standing at the top of the steps waiting to greet them was Miss Shuttleworth the Matron and her uniformed colleague, Sister Dorothy Lee. The Matron looked absolutely fearsome. She had a deep frown which caused her thick eyebrows to meet in the middle of her wrinkled forehead. Her facial expression showed a scowl and by the look of her Phil wondered if he'd have to raise his hand to ask, when he needed to go to the toilet.

However, looks could be very deceptive. Matron came down the steps to the pavement and greeted him with a very warm welcome. She was joined by the equally charming Sister. Matron clicked her fingers and Donald picked up Phil's case. "*Room five one nine!*", said Matron. Donald then disappeared into the building with the case. Matron and Sister then returned up the steps. Phil was instructed by Sister to follow Matron into her office, to be formally received, after which he was to make along to the surgery for Sister to complete other formalities.

Phil entered Matron's oak panelled office which overlooked the sea and was asked to sit down and make himself comfortable while Matron, sitting at her large desk, went on to explain the 'rules of the house' together with all the dos and don'ts! "*All patients must be in by ten forty five pm and under no circumstances whatsoever will alcohol be allowed on the premises*", droned the Matron. "*If you wish to bring a guest into the home, make sure he or she is booked in and they must be out of here by nine pm*", Phil was informed. "*Please keep quiet as there are some serious, even terminally ill patients here, and remember at all times, you are a Police Officer, and we expect you to behave as such*". Finally, Phil was given his last instructions, "*Do not use the lifts whilst wearing wet shoes or clothing, also we have a no smoking policy here as well*", said Matron and went on to inform him of the dire consequences which would befall anyone who disregarded the rules of the house, especially any blatant infringements with regard to alcohol or breaking curfew times.

Phil was told that there had been one or two cases where

officers had been 'RTU'd (returned to their force forthwith) for their sins. At last Phil was allowed to go and see Sister along the corridor. On reaching the surgery door, which was closed, Phil knocked and sought admittance. The sound of muffled voices from within told him to sit on one of the chairs near the door and wait until he was summoned.

Eventually the door was opened and Phil was greeted by the friendly Sister. *"Come in and sit down, sorry about that, I was on the 'phone"*, explained Sister. A nearby radio with its volume turned down low, was switched off and Sister explained that she would take a few details before weighing Phil and taking his blood pressure. Before her, lying open in her desk, was Phil's file containing his medical notes. Phil tried to read them but gave up as they were upside down to him.

After a few questions and answers, Sister said, *"Right! You prefer Phil not Phillip then?"*, then went on to ask him to unbutton his jacket whilst she retrieved his right arm from out of the garment. *"I just want to check your blood pressure before I weigh you"*, she said. She rolled Phil's right sleeve up above his elbow then applied the apparatus and commenced her check. Mission completed and Sister said, *"That's fine"*, she then handed Phil a glass jar and said, *"Do you think you could pop in there (indicating a small ante room toilet) and provide me with a sample please Phil?"*. She then replaced the blood pressure apparatus (the sphygnamometer) back into its box and proceeded to scrutinise the papers concerning Phil's injuries, treatment and medication, together with eventual physiotherapy. An embarrassed Phil, having duly obliged the Sister by supplying a specimen of urine, had difficulty trying to stop! He handed Sister the jar, hoping she wouldn't notice the fact that he had dribbled down the front of his trousers and onto his shoes. Sister Lee thanked Phil and informed him, *"You'll be seeing the doctor, Doctor Prout, in the morning, until you have seen him you will not be able to go out"*. *"That's okay, no problem Sister"*, replied Phil. Sister was amazed. *"Gosh that's a change, most bobbies get very annoyed because they have to stay in until he allows them out"*, she remarked. *"It doesn't bother me Sister, honest!"*, said Phil.

Sister Lee accompanied Phil up to his room on the fifth floor and assisted him to unpack and change. When this was done she left him to make his own way down to the lounge and acquaint himself to those of his fellow patients who were not sitting in the sun outside the home's beach hut, opposite the convalescent home.

As the afternoon wore on, those who had been relaxing in their deck chairs at the beach hut, taking advantage of the warm sun, returned slowly, drifting in one by one. As each entered the lounge to 'see what was doing', before making to their rooms to prepare for dinner, those who spotted the newcomer went to Phil and introduced themselves. Some patients included 'premature' pensioners, those who had been forced to leave the service through ill health or injury. Others had retired many years ago at the conclusion of their long and eventful careers.

One poor girl in her early twenties, was confined to a wheelchair due to terminal illness. However, she still managed to smile at Phil when she caught his eye. She propelled herself over to him and again gave a wonderful smile. She was a beautiful young woman but the wan look of her drawn face gave away the fact that she was a very sick young lady. *"Hello, my name's Hazel, I'm......, or I was, a probationer from Cumbashire Constabulary, can't see me going back now though, anyway what's your name?"*, she asked impishly. Phil took to her in an instant and hoped he reciprocated her warmth and friendliness. Phil extended his hand and took hold of Hazel's cold hand at the end of her thin white delicate arm. *"Phil Clayton, Warbreckside"*, he announced, embarrassed at his own temporary disability in comparison to hers. *"What have you done to your poor arm and face? Have you been in a motorbike accident or something?"*, asked the nosey but sympathetic Hazel. *"No, it took three drunken pieces of pond life in their Doc Martens to do this, at the back of a pub one Saturday night"*, informed Phil.

Referring to herself Hazel said bravely *"I've got the big C. The doctors think my tumour was caused by a kick in the stomach when I was beaten up by two shoplifters I was trying to hang on to. I know it's terminal, but they, the doctors, keep trying to kid me that things might improve. They must think I'm stupid!"*. Christ she's got guts thought Phil, not knowing what to say. The two chatted and everyone who entered the room made a fuss of the young policewoman. It was obvious to Phil that she was the jewel in the crown among the patients and staff here at the home. Others present in the lounge, after rummaging among various magazines that were lying around, decided it was time to prepare for dinner and left the room.

"C'mon Phillip, let's go down and wait for the bell", suggested the mischievous wheelchair pilot, knowing full well it was absolutely taboo to hang around outside the dining hall before the bell rang, adding, *"We'll be first in for dinner then!"*. The two squeezed into the confines of the lift and Hazel pressed the button to taken them down to the ground floor. *"We'll go over the road after you've seen the doctor tomorrow an' I'll show you our beach hut"*, promised Phil's new mentor.

Hazel explained that patients must not enter the dining hall before the bell under any circumstances, as to do so would invoke more than Matron's wrath. *"You're not to hang around in the foyer either"*, said Hazel, adding, to dispel any apprehension Phil might have, *"We'll be alright though, so long as Matron doesn't catch us!"*. The two left the lift and Phil pushed Hazel along until they reached the dining hall. They stood chatting opposite a little counter with its shutters down. This served as a little shop for the sale of stamps, sweets, cards and a few souvenirs during the mornings.

Suddenly, like a peel of unexpected thunder, Matron's booming voice demanded, *"What, may I ask, are you doing here Miss Tunstall, and you Mister Clayton?"*. Before Hazel had time to think of an excuse, Phil replied, *"I was just calling to ask you if I could push Miss Tunstall round the block after dinner Matron!"*. Miss Shuttleworth glared at Phil and snapped, *"ALL new arrivals must remain inside the home until they have been seen by the doctor, and that includes you Mister Clayton"*, then turning to Hazel, Matron asked, *"And what's your excuse for hanging round down here young lady?"*. Hazel replied wryly, *"I'm on my way to Sister for an aspirin, I've got a headache!"*. Due to Hazel's impish cheek in implying that an aspirin would assist or cure her ills, Matron couldn't help but be impressed, and totally amused but felt a lump in her throat at the brave girl's sarcasm. Matron grinned and said, "*Aspirin indeed, you cheeky bugger!*". Before any further admonishment could be administered to the two heinous, perpetrators of the pre-dinner bell parade, the loud, continual clanging of the dinner bell announced to all that it was dinner time, as well as well as dislodging the wax in Phil's ears.

Phil and Hazel entered the large dining hall. Its five highly polished Mahogany tables resplendent with their silverware and cutlery. Hazel winked at Phil and said, "*See you later*", then propelled herself to her place at table B, the second table in the room. A smartly dressed middle aged steward indicated to Phil which was his place at table D. The steward approached Phil and lisped in a very effeminate voice, his hands held tightly together under his chin, head slightly tilted to one side, "*You mustn't sit down 'til we've had grace!*", then he minced away to join his two colleagues who were stood chatting at the serving hatch.

One of them wiped his spectacles with a tissue, which he then replaced into his top pocket and donned his glasses, the other stood holding his left elbow in the palm of his right hand while the little finger of his left hand was poking into his mouth. It was obvious that all three stewards were gay, a fact which was very soon confirmed to Phil by his fellow patients. However, each steward, Rupert, who had taken the trouble to enlighten him about not sitting down before grace, and his two colleagues Michael and Norman, were very well liked by all of the staff and patients alike.

Phil and two other new arrivals were asked to stand during the meal and introduce themselves to all present. Things were very pleasant there and all at the home wanted for nothing. The following day, seeing the doctor and completing the remaining formalities consumed very little time and Phil was then allowed to 'play out'.

Time flew by and Phil spent a lot of time in the company of Hazel who, despite her condition, was partial to setting up or organising the occasional prank. Phil was proud to have befriended such a nice person. Unfortunately Hazel's health deteriorated rapidly after the first week he was there. He had become quite close to Hazel and each had promised to keep in touch once they had left Dansford.

As is par for the course, there was a young officer from the Metropolitan Police who cared not for others. He was frequently being rebuked by staff and his co-patients alike for being rowdy, playing his radio very loud to the annoyance of those trying to rest, switching channels while people were watching a programme and generally being a nuisance by misbehaving. An officer from the Birmingham force grabbed him one day and said, *"I don't know who the hell you think you are, but there's other people here as well as yourself, which force are yer from?"*. The officer cockily replied, *"The Met, it's magic!"* Brummie curtly informed him, *"That's certainly true, I've worked with pricks like you from the Met. When you lot are about, everything disappears!"*, and ended by adding, *"I've bin longer on a bloody message then you've got service!"*.

Phil's arm took its time healing but welfare were definitely right, the atmosphere itself, not to mention the wonderful and caring staff were certainly therapeutic down at Dansford. Poor Hazel continued to give cause for concern and was eventually transferred to a hospice near to her home in Luckton.

His beneficial stay now over, Constable Clayton returned home to the welcoming arms of his wife and daughter Samantha. Slowly but surely Phil's arm grew stronger as he climbed his way back to fitness. Two weeks after returning home, Phil decided to ring and see how his friend Hazel was getting along. He rooted for the piece of paper on which Hazel had scribbled her number. He had rang once or twice but as yet he hadn't been able to get any answer. Today however, success! A woman's voice, not Hazel's, answered and said, *"Double three four two, Missus Tunstall speaking"*. *"Oh hello, it's Phil Clayton here, I'm ringing............"*, he was interrupted by the lady at the other end of the line. *"Oh you're Phillip, the boy from the convalescent home at Dansford? I'm Hazel's mother Nora. Hazel never stopped talking about you Phillip. She insisted that you enhanced her stay considerably, I'm so grateful to you.................!"*, the line went quiet. Phil wondered if they had been cut off. *"Hello! Hello, Mrs Tunstall are you there?"*, he asked. He heard something, like a sniff, a sob, then a cough, *"Ahem!, I er, I, I'm so sorry Phillip, I'm afraid I have to tell you that Hazel, my lovely daughter, passed away yesterday morning. Please, I know Hazel had your number but could you give it to me again please and I will ring you back"*. Phil was choked. He did what he was asked and Mrs Tunstall said, *"Please forgive me. I'm sorry, I will stay in touch and inform you of arrangements"*. Then, CLICK, the 'phone went dead.

Minutes later Denise entered the room saying, *"D'you know what this little madam has just done?............"* then broke off when she witnessed the very rare sight of her husband dabbing tears from his eyes. *"............Oh Phil, what on earth's the matter? Is it your arm love? I'll go and get you some pain killers"*, she said most concerned at her husband's distress. Phil looked up at his wife, who was just a little older than Hazel's twenty two years. His red rimmed eyes glistening as tears continued to trickle down his cheeks.

"No, no, It's worse than that. Hazel, the girl at the home, she died yesterday", said a very choked, and angry Phil. *"The bloody crap and low life who live 'til they're eighty, an' a lovely girl like her dies at twenty two years of bloody age, and through some bastard kickin' hell out of her who'll never have to answer for it"*, he seethed. Denise was also upset at the news, as Phil had been praising Hazel to high heaven for her courageous efforts, ever since he had returned from Dansford, so much had he been impressed by her.

Mrs Tunstall eventually regained her composure and telephoned back with her sincere apologies. It was Denise who answered and had a lengthy chat with the inconsolable mother. Phil was summoned to the phone and he and Mrs Tunstall spoke for some time. Phil informed Mrs Tunstall that he and Denise would attend Hazel's funeral. He and Denise were invited to the Tunstalls' home after this was over.

It took nearly three months for Phil to recover sufficiently enough to return to his duties at Angel Street. The three youths responsible eventually appeared before Warbreckside Crown Court where Phil and his colleagues were required to give evidence. The three were found Guilty of a number of serious charges and the Judge, Mr Justice Foxglove remarked as to how society owed a large debt to the brave men and women of the police service, who day and night, selflessly go about their duties for the protection of the public. He, like most law abiding citizens, appreciated the efforts of those gallant officers. He sentenced each of the three defendants to three years imprisonment.

It wasn't long before Phil was back into the swing of things. His Sergeant, the Gay Marine, had missed the hurt one of his flock, and was pleased to have him back into the fold. Phil would never forget the privilege of his having met and befriended Hazel, but what a sad, sad waste he thought, the injury she received from that kick would no doubt be classed as 'one of the hazards of the occupation!'

It comes to he who waits!

The rain poured down in sheets at the large container ship, the 'Rapid Conveyor', assisted by tugs was eventually secured at her berth in Blangton Dock. It was a filthy night and high tide was at midnight, in one hour's time. Now that all the major work had been completed, the actual unloading of the many containers from the Conveyor's decks wouldn't start until some hours later in the morning.

Some of the ship's crew were local men, many were of foreign nationality. The 'Rapid Conveyor' had just crossed to the U.K. from Rotterdam. Two of the crew, Teddy Elkington and his mate, Danny Banks had obtained a large amount of heroin after lengthy negotiations with a major drugs syndicate over in Rotterdam. However, the two were but minnows and were acting for a 'Mister Big' here in England. The drugs they had acquired, had been secretly loaded into a container full of paint, grease and thinners prior to its transportation to the docks where it was then hoisted aboard the Rapid Conveyor. The container was addressed to McLelland and Sons, Viaduct Motors, at the railway arches, Senton. This was a seedy area where there was a small 'industrial' estate among the arches of the railway bridge, the almost derelict area contained a couple of scrap metal merchants, a car breakers yard and McLellands' yard, a grotty little car repair and respraying premises. Each 'business' in the area was run by its devious and ex-criminal owners. The Police gave the area a wide berth unless they were specifically called.

As the routine work was being carried out at the quayside, the only other nocturnal activity was the arrival of a black cab. It stopped at the end of the gangway of the newly arrived 'Conveyor'. Out into the rain stepped Helen Marshall and Pauline Rothwell, two of Angel Street's well known prostitutes. After they paid the driver the taxi swished away and vanished into the night in a cloud of spray. The two girls pulled their coats tightly about them and huddled together under the overhang of a nearby dockers' hut. It was still raining heavily, the powerful overhead lighting illuminated the scene as though it were daylight.

It wasn't long before the two were spotted by a member of the Conveyor's crew, which was the sole purpose of their visit! *"Hey!, Vy don't you come aboard ant haff a drink?"*, asked Klaus Mueller. *"C'mon Helen, we don't need to be asked twice, I'm friggin' soaked already"*, said Pauline. Klaus's shouts were heard by his crew mate Jurgen Lostein who joined his mate at the ship's rail.

The two women were helped aboard and quickly smuggled into the crews' quarters. Although it was cramped, it was warm and comfortable. Klaus went to take Pauline's wet coat and said, *"Let me take your vet clothes ant I vil dry dem"*. Pauline brushed his arm away and said sharply, *"Hey!, if there's any clothes cummin' off, I'll take 'em off, don't touch anythin' yer not gonna pay for"*. In no time all four were drinking a variety of spirits. As the women sat drinking their senses were becoming dulled by the amounts of strong alcohol the two men were plying them with. Helen sat with her legs crossed and sitting directly in front of her was Klaus, who could see the white of her panties and a generous bit of white thigh above her stocking tops. As the night wore on Helen's head and shoulders dropped and leaned more forward as time went on. Both men were treated to a wonderful view of her bra-less breasts and each nudged each other in lustful anticipation of what they hoped was to come.

Pauline started to encourage Jurgen, hoping ultimately, to increase the dimensions of the wallet she carried in her handbag. She didn't mind what she had to do, within reason, or with whom, punters were punters!

Eventually Jurgen suggested that he and Pauline went to another cabin and the two then left to indulge in a lustful few hours of debauchery. Once they were alone, Klaus decided it was time that he 'got down to business' with the now almost unconscious Helen. She was completely unaware of what was going on as Klaus picked her up and transferred her to a nearby bunk. He lay her on her back and as he did so Helen stirred. *"H-hey!, w-wha' yer doin'?"*. Klaus reassured her softly, *"It's okay, it's okay!"* he said as he took the thin straps of her white cotton dress and pulled them down her arms, exposing her large breasts as he did so. He saw that she had a tattoo of a butterfly above her left nipple. Klaus then slid his hand up between Helen's thighs. When he reached the top Helen reacted with a jump. *"Hey!, w-wha's goin' on?, gerrout!"*, she slurred and feebly tried to move Klaus' hand away with her own.

Klaus was not however, going to be deprived now he had got this far. He moved her dress up above her feebly struggling hips then took hold of her panties. Helen protested and struggled a little stronger this time, but the powerful Klaus persisted. He tore the garment from her and caressed her naked thighs then tried to remove her suspender belt. He had difficulty doing this so he ripped this also and was beginning to get himself into a frenzy.

Due to the rough treatment she was being subjected to, Helen started to sober up a little. She started to put up more of a struggle to try to prevent the matelot having his wicked way with her. The fact that she was a prostitute had been eliminated by her alcohol consumption, it was now a case of fighting for her dignity and 'honour', it was a case of self preservation!

The rampant seaman's attitude had now changed completely, his frustration assisted by his own consumption of alcohol. The struggle was becoming more serious, he had an erection and an uncontrollable urge to penetrate his anaesthetised 'guest', either with or without her consent! Helen continued to try and thwart his efforts and in doing so she scratched his cheek with her long fingernails. Klaus went beserk, he punched the hapless woman violently in the face knocking her completely unconscious and blood poured from her nose and mouth. As she lay there out cold, Klaus removed every item of her clothing then shed his own. He grunted as he climbed on top of Helen and mercilessly raped her as she lay there helpless.

As she was lying on her back Helen started to choke on her own blood and started gasping. After he had done with her Klaus got dressed and made attempts to clean up Helen's by now very swollen face. He attempted to restore Helen to her former self by replacing her (torn) clothes. He dabbed her cheeks and forehead with water and wiped the blood from her lips. – He didn't know that there was blood somewhere else!

Helen eventually woke up. She started to sob and seemed unable to speak. As the light started to appear over the Eastern horizon and the brass cabin clock showed five thirty, Pauline appeared with a very dishevelled Jurgen. *"Bloody 'ell!, wha'ra night that was................."* She caught sight of her friend and stopped horrified. Then she gasped, *"Friggin' 'ell!, what in God's name's 'appened to you?"*. Helen started sobbing and again, she could not speak. Pauline turned to Klaus and snarled, *"Wharrave you done to 'er?"*. Klaus shook his head and shrugged his shoulders, denying any knowledge of the state of her friend. The side of Helen's face was puffed up like a football and although she couldn't speak, Helen made a fist and shook it in front of her then pointed to Klaus and then pointed to her jaw. Even Klaus's shipmate Jurgen was put out by Helen's disturbing revelations.

Pauline ranted, *"You bastard!, what 'ave you done? Look at 'er, look at 'er clothes!"*. She took hold of her friend and retrieved her coat and handbag and said, *"C'mon Helen, let's get out of 'ere!"*. Even Jurgen apologised profusely, but Pauline snapped, *"Take it from me, 'e's right in the shit 'cos I'm takin' er to 'ospital then ringin' the Police"*. Klaus defiantly replied, *"I haf not done anysink wrong, she has been paid for vot ve did!"*. Pauline glared at Klaus and spat out venomously, *"Oh no mister, don't you kid yer friggin' self, you 'aven't paid anything yet for what you've done to 'er!"*. Klaus poured himself another drink and sat there bleary eyed. His crewmate, Jurgen meanwhile sheepishly escorted the two women down the gangway and onto the quayside. Pauline put her arm around her distressed friend and they both made their way to a nearby 'phone box outside the dock gate on the main road where Pauline summoned a taxi.

A short time later their taxi arrived and the two climbed into the back out of the rain, which had reduced to a fine drizzle after

82

the night's heavy downpour. *"Warbreckside Infirmary please"*, instructed Pauline. The taxi quickly conveyed the two women through the town and on to the casualty department at Warbreckside hospital. Helen, although still not fully sober was taken through to X-ray after a brief explanation to the casualty Sister by Pauline. Helen's face needed no explanation that serious damage had been done. The X-rays revealed that she had sustained a badly fractured jaw as well as losing two teeth. Helen managed to report the fact that she had also been severely raped during her attack.

Sister Rutherford immediately reported the rape allegations to Angel Street police station and was put through to Detective Sergeant Foster. In no time, Frank and his colleague, Detective Policewoman Vicky 'Les' Bienne attended at the hospital. Although Helen was still being treated for her injuries and was also under sedation, Pauline enlightened the Sergeant as to the circumstances relating to them both being on board the 'Rapid Conveyor'. Both girls were well known to Frank, especially Helen, as she had acted as a 'snout' (informer) for Frank on many occasions.

Frank listened patiently while WDC Bienne meticulously recorded every detail in writing. The Police surgeon, Doctor Plessey, was summoned and attended a short time later. Eventually Dr Plessey was able to examine the injured and still traumatised Helen to enable him to compile a full and comprehensive report of his findings for Sergeant Foster, as well as obtaining DNA samples for comparisons and evidential purposes. Prostitute or not, Helen still had the right to say no and Frank was damned if he was going to allow a lustful, foreign sailor to come over here and violently rape and abuse any female he chose, just because she was a prostitute. Enquiries revealed that the 'Rapid Conveyor' would be berthed at Blangton Dock for at least a week as she was having repair work carried out on her rudder as well as discharging, before taking on more cargo.

The following day Helen was still shocked and very distressed, however, Frank managed to have a brief chat with her at her bedside. After this Frank decided to visit the dock and the ship, and after briefly putting Detective Constable Wainwright in the picture regarding the unsavoury incident, the two drove along to the dock estate. The two arrived at the dock amid intense activity as large containers were being unloaded from the 'Rapid Conveyor' then transported across the quay to be stacked ready for their subsequent removal to various near and distant venues. A smaller ship, the 'Sea Star' was moored astern of 'Conveyor' and was taking on timber. Dock traffic was heavy and dockers swarmed everywhere like ants. *"Christ!, it's bloody chaos 'ere Sarje"*, commented Ronnie. *"You can say that again"*, said Frank and went on, *"I'm gonna 'ave this bastard Ron, she may be a cow, but she's entitled to keep what's in 'er knickers to 'erself if she wants to, I'm not goin' to let some bastard break 'er jaw an' get away with it that's fer sure"*. *"Too bloody right!"*, agreed Detective Wainwright.

"Hey, Frank!, look who's over there", said Ronnie grabbing his Sergeant's sleeve and indicating a figure well known to both of them, Danny Banks, as he walked along near a number of stacked containers. *"Where?"*, asked Frank. *"Over there, walking past the containers"*, said Ronnie pointing him out. *"Bloody hell, well, well, well!"*, said the surprised Detective Sergeant and continued, *"Danny Banks! Yer can bet yer bottom dollar 'e'll be up to no good"*. *"What d'yer reckon the little toe rag's up to Sarje?"*, asked Ronnie. Neither knew that Danny was a member of the 'Conveyor's' crew. It hadn't escaped Frank's observations that Banks was carrying a brown, wrapped parcel..., *"Dunno"*, replied Frank, *"but you can bet the devious little bastard's up to something, we'll 'ave to see what we can find out eh Ron?"*. Detective Wainwright shrugged his shoulders and nodded his agreement. Both officers remembered Banks only too well from his involvement with Frank Mayhew and his gang when Vipers Club was in full swing.

Frank sat there pondering, *"Mmmmm, He's too well dressed to be a docker, an' anyway, what little work they do do, would bloody kill 'im"*, he muttered. *"Perhaps Mayhew has opened a club on the dock estate?"*, joked Detective Wainwright. *"That wouldn't bloody surprise me either, knowing Mayhew"*, replied Frank as he sat there wondering what it was that could have enticed Banks to the docks.

"*Let's go an' 'ave a word with the captain of the 'Conveyor'*", said Frank. The two then locked their vehicle and wandered over to the large container ship. As they walked up the gangway they were met at the ship's rail by a scruffy looking crewman who asked them the reason for their presence. Frank introduced himself and his colleague, and asked to see the Captain. The crewman instructed the two to follow him. After leading them through a labyrinth of passageways they came to a highly polished oak door in which was a brass rimmed porthole, but a drawn curtain on the inside prevented anyone from seeing inside. A large sign bearing the words 'Captain Hans Larsen' was affixed below the porthole. The crewman knocked, and after a grunted command from within opened the door and vanished inside. A short time later the crewman re-appeared and was dismissed by a large bearded man wearing an open, double breasted navy blue tunic bearing four gold rings on the cuff of each sleeve. He had no tie and his white shirt was open at the neck showing a thick clump of black hair at the base of his throat.

He held out his hand and said,"*Gentlemen, I am Captain Larsen, Vot can I do for you?*". Frank took the Captain's hand and shook it warmly, then introduced Ronnie and himself. "*Zer Politzie, Vot do you vont vis me Sergeant?*". Frank went on to elaborate as to how, during the early hours of the previous day, two females had been on his ship and one had been raped and badly injured. To emphasise the gravity of the situation and hopefully dispel any loyalty the Captain may have had to the crew member responsible, Frank said slowly, "*What he did to that woman, carries life imprisonment in this country!*". Captain Larsen was visibly shocked by the Sergeant's revelation as to what had happened on his ship, under his very nose, a short time earlier.

The Captain assured Frank of his utmost co-operation to bring about the speedy apprehension of the offender. The description Frank had been given very soon resulted in Klaus and Jurgen being arrested and removed from the ship. The two were taken to Angel Street and interviewed at great length. At first, Klaus maintained his arrogance and didn't see the seriousness of the situation, as he said, "*She vos only a prostitute, vy all zer fuss?*". However, he soon changed his tune when he realised the gravity of the position that he had placed himself and his crew mate Jurgen into. To spare his mate, Klaus decided to change tack and admit what he had done. Jurgen would be in enough trouble as it was for having a woman, an unauthorised female, aboard the vessel.

Frank, Ronnie and a photographer made a couple more visits to the vessel, accompanied by Jurgen, to take a number of photographs of the 'scene of the crime' and gather items for evidence. During one of these visits, Frank again saw Danny Banks as he scuttled to a car with a parcel under his arm. The rear door of the car, a large Jaguar, opened and Banks dived inside. The car then sped off and Frank noticed that there were other men in the car beside Banks and the driver. Frank noted the registration number of the car, he'd get a PNC check on the vehicle later!

Some days later, in the late afternoon, Constable Vinny Andrews was driving his patrol car along Dacre Street when all of a sudden a large, dark blue Jaguar pulled out into the officer's path from the railway arches at Senton, causing the officer to swerve and brake violently to avoid a collision. The Jaguar did not stop, and accelerated away at high speed. Constable Andrews gave chase but it was obvious that he would not catch the rapidly disappearing Jaguar. The officer had noted the number however, and circulated its number and direction of travel over the air, hoping the vehicle would be intercepted and stopped.

Sitting at his typewriter upstairs in Angel Street CID office, Detective Sergeant Foster heard Constable Andrews' transmission on his radio, which was lying on his desk as he typed. Frank's ears pricked up on hearing the registered number and the fact that it was a Jaguar. He rooted for the piece of paper in his jacket pockets, he'd forgotten all about the Jag at the docks, having been preoccupied with Helen's rape. Eventually he found the crumpled piece of paper on which he had noted the vehicle's number, it was in fact a 'Visa' payment receipt for petrol, it was lucky he hadn't thrown it away! Frank picked up his radio, "*CID to control, could you relay the number of the Jag referred to in the last transmission please, over!*". The number was again recited and, bingo! It referred to the same Jag at the docks that Danny Banks and his brown paper parcel had dived into. The Detective Sergeant asked to be kept informed, and also requested that Constable Andrews see him as soon as he was able.

The Jaguar was intercepted and stopped in Pender Vale as it made its way out of town. The driver, Martin Housley, had been drinking. He was asked to provide a breath test and on his doing so, it proved positive and he was arrested. A subsequent check via the PNC (Police National Computer) revealed that the registered owner of the expensive vehicle was Marjorie Housley, sister of the arrested driver.

On being informed of developments, Detective Sergeant Foster was not happy with the way things looked. The Jag was removed to Angel Street and thoroughly searched. A sharp eyed Detective Constable 'Randy' Walker found a large quantity of heroin wrapped in brown packages, secreted in the wheel well under the spare wheel.

When the packages were opened and evaluated it was revealed that at least £85,000 worth, at street value, had been intercepted and recovered. Frank noticed that the brown wrappings resembled those which he had seen Danny Banks carrying on the day he had seen him dive into the back of this very same Jag.

Things started to move very quickly, Housley was kept in custody and his sister Marjorie was asked to attend Angel Street to collect her car. She attended as requested, unaware that her brother had been arrested or that drugs had been found in her vehicle. Marjorie was taken to an interview room and spoken to at great length by Detective Sergeant Foster in company with Detective Constables Walker and Woman Detective 'Les' Bienne. Frank's skilful questioning uncovered a tissue of deceit. Marjorie was a travel courier and constantly visited many countries. More important, and to Frank's surprise, she was also the mistress of Mr Frank Mayhew! Indeed, the Jaguar was finally established as actually belonging to Mayhew. Mayhew registered the vehicle in Marjorie's name as she and her brother sometimes travelled over to the Continent in it before returning with unaccustomed goods, and yes, she admitted, they were usually drugs! Danny Banks, Marjorie informed, would then distribute them for Mayhew.

Frank was over the moon as neither Marjorie or her brother had ever been subject to any Police suspicion or scrutiny, let alone been connected with the notorious and deviant Franklyn Mayhew esquire. This was indeed a turn up for the books!

In a very short time, Danny Banks was sitting in Angel Street, cockily demanding the reason for his presence there. Sergeant Foster gladly obliged by showing him one parcel of heroin. *"We're gonna turn your 'ouse over, so if we find more, an' you know nothin' about it, your wife will be brought in an' charged"*, said Frank. *"Okay!, okay!, but there's only a bit, I'm mindin' it for mister Mayhew"*, whimpered Banks.

Two parcels were recovered from Danny's house to the complete surprise of Danny's wife Nora, who, Frank believed and accepted, was not aware of his dealing in this particular type of 'filth'. To save his own skin, Danny sang like a canary. CID and uniformed officers went to the railway arches at Senton and carried out a detailed and meticulous search of all premises there. A large container, secreted inside a derelict and debris strewn arch, which had crudely been painted with black paint in an unsuccessful attempt to hide its original orange colour, was forcibly opened and searched. Constable Clayton drew Sergeant Foster's attention to a label which had been missed by the container's 'painter'. It bore the name 'Rapid Conveyor'! Andy Mclelland, the owner of Mclelland Motors, shook with fear as events unfolded.

The container was emptied of paint, grease, and thinners, and a large stack of brown parcels could be seen half hidden under some pallets, having been sniffed out by one of the dogs. When she was made aware of the very serious developments, and possible repercussions to herself, the very co-operative, and very frightened Marjorie Housley decided that self preservation completely outweighed her loyalty to her devious lover Frank Mayhew. As she became aware of more and more people being apprehended, and the astronomical scale of the drug's value, she decided to reveal all in sheer desperation.

She revealed where documents relating to the sale of drugs, their whereabouts, hidden places where stolen property, including part of an imported consignment of cigarettes and tobacco, lay hidden, and lists of addresses and telephone numbers, ... all relating to, and stemming from, the Mister Big, Mister Franklyn Mayhew! To Detective Sergeant Frank Foster, Christmas had arrived early this year!

Frank and his team worked non stop in gathering and compiling all the incriminating information received. More property was recovered and more of those apprehended decided to assist the police as it was obvious that to resist further would be futile.

Finally at three o'clock in the morning a very tired and exhausted, but very elated, Detective Sergeant Foster, together with a number of colleagues, including members of the dog section, made their way quietly to the front door of Frank Mayhew's illuminated, large and impressive house out in the wilds of the neighbouring force area, whose officers were also assisting this morning's operation. The deep bark of Mayhew's German Shepherd dog Major could be heard from the bowels of the large house, which was then accompanied by Mayhew's Westie Jock, as he yap, yapped in unison with his big cousin.

An upstairs window opened and Mayhew's head leaned out over the flowered window sill, *"What the hell's going on for Christ sake?"*, he snapped .... then he spotted Frank. *"Oh Christ, Foster! What the fuck are you doing on my property?"*, he snarled menacingly and added, *"I'm calling my lawyer Mister Smethurst, now! He'll sort you out"*. The Detective Sergeant, was still under the anaesthetic of 'apprehensional enchantment' having built a water-tight case against Mayhew and his gang, and longed for a confrontation with his old adversary, the unpopular and unscrupulous barrister, Mr Brian Smethurst, especially at this time of the morning. Frank replied, *"Mister Mayhew, you're goin' to well an' truly need yer lawyer this time, I'm 'appy to say. In the meantime, get yer coat on now, my patience is runnin' out!"*. A short time later, bolts were drawn, chains rattled and hasps unlocked. Finally Mayhew stood there in his housecoat and slippers. *"Get dressed, I'm takin' you in"*, said a delighted Frank. *"What are you talking about? I'm ringing my lawyer"*, said Mayhew. The Detective Sergeant put his face against Mayhew's and growled, *"Listen bollocks, I've now got enough on you to put you away for the rest of your natural, so get dressed, I'm takin' you in.*

You can ring you lawyer from Angel Street, for all the good it'll do yer!"

Mayhew was taken in and again his sumptuous mansion was searched. This time however, incriminating documents were recovered and placed with those supplied by Marjorie Housley. Smethurst's eventual pompous attendance at Angel Street was soon deflated when part of the overwhelming evidence against his client Mayhew, was divulged. A very white faced Mayhew was left talking to his equally apprehensive lawyer. Oh how Frank had lived for this day! He felt the same amount of pity for Mayhew as would a Ferret for a Rabbit!

The case turned into a long, drawn out saga, no doubt to the financial delight of Mayhew's barrister Smethurst, but eventually, after many months had passed, Mayhew and his despicable ilk received their just rewards! Mayhew was sent to prison for twelve years, and those others involved received proportionate terms from twelve months to three years. The whole successful operation was brought to fruition by the instigation of the alert Constable Vinny Andrews as he had been diligently patrolling his patch. It was the CID however who received the accolade!

The Blangton Dock rape was eventually concluded when the vicious Klaus Mueller received eighteen months imprisonment.

Frank Foster continued to bath in the 'asp's milk' of his success regarding Mayhew, and as he raised his pint glass to his lips in the Hornless Goat, he said to his colleagues, Ronnie Wainwright and Randy Walker, *".........Ah!, it always comes to he who waits!"*

The Devil's Apprentice

The smoky and grimy atmosphere of the Angel Street division didn't enhance the enthusiasm of budding botanists residing in the area to say the least. Indeed, although the area was not blessed with much greenery, there was one 'jewel in the polluted crown' where people could retreat for some semblance of fresh air - Greenacres Park.

Although it was called a park, it was in fact a mixture of football and cricket pitches and run-down bowling greens, with their vandalised pavilion. Allotments bordered one side, secreted behind a screen of tall poplar trees. A swing ground and play area was situated just inside the gates at the main entrance near to a small lake. A number of ducks, moorhens and Canada geese drifted aimlessly about its surface, negotiating numerous obstacles protruding from below, old washing machines, tyres, shopping trolleys and other equally enhancing traps for the unwary - discarded and dangerous items waiting to snag feathers or fur!

Situated near to the entrance, accessible from both inside the park and the pavement outside, were the public toilets. Unfortunately, these premises were the regular haunt of society's deviants as well as innocent children from the park. The more sinister visitors using the conveniences would visit the venue in many guises, taxi drivers, sales reps and many others whose visits were for one purpose only, to importune others of their ilk thus enabling them to indulge in various lustful forms of indecency and self gratification, sometimes their offensive and despicable behaviour was even witnessed by children using the toilets. Many unsavoury incidents occurred in and around the confines of Greenacres Park!

A chilly Monday morning saw two ten year old pals, Ronnie Tucker and Michael Evans making their way to school along Park Road which bordered Greenacres Park. Young Mickey carried his school dinner money in his trouser pocket. Ronnie's dinner was in his school bag, consisting of sandwiches, crisps and a can of 'Coke'. Both lads chatted merrily as they made their way along to their school in Dulcie Street, at the top of Dykin Road.

Just as they were passing the park gates, out stepped the local bully, Danny Casey, feared by most of the children in the neighbourhood. Casey was two years older than Ronnie and Mickey and big for his age. He had been in trouble with the police many times in his young life already for stealing and beating up local kids as well as continually harassing people by damaging their property. His family were well known and disliked, both of his parents having been in trouble with the police for stealing, and offences of G.B.H. (grievous bodily harm) by his equally bullying father. Not to be outdone, Casey's elder brother Terry was presently serving a prison sentence for burglary.

"*C'mere you two*", commanded Casey baring his yellow, decaying teeth in an intimidating snarl. The two terrified youngsters did as they were told. "*Worrave yer gorron yer?*", snarled the juvenile footpad. "*Nuthin', only me butties an' comic*", said Ronnie. "*Empty yer bag an' let's see then*", ordered Casey. Ronnie was only too pleased to oblige the bullying tyrant and emptied the meagre contents of his canvas school bag onto the pavement. His pack of corned beef sandwiches spilled from their loose Daily Mirror page one newspaper wrapping into the gutter and his can of Coke rolled after them, being halted by a large dollop of dog dirt. His treasured comic, the Dandy fluttered away as the breeze separated the pages, sending them one by one along the road and into the air.

Ronnie stood and said nothing, he was too frightened. Casey turned to Mickey, who was standing there trembling in anticipation of what was to befall him. "*Worrabout you?*", he asked. Fearing he would be beaten up if he didn't appease the intimidating young thug, Mickey owned up to having three one pound coins and a fifty pence piece in his pocket. "*Give 'em 'ere*", ordered Casey holding his clenched fist menacingly under

Mickey's nose. The terrified Mickey instantly emptied his pockets, producing a penknife and the coins. Casey snatched the coins and the knife, a swiss army knife. *"Anythin' else?"* snapped Casey as he pocketed Mickey's dinner money and (his dad's) knife. *"No, honest Danny, that's all I've got, it's me dinner money!",* cried Mickey. *"It'd better be or else, now fuck off before I 'it yer",* snarled the bullying youth, then added, to Ronnie, *"Clean the shit off that can o' Coke an' give it 'ere!".* He made Ronnie wipe the can clean on his coat then Casey inspected it before taking it from him, again telling the two, *"Now fuck off!".*

Both boys, grateful to have escaped being beaten up then ran off as they were ordered, Ronnie hurriedly retrieving his school bag, but leaving his sandwiches in the roadway. The delighted Casey checked the can of Coke again, making sure there was no dog shit on it then placed it into his anorak pocket before he sauntered off, wondering how he could idle away the rest of the day, as her had no intention of going to school. He was the bane of the teachers and his co-pupils at Gilbey Lane Comprehensive School at the other end of town, and he was only in his second year!

A short time later the two terrified and exhausted victims of Casey's intimidation staggered panting and gasping into their classroom and eventually poured out their alarming tale to their teacher Mrs Errington just as she was about to start the morning's lessons. Mrs Errington was very sympathetic and also very cross at the thought of what that wicked youth had done to her pupils, she would certainly ensure that both boys' parents were made aware of the incident as soon as she was able.

In the meantime Casey, three pounds and fifty pence richer, meandered along, undecided what to do with his new found, ill-gotten wealth. As he wandered along, aimlessly thinking as to how he could spend yet another day's truancy, his attention was drawn to a child sitting strapped in her pushchair outside Nessie's hairdressing shop in the Grange shopping precinct. The little mite, dressed in her pink woollen bonnet and maroon siren suit, her little mittens dangling on cords at the ends of her little sleeves, cooed contentedly as she cuddled her little teddy bear while her mother, Shirley McKenzie was inside the shop booking a hair appointment for the following day. For no other reason than sheer devilment

Casey took the pushchair and wheeled it away, little two year old Stacey none the wiser and completely ignorant of her forthcoming unauthorised outing. Casey made his way through the streets and although he drew one or two stares, nobody's suspicions were aroused sufficiently to cause him any concern.

Eventually Casey turned off Tarran Road and onto the 'Moors' an area of grassy wasteland, bushes, debris and unauthorised tipping, through which ran a footpath leading to Frodsham Street, half a mile away. The path passed a large pond where local anglers sometimes sought peace and tranquillity, and where kids played or picnicked. At night the area was frequented by courting couples or prostitutes with their 'punters'. Further along, the path passed the rear of the Hudson Lane animal clinic.

Brrrrrrrrm!, Brrrrrrrrm!! Casey started to run with the buggy, playing 'buses', as he negotiated the twists and turns of the footpath, stopping now and again at imaginary bus stops, then continuing on along his 'route'. He splashed through puddles and bumped along the lumpy and pitted path. Suddenly little Stacey's beloved teddy bear slipped from her grasp and fell onto the wayside. Casey continued along, leaving the treasured little bear at the side of the muddy path. Stacey couldn't bear to be parted from her fluffy friend and started to cry and scream hysterically.

There was nobody about to hear the child's demented and pitiful screams. Casey stopped and hurled abuse at the child. *"Stop yer fuckin' screamin' will yer!"*, he ranted. Poor Stacey would not be silenced and continued crying broken heartedly for the return of her fluffy little pal and bedmate. Casey's game of 'buses' came to an abrupt end. The evil twelve year old wondered why on earth he had taken the hysterical little cretin in the first place. He now became acutely bored, having exhausted his nasty little escapade with someone else's beloved little offspring.

Seeing the pond behind the bushes, Casey dragged the buggy and its crying passenger across the grass near to the water's edge. The child was still strapped in its carriage crying and sobbing profusely. Suddenly Casey's temper flared as his patience snapped. He shouted into the face of the hapless child, *"Fer fuck sake, shurrup will yer?"*. This made the purple faced little infant worse. She was terrified and wanted her mum, and her teddy!

The nasty and vindictive youth then pushed the carriage and baby down the grassy slope and into the cold, muddy waters of the pond until only the red plastic handled tips of the buggy remained visible. Stacey's fluffy, pink woollen bonnet floated on the surface into some nearby reeds. Realising the gravity of what he had done, Casey panicked and ran along the deserted footpath to put as much distance as possible between himself and the unforgivably foul deed he had so mercilessly just perpetrated. He made for Commerce Street railway station hoping to get a train to anywhere which was far enough away from the scene of his horrific crime.

Eventually he arrived exhausted at the station. Seeing an advertised half fare return for £2.95p which would take him out into the sticks to a little village called Leighton, Casey purchased his ticket and eventually set off on a ride into the country. Some time later and many miles up country Casey's train arrived and deposited him at Leighton Halt, the small station nestling in the popular little picturesque village of Leighton, well inside the boundaries of the Lymphonshire County Constabulary.

Back at Nessie's hairdressing shop the unsuspecting Mrs Mckenzie, having made her appointment, bade young Joanne the hairdresser and receptionist goodbye. Having only been in the shop a matter of five minutes or so. Opening the door for her client, Jo said, "*Before you go I'll just slip out to see the baby*", then accompanied her customer outside. All of a sudden Mrs McKenzie let out a piercing shriek and screamed, "*My baby!, My baby!, ---- she's gone! Someone's taken my baby!*". The panicking, hysterical and totally distraught mother staggered round in circles, her hands to her head, sobbing uncontrollably. Young Jo, herself deeply shocked, took hold of the inconsolable young mother and gently guided her back inside the shop. The three other women customers in the shop, in their various stages of perms and highlighting, came from under their driers to comfort Shirley as she sat and sobbed. Jo had the presence of mind to tell her two colleagues Beattie and Fran to make some tea while she contacted the police. Marjorie Turner, the manageress from the cake shop next door came in to see what all the commotion was about.

The police were informed of the apparent abduction of the young child and the call was put through to the CID at Angel Street

95

police station. Randy Walker and his colleagues, Vicky 'Les' Bienne, Ronnie Wainwright and Sergeant Frank Foster were busy sorting and allocating the previous night's 'jobs' whilst consuming their mugs of tea before starting their day's labours. Randy was nearest the 'phone when it rang, having again failed his initiative test! He picked up the receiver and spoke into the mouthpiece, *"Hello, CID Angel Street, Detective Walker speaking"*. For some unknown reason, CID officers below the rank of sergeant never seemed to give their full title when speaking to Joe Public, perhaps their ego didn't like to acknowledge that those who were constables were of exactly the same status at the uniformed man who walked the beat, in actual fact, the man on the beat had far, far more responsibility if the truth were known! Wives of CID officers were the biggest offenders.

"Call for you", said the crisp unemotional voice of the female operator manning the headquarters switchboard. Randy again announced himself, *"CID Angel Street, Walker speaking"*. *"Oh hello"*, said the timid voice of young Joanne Foxglove, *"I'm Joanne Foxglove and I'm ringing to report a baby missing from outside our shop in the Grange Precinct"*. Randy could clearly hear the distraught sobs emanating from Shirley McKenzie as she sat nearby being comforted by all those present in the shop. Randy ascertained full details and particulars of the incident and reassured young Jo that the police would be along in minutes. Randy jumped up and grabbed his coat, *"There's a toddler bin snatched from the precinct ten minutes ago"*, he informed all present. *"Right, take 'Les' and give us an update as soon as yer can,"* instructed Frank and proceeded to telex what scant details had been obtained by his subordinate through to headquarters for general circulation.

On attending Nessie's shop the detectives had to run the gauntlet of a large number of people who had gathered by this time. As was par for the course, speculation was rife among those who were unaware of what had actually happened.

Randy and his colleague managed to get the still sobbing Shirley into a small, empty store room at the back of the shop, offered by the sensible young Jo, whose father was a police sergeant in another division. Jo outlined what she had gleaned from Shirley's sobbed and partly incoherent story. W.P. Bienne delicately eased the full circumstances of the morning's outing and the subsequent parking of little Stacey's buggy while her mother went into the shop to make her appointment, from a slightly more subdued Shirley. "*I was only in 'ere a couple o' minutes or so*", sniffed Shirley as though trying to justify herself while she dabbed her eyes which were now red and bloodshot with her continual crying. "*I only took me eyes of 'er for a second, I was watchin' 'er all the time through the window, an' the next thing, I wen out an' she was gone!, just ....gone!*". Shirley lost control again and sobbed bitterly. "*Okay, there, there, I'm sure there's going to be a logical explanation*", said Policewoman Bienne as she tried to console the frightened and despondent woman by placing a comforting arm around her shoulders.

Shirley held her almost empty (third) cup of tea in both hands and sipped its contents. "*First we'll 'ave a cruise around town to see if we can find little Stacey eh? Then, if we 'aven't bin successful we'll call at Angel Street to complete some formalities, is that okay Shirley?*" asked Randy gently. Gathering her composure and once again drying her now 'raw' red eyes Shirley handed the empty cup back to Jo and stood up, "*Ye, yes, okay*", agreed Shirley, keen to get things under way.

Young Stacey had been taken at about nine forty five and by eleven thirty the youngster's full description had been supplied to the press, radio and television for inclusion in their next bulletins. Enquiries were commenced in the area and once news of the abduction had been released by the media people started ringing in reporting their various, possible, sightings of what could have been the missing Stacey earlier that morning.

A Mrs Duffy was first to contact the police. She rang to say saw 'thought' she saw a young boy pushing a child's buggy at around ten o'clock or so but for the life of her she couldn't remember exactly where it was she saw them. All she remembered was that she thought it unusual for a child to be out in charge of a baby when all the kids should have been at school. She only caught a glance of the two as she passed by on the bus. The direction of travel, the bus's route number and the approximate time of the sighting was noted as these bits of information would eventually give a rough guide to the venue of the sighting. An immediate search of the bus's route was instigated by mobile patrols. Other 'sightings' followed and all information thankfully received was duly acted upon in an effort to trace the missing youngster.

Later, at Dulcie Street Primary School some of the teachers were relaxing in the school staff room during their lunch break. Some were reading, others just lounging in their chairs. Some, including Mrs Errington, were watching the lunch time news on television. News of little Stacey Mckenzie's disappearance was related and a picture of the missing child appeared on the screen. The venue of the taking was given, as well as a vague description of a possible youth who may have been seen pushing the little girl in her buggy. Suddenly the hair stiffened on the back of Mrs Errington's neck! Remembering the incident earlier that morning regarding the late arrival of the terrified duo Ronnie Tucker and Michael Evans after the latter had been subjected to the trauma of having his dinner money stolen by Danny Casey, Mrs Errington pondered. Casey had previously been a very disruptive and unruly pupil of Dulcie Street before moving on to the Gilbey Lane school once he had reached the age of eleven years.

Although Mrs Errington didn't know what Casey was wearing that day, the 'abducting' youth's vague description could possibly fit that of young Casey. Mrs Errington left her colleagues recuperating from the rigours of the morning's lessons and went to the playground in search of young Ronnie and Michael. Among the noisy hulaballoo of the crowded playground the eagle-eyed teacher soon found young Tucker as he played 'hopscotch' with some of his classmates. She then spotted young Evans as he dived this way and that on the concrete floor as he attempted to prevent his mates from scoring goals between the chalked goal posts on the outside wall of class 5C's classroom, thus adding to the already large number of holes in his tatty jersey. Mickey finished emulating his England hero David Seaman and promptly answered his summons from Mrs Errington as she stood beckoning him, surrounded by a large group of inquisitive children, eager to know what Tucker and Evans had been up to.

Mrs Errington dismissed the gathered throng ordering them to go away and play. *"It's alright boys"*, Mrs Errington reassured the apprehensive two who were wondering what on earth they had done to cause a teacher to interfere with the sanctity of their play time. *"I just wondered if you could remember what Danny Casey was wearing when you both saw him this morning, can you remember?"*, Mrs Errington went on.

Between the two of them little Ronnie and Mickey furnished a reasonable description of their assailant. He wore his usual intimidating black baseball cap (back to front), dirty grey anorak, jeans jacket underneath, *"An' I think 'e 'ad a red jersey on"*, said Ronnie, and, not to be outdone, Mickey volunteered, *"E 'ad new white an' blue trainers on an dark brown pants"*. *"Long or short trousers?"*, asked the teacher, *"Long!"*, replied both boys in unison. *"Yer won't tell 'im we snitched on 'im will yer miss?"*, asked the frightened Mickey, terrified that he may suffer further repercussions for reporting the matter. *"No, of course not, don't be silly. Okay, that's all for now, go along and play"*, instructed the teacher before making her way back to the staff room.

Mrs Errington rang Angel Street Police and contacted Sergeant Royle, with whom she had dealt with in the past. The sergeant had attended the school to deal with numerous matters concerning some of the errant pupils and Mrs Errington was always impressed with the way he pursued matters, she also like his being a stickler for discipline. The teacher was always assured of the sergeant's undivided attention whenever she contacted him with a problem, irrespective of whether it be major or minor.

The lisping voice of the Gay Marine came through and asked the excited teacher what it was that he could do for her. Mrs Errington began, *"Er, I don't know if my imagination is running riot Sergeant, but do you think you could spare me a few minutes of your time and call to see me here at Dulcie Street please? I need to talk to you urgently, although.......it may be nothing!"*. *"Right ma'am, on my way"*, replied the Gay Marine. He radioed for W.P. Perry, the 'red onion' to meet him outside Dulcie Street school in twenty minutes, the sergeant always preferred a policewoman in his company when he dealt with small young children, and that's what he presumed he would be doing if Dulcie Street's past enquiries records were anything to go by.

The sergeant and his woman constable arrived at the school with half an hour to go before the afternoon lessons started. They quickly found Mrs Errington who, as usual, ensured that the two officers and herself were in possession of a cup of tea before she outlined her reason for their attendance. When all three were sitting comfortably the Gay Marine asked politely, *"Now Mrs Errington, what can we do for you?"*. Mrs Errington related the story of young Tucker's and Evans's exhausted arrival at school that morning and reiterated their story of having been robbed by Danny Casey, *"Who, no doubt, you know very well?"* said the teacher. *"I certainly do!"*, confirmed the Gay Marine, adding, *"Who doesn't know that family? Anyway, carry on ma'am"*. Mrs Errington went on to voice her concern at having seen the news on television a short time before concerning the missing child, taken from the Grange Precinct. *"I'm not saying that the person responsible was Casey, but it could well be, and I thought I should voice my concern to you"*, concluded Mrs Errington. *"Indeed, you were quite right to send for us, may we see the two lads please?"*, then asked the sergeant politely. The Gay Marine knew the Casey family well, having dealt with them all at one time or another! Although kidnapping? That's certainly something new from the family thought the sergeant. However, nothing would surprise him as to what that despicable family of 'pond life' would resort to.

Some minutes later the two nervous boys stood in front of the three and again their tale of woe was repeated concerning the taking of little Mickey's money........and the knife! His dad's knife! As soon as the officers had obtained all that they needed for the time being they left the co-operative teacher and her pupils and returned to Angel Street to convey all to paper as an official report of a robbery. Even if there was no connection between Casey and the missing baby the Gay Marine was going to do his damndest to get that young bastard before the courts, and hopefully, someone with courage who might possibly consider the sentiments and welfare of the victim instead of the perpetrator might ensure that the piece of juvenile low life is put away for a change.

As they drove back to the station Sergeant Royle turned to his colleague and said, *"Jer know what Vee? Bastards like Casey an' 'is family should be exterminated, they're just a bloody cancer in society that should be surgically removed and disposed of!"*. He ranted on, *"Neither of 'is bloody parents 'ave ever done an honest day's work in their lives an they breed like bloody rabbits for the rest of us to pay for"*. Vera looked to her sergeant and nodded her whole hearted agreement at the Gay Marine's sentiments. The two eventually arrived back at the station and sought an update on young Stacey. A widespread search included the use of police dogs, horses and the neighbouring County force's helicopter went on throughout the day but no trace of little Stacey could be found.

Meanwhile, later in the afternoon, in far away Leighton, an alert young county police officer was walking along wheeling his bicycle as he made his way round his rural beat on the outskirts of the little village. He noticed that someone was in the phone box near the entrance to Leighton Parish church.

As he drew closer, Constable Kevin Rothwell saw that the occupant of the kiosk was in fact a boy, who as yet had not noticed the officer's approach. Constable Rothwell saw that the boy was not using the phone and a closer look revealed to the amazed young bobby that the boy was in fact urinating over the phone and its mechanism. Constable Rothwell wrenched the door open and the startled boy stood upright, putting himself back into his trousers and pulling his zip closed but unable to stop urinating down his leg in fright. Before the officer could say anything, the boy, none other than Danny Casey the little tyrannical 'evacuee' from Warbreckside, spluttered, *"I 'aven't dun nuthin mister!"*, as he stood in a widening pool on the floor in his wet and muddy blue and white trainers.

"What's yer nirm lad?", asked the county 'woolyback', completely ignorant and unaware of Casey's criminal pedigree, never having been aware of him or his family's notoriety back in the 'real' world! *"Billy Fisher sir"*, lied the streetwise young thug. *"Wrrr d'yer cum from, yer nor, what's yer address?"*, persisted the officer. *"I'm stayin' at me aunties down there"*, stuttered the little thief, ... and killer! Casey started to cry, hoping to obtain a sympathetic ear from the unimpressed Constable Rothwell. *"C'mon son, we'll 'ave a little talk an' you can tell me what you're doin' 'ere an why you're not at school and the reason for using the phone box as a bloody pisshouse!"*, said the not too pleased officer. *"Me mum an' dad 'ave died an' I'm stayin' at me aunty's"*, lied the now sobbing young 'oscar' seeker, hoping his little act would influence the constable to feel sorry for him and let him go.

However, Constable Rothwell was anything but impressed. He'd seen it all before. If he had a pound for every truant he had caught and returned to school, he'd certainly have a few bob, he thought. *"C'mon, stop your cryin' and tell me the name and address of your aunty"*, insisted Rothwell. *"Mrs Blakely"*, replied Casey, forgetting to sob this time, a point not missed by the constable, neither were the 'dry' eyes! *"What did you say your name was again?"*, asked the constable. *"Eddie Fisher sir"*, replied Casey. *"Oh it's Eddie, not Billy then eh?"*, said Rothwell instantly picking up on Casey's blunder. *"Er, no, me name is Billy, they call me Eddie fer short"*, lied the little cretin as he underestimated the officer's intelligence. This time Constable Rothwell's voice changed. *"C'mon, stop messin about lad, what's yer name? Yer real name? An' where does this auntie of yours live?"*.

Casey, realising he was not getting anywhere and remembering what he had done earlier, kicked the constable's leg and tried to force his way past him out of the kiosk in sheer panic. *"Hey, yer little bastard, not so fast"*, snapped Rothwell as he grabbed Casey's arm in a vice like grip. *"Ow, ow, yer irtin' me arm"*, cried Casey as his arm hurt, this time bringing genuine tears to the boy's eyes. *"I'll hurt more than your bloody arm if you try that again"*, promised the angry constable.

The officer spoke into the microphone of his personal radio which was clipped to his lapel. He requested transport for *"An unidentified male juvenile found wandering in Leighton"*. *"While we're waiting, empty your pockets"*, Casey was ordered. *"Where are we goin?"*, asked the by now frightened Casey. *"I'm taking you in to the station, we can sort everything out there"*, replied the officer. Casey produced some coins, an elastic band, a penknife and a return rail ticket from Commerce Street to Leighton Halt. Constable Rothwell took the ticket from Casey and examined it. *"When did you come up 'ere to your auntie's?"*, he asked. Casey was really crying now! He sobbed his reply, *"Last week when me mum an' dad died"*, answered the young liar, not realising that the tell tale little document in the palm of the officer's hand was dated, - with this day's date! *"Right, well we'll get back to the office an' find out who you really are shall we? I'm not arsin' about any longer. You must think I've come up the Clyde on a bloody bike lad"*, said the angry constable as they awaited their transport back to the nick.

A short time later, a patrol car arrived and Casey was placed and locked into the rear of the vehicle. As the vehicle drove off Constable Kesteven, the driver, turned to his colleague and asked, *"What 've yer got 'ere Kev?"*. *"Dunno yet, but 'ees a bloody little liar!"*, replied Rothwell. Casey was taken to the little police office built onto the side of Constable Rothwell's police house next door to the village's fire station. He was then sat on a high chair at Rothwell's desk while Constable Rothwell placed Casey's meagre possessions onto his desktop blotting pad. Constable Kesteven proceeded to assist events by brewing up tea for the trio.

Although Casey had stopped crying, he still uttered the occasional sob for dramatic effect, which was completely ignored by both officers. The true gravity of what Casey had done had still not hit home to the delinquent youngster. Constable Kesteven stood with his bottom resting on the back of a chair, his arms folded across his chest as he awaited the kettle's signalling whistle. Rothwell sat down opposite the detained youngster, sighed a long drawn out sigh then yawned before leaning back and placing his hands behind his head then said, *"Right young fella me lad, let's start again. This time I want the truth! D'yer 'ear?"*. Once again Casey was asked, *"What's yer nerm?"*. Casey played with his grubby, nail chewed fingers as he looked at his feet which were a good six inches from the floor. *"Fuckin' told yer me name, it's Eddie, Billy, I mean Eddie Ca...Smith!"*, stuttered the now confused little truant. *"Stop pissin' about will yer, I want yer real name!"*, snapped Rothwell, his patience rapidly evaporating. His loud outburst even made Bob Kesteven jump! Bob then asked his colleague, *"What's that ticket there Kev?"*, pointing to the rail ticket on the pad. *"It's a return ticket to Commerce Street from 'ere"*, replied Rothwell. *"When's it dated?"*, asked Kesteven. *"Today, an' the lyin' little bugger told me 'e came up 'ere last week!"*, informed the angry Rothwell at the thought of a young kid trying to pull one over on him. *"Hmmm!"*, sighed Kesteven, then asked, *"Isn't Commerce Street Station on Warbreck's patch Kev?"*, and not waiting for confirmation he suggested, *"Contact Warbreckside an' ask 'em what station covers Commerce Street railway station, then give 'em a bell to see if they know this little tyke. P'raps 'es bin reported missin'!"* "That's an idea", acknowledged Rothwell and was about to ring through to Warbreckside, the neighbouring force, to make the suggested enquiry when the welcoming sound of the kettle's whistle interrupted proceedings.

Constable Kesteven turned to perform the ritual of furnishing all three with a nice hot brew and Constable Rothwell abandoned his telephone and said, *"Right then!, we'll 'ave a cuppa first then I'll ring Warbreckside eh?".* Constable Kesteven nodded acknowledgement and started to pour. Turning to Casey he asked, *"Jer wanna cup o' tea lad?",* *"No I don't",* snapped the aggressive, anti-police youth. *"Please yer bloody self, yer won't be asked again, that's fer sure",* said Kesteven. The two officers sat and consumed their nectar and Constable Kesteven then produced a battered green Rizzla tobacco tin and removed the lid before taking a liquorice coloured cigarette paper and sticking it to his lip while he took a pinch of tobacco from the tin before rolling it into what was supposed to be a cigarette inside the dark brown paper. Finally, after running the end result along the tip of his tongue, he ignited his fag and blew a pall of blue smoke across the room, returning his battered tin and lighter to his pocket as he did so.

Further questioning of the youth proved futile and eventually after establishing that Angel Street police station covered the area of Commerce Street railway station, Constable Rothwell was finally put in touch with his counterpart, Constable Barry Smith, (Plums!), who was manning the enquiry desk at Angel Street. Kevin introduced himself to his opposite number, *"Hiya mate, it's Constable Rothwell 'ere, Kevin Rothwell, County Police at Leighton. 'Ave you got any recent MFH's (missing from homes) in your area? We've got a right little toe-rag up 'ere that we think may be one of yours".* "Fuckin' right, 'aven't you 'eard?" replied Plums, *"A baby's gone missin' from our local shoppin' precinct this mornin'........".* "Yes! Yes, I'm aware of that", interrupted Kevin and added, *"No, we've got a lad 'ere about twelve or thirteen years. 'E's a right little bastard an' no mistake, 'es in possession of a return ticket to Commerce Street that was purchased down there today".* "Give us a description please", asked Plums, then proceeded to write down Constable Rothwell's description of the detained youth they had up there in Leighton.

As Plums was busy writing down the details related to him over the 'phone, in walked the Gay Marine who peered inquisitively over Plums' shoulder as he walked behind him. Suddenly Sergeant Royle froze as he noted the contents of his subordinate's scriptures. The sergeant tapped Plums on the shoulder and whispered, "*Can I 'ave a word with whoever that is Plums?*". Barry finished noting Constable Rothwell's description and said, "*Just a minute 'offs', my sergeant wants a word with you*", before handing the receiver over to his sergeant, his hand covering the mouthpiece and saying, "*Constable Rothwell, County Police at Leighton*". The Gay Marine took the receiver and lisped into the mouthpiece politely, "*Hello, Sergeant Royle here. What's the circumstances relating to the youth you've just described to my officer please?*". Sergeant Royle had not considered young Casey as a serious contender in the disappearing baby case yet, but it was just possible! At present, the Gay Marine wanted the little bastard for robbing young Mickey Evans.

The sergeant's colleague out there in the county outlined the circumstances of his earlier discovery of the cocky youth, sitting opposite him chewing his grubby fingers, "*I caught 'im 'avin' a piss in a 'phone box. E's lyin' through 'is teeth an' won't tell us 'is name*", concluded Constable Rothwell. "*It sounds as though 'e's the little twat I'm lookin' for*", said the Gay Marine, then went on, "*The lad I want is about four foot, four foot three, 'is name is Daniel Casey, Daniel Stephen Casey to be precise, born and crawled from slime on the thirteenth of April nineteen eighty six here in Warbreckside. He's a pupil of Gilbey Lane Comprehensive School, when the bastard's there. I'll get back to you in a minute, I'll just 'ave a word with our collator an' see if he's got anything further for you, give me a couple o' minutes will yer?*". Sergeant Royle then dashed through to Alec Hughes the collator. Although the Gay Marine didn't have a lot of time for the constable, due to his reputation for constant snivelling to senior officers, the sergeant none the less conceded that he was a good collator and his intimate knowledge of many villains had without doubt led to their incarceration and the clearing up of many of their crimes.

Ten minutes later the Gay Marine was again on the line to Lymphonshire County Constabulary at Leighton. *"Is that Constable Rotherwell?"*, lisped the sergeant.*"Sergeant Royle again, sorry to keep you waiting...........!"*, *"'Ang on a mo' Sarje I'll get 'im, it's Constable Kesteven 'ere!"*, said Bob having picked up the receiver. He handed the receiver to Rothwell, *"Sergeant Royle from Angel Street for you Kev"*. Rothwell took the receiver from his colleague, eagerly awaiting the sergeant's update, *"Hi Sarje, P.C. Rothwell, anything tasty?"*, he asked. The Gay Marine perused the collator's file before him then asked, *"'As that little bastard got a big, really dark brown mole about an inch long by three quarters of an inch wide on the back of 'is right arm just below the shoulder?"*. *"Dunno sarje, 'ang on though, I'll 'ave a look"*, replied Constable Rothwell enthusiastically. The P.C. lay the receiver on his desk and moved round to the back of the unsuspecting Casey's high chair. Rothwell pulled down the collar of Casey's anorak, jacket and jersey roughly, almost tipping the youth over the back of the chair as he did so. Bingo! There for all to see was the tell-tale, almost black blemish of a large mole on the youth's arm just below the shoulder amongst numerous pimples and blackheads which would no doubt have been eliminated with the constant and regular use of that which he was undoubtedly unfamiliar with, soap! *"Gerroff!"* squealed the cowardly young thug, pulling himself from the officer's scrutiny, unaware that his true identity had just been confirmed.

Rothwell returned to the 'phone, giving a wink to his mystified colleague, Bob, as he punched the air in ecstasy. *"Bingo sarje!, just as you described"*, he confirmed to the far away sergeant. *"Great! That little bastard is a well known little thief, robber, burglar, and persistent vandal of ours. His full name is Daniel Stephen Casey, born Warbreckside thirteen, four, eighty six, his hovel is at 18A Seldom Street on our more salubrious Meadowfield Estate, he does have a record number, it is WAR/ 7834 of '97. His old fella's just done a stretch for GBH (grievous bodily harm) an' 'is mother's got form for shopliftin'. They're a very charming family"*, concluded the sergeant's gleeful recital. *"I'll come out there an' collect the little cretin as soon as I can arrange a car"*, said the Gay Marine. *"Right sarje, 'look forward to meeting you later then"*, replied Rothwell and replaced the receiver. Turning to Casey, Rothwell said, "*Right Daniel Stephen Casey, I've 'ad enough shit from you, I'm putting you in the detention room to await the arrival of a nice sergeant from a place called Angel Street. He's just dying to see you!*". Rothwell took Casey's arm and escorted him into a nearby ante-room where he deposited his angelic little charge before locking the door. Casey kicked and banged at the door as he shouted, "*I'm gonna report you fer fuckin' police brutality!*". Constable Rothwell returned through to the office, closing the dividing door behind him to minimise the sounds from the irate youngster as he banged and shouted his dissent, accompanied by a variety of profane rhetoric. "*Right! Let's 'ave another brew before I leave you Kev*", said P.C. Kesteven and again furnished two mugs of tea before resuming his mobile patrol.

Back at Angel Street there was still no news of the missing McKenzie baby. The far away detention of young Casey was now widely known throughout the station but not a lot of attention was given to him regarding the missing child enquiry as it wasn't thought that Casey, being apprehended 'solo', far away, would be involved with the taking of a child. Casey's claim to notoriety was for the taking of cars, burglary, assault and robbery, none of his family were deemed baby-snatchers. The Gay Marine however, intended to see what the young yob had been up to that day before P.C. Rothwell had caught him pissing in the 'phone box, out in the 'sticks'.

During the whole time spent awaiting the officers from Angel Street, not once did Casey change his story, or his false name, such was the calibre of the young thug.

It was dark when the Gay Marine and policewoman Perry eventually drew up outside the village police house cum office in Leighton. "*Bloody 'ell sarje, imagine workin' out 'ere in the sticks eh? It'd be great!*", enthused the 'red onion'. "*Nar, not for me, Vee, I don't fancy gettin' covered in cow shit an' sheep dip every day*", replied her lisping sergeant. The two walked down the concrete flagged path to the single story extension built onto the side of the grey, pebbledashed house and rang the bell marked 'press for attention' under the blue, spherical lamp, which cast its eerie glow over the nearby privet hedge bordering the little garden which separated the garden from the adjacent roadway. As he rang the bell, the Gay Marine noticed two empty milk bottles at his feet by the side of the doorstep. Protruding from the neck of one of the bottles was a note for the milkman, while sitting on top of the other were two fifty pence pieces, topped with three twenty pence pieces, the order, and cash, for the following morning's delivery. The red onion couldn't believe what she saw! *"Christ Sarje, imagine that 'appenin' on our patch!"*, she said with utter amazement. and added, *"I wouldn't 'ave believed it if I 'adn't seen it with me own eyes!"*. The Gay Marine replied, *"There are some decent people in this world Vee, it's just that we've got all the shite on our patch back home!"*

The door was opened by Constable Rothwell in answer to the Gay Marine's ring. Rothwell was the epitome of a country bobby, his blue shirt (Warbrecksides' shirts were white) undone at the neck and minus his tie. Braces supported his trousers and the young officer's weather-beaten face resembled a 'smacked arse' thought the Gay Marine as he eyed his county subordinate.

After formal introductions were completed, Constable Rothwell, having his priorities right, brewed up and furnished his 'guests' and himself with a mug of tea and a newly opened packet of chocolate biscuits. *"I've just checked the lad sarje, he's still alive!"*, said Rothwell. *"Pity, yer should 'ave smothered the little bastard an' done society a favour"*, replied the Gay Marine, adding, *"Let's 'ave a quick butchers while me tea cools, 'better make sure it is 'im!"*. P.C. Rothwell took the sergeant through to the securely locked interview/detention room and reached for his keys as the Gay Marine peered through the little hatch window in the door. Casey was sitting on a chair with his arms round his knees which were up under his chin, his bored expression showed the contempt in which he held his 'captors'. *"Yes, that's the little twat!"*, confirmed the sergeant, gesturing with his hand for Rothwell to put his keys away, adding cynically, *"S'alright, let the little bastard stew for a bit longer, we 'aven't 'ad our tea yet!"*.

Both then returned to the little office where W/P Perry was sipping her tea as she sat, fascinated, reading the station's incident book. She noted some of the entries with amused interest. As Rothwell and the Gay Marine sat and drank their tea, the red onion looked over to her sergeant and said with a grin, *"E'are* sarje!, 'ere's one for yer. The theft of half a dozen eggs from the Reverend Barnaby Alcock's hen shed at the back of the vicarage!". Rothwell looked at his female colleague and replied seriously, "We got the buggers for that 'job'! But unfortunately we didn't recover the vicar's eggs".

Rothwell was oblivious to his 'townie' colleague's scorn at what she obviously considered such time-consuming police duty trivia, and went on, "We forensically matched the henshit from the shed to the two fellas' shoes!". "Well done Kevin", lisped the Gay Marine, "What with yer eggs enquiry then catchin' young Casey pissin' in a 'phone box, you're certainly clearin' up some crime", went on the sarcastic sergeant in friendly banter. "Well at least we've caught one of your 'invading' pieces of low life from Warbreckside though Sarje", replied Rothwell to justify his existence. The Gay Marine slurped at his tea and crunched at his chocolate wholemeal then said seriously, "You never know young Kevin, you may well 'ave opened a can of bloody worms up 'ere, catchin' that piece of shit. 'E could 'ave bin up to anythin' as 'e wandered round 'ere!"

Eventually the Gay Marine decided to make their long way back to Angel Street with their juvenile 'quarry'. They'd certainly log a few hours overtime (or 'time due' if the Chief Super has his way) by the time they both returned and booked off duty at their home station, thought the sergeant.

Casey was brought out rubbing his tired, ferret like eyes that missed absolutely nothing that was opportune. "Put yer coat on, yer goin' 'ome to Angel Street", lisped the sergeant, and, not taking any chances he produced a pair of handcuffs. "Ere, put yer 'ands out, juvenile or no juvenile, yer 'avin' these on yer 'til we get back", he said, surprising his county colleague by his not too gentle treatment of someone so young. Noticing the muddy trainers on Casey's feet the Gay Marine asked, "Where jer get all that shit from on yer new, expensive, knock off trainers?". "Nowhere!" grunted Casey. Sergeant Royle added, "What's all this about you bein' Billy Smith, an' yer mum an' dad dyin? Christ, I wish they bloody 'ad!". Casey stood with his shoulders hunched, keeping his hands up inside the cuffs of his anorak, portraying to all that he was cold. Noticing this, the Gay Marine made a mental note to put the cooling fan on once they were in the car on their long return journey!

Questioning of Casey revealed nothing but lies and cheeky abuse and he was unceremoniously placed into the back of the Gay Marine's car. After final formalities were completed the sergeant and his policewoman colleague thanked Rothwell for his hospitality and bade him farewell before they drove off into the late evening darkness heading for the bright lights of the distant Warbreckside.

During the absence of Sergeant Royle and the red onion, there had been some developments in the Stacey McKenzie disappearance. Officers had been sent to an address out of town where a child answering Stacey's description had been seen on a new housing estate. Unfortunately, hopes were dashed when it was established that the call was a false alarm with good intent. The baby concerned was the legitimate child of a young couple who had moved into their new house on the estate that very afternoon.

However, an eccentric old lady who was known throughout Warbreckside town centre area as 'Effin Nellie', due to her every other word being the quaint old anglo saxon expletive, and who insisted on feeding anything and everything from the bird and animal kingdom, from her tatty bag of stale bread she permanently carried, stated that she saw a boy wheeling a baby in a pushchair as she fed a 'fox' with some of her bread in busy Upper Carswell Street. This information was gleaned from her by Dolly Keffer the traffic warden when she had asked the old woman if she had seen such a duo about. At first Dolly didn't attach much credence to old Nellie Walker's reply due to her senility and eccentricity, especially as she had insisted she had been feeding a fox on such a busy thoroughfare - with bread!

Dolly thanked Nellie and continued on her 'motorist harassing' patrol. Old Nellie's insistence bugged Dolly however, what if she had seen the two as she said in her ramblings? The more Dolly thought about it the more she was disturbed as she made her way through the town's sinning motoring fraternity. Nellie's ready reply, *"Yeah!, I saw a fuckin' lad pushin' a fuckin' pushchair before"*, kept echoing in her head.

Just after her last booking of the day, Dolly started to make her way in to Angel Street to book off duty at five. She ambled along past the old 'Vipers' Club in Liverhead Road as a patrol car drew alongside her. The driver was the popular, recent transfer to the Angel Street division, Sergeant Nigel 'Pepsi' Coaler. *"Fancy a quick runaround before you go off duty Doll?"*, asked the courteous sergeant. *"Thanks sarje, I'd love to, it'll take the weight off me feet for a bit"*, replied the grateful warden as she got into the vehicle. Not a lot of police officers offered such kindness to the station's traffic warden, especially Dolly, who had, on occasions 'inadvertently' booked cars belonging to members of the constabulary!

As they drove around, Pepsi mentioned the missing child, *"Bloody shame, 'thought we'd found her before but it was a 'joey' (false alarm). Somebody thought they'd seen her over on the Foden Estate. Christ, I 'ope she turns up soon"*, he sighed. *"Funny enough Sarje, I was speakin' to one of our 'nutters' before, ol' Effin Nellie, she said she was feedin' a fox in Upper Carswell Street of all places?, - an' she insists that she saw a lad, I think he had a pink hat on, pushin' a buggy"*, offered Dolly. *"Christ Doll, the missing baby was wearin' a pink hat! Let's go an' see if we can find this nutter of yours. What's she look like, this woman?"*, asked the sergeant. *"Christ, she could be anywhere by now. She's bloody crackers I'm tellin' yer sarje"*, replied Dolly. *"Nevertheless, let's see if we can find her"*, insisted the sergeant. *"As well as bein' crackers, she's bloody filthy an' stinks of stale pee"*, volunteered Dolly as an afterthought. The two scoured the town without success. Finally Pepsi had an idea, *"I know! The ol' girl might be hungry an' cold, let's try the buffet at Commerce Street Station"*, he suggested. *"I doubt if she'll be there sarje, they won't let 'er in, I'm tellin' you, she really honks!"*. Not to be deterred, Sergeant Coaler headed for the railway station and as he did so he put out a call over the air requesting anyone who sighted the old lady to inform him immediately.

Commerce Street Station drew a blank as Dolly had prophesied and after further fruitless searching Sergeant Coaler realised that it was high time that Dolly was back at the station to book off at the conclusion of her day's tour of duty. As Dolly had furnished the sergeant with a very detailed description of the elderly 'Effin' Nellie, ex-barrow woman and now nocturnal shop doorway proprietress, or other suitably convenient residence

111

dweller of this parish, Pepsi decided to make further attempts to trace the lady in the slight hope of furthering the search for the missing Stacey McKenzie. Unfortunately, the sergeant's continual efforts were proving unsuccessful. Eventually six o'clock drew near, half of the section would then be in for their 'scoff' (refreshments) thought Pepsi, but he decided to stay out and continue his search for the elusive, eccentric old lady, 'Effin' Nellie'.

At six thirty, Pepsi's persistence bore fruit. He spotted the old lady as she sat in the drizzle on a bench in Pender Vale. Another sharp eyed patrol, Ged 'Mule' Train spotted the old lady at the same time. Sergeant Coaler utilised Mule's presence to enable him to show the constable a visit with a record in the officer's notebook. Ged informed his sergeant, *"There she is Sarje, Effin Nellie. She's all yours! I'll piss off if yer don't mind, I don't want to spoil a good thing for yer!"*, jested Ged and added, *"Don't forget yer mask an' yer D.D.T.!"* Pepsi thanked Mule for his kind advice and comments then allowed him to resume his patrol. The sergeant drove over to the old lady, a plastic carrier bag adorned her lice infested head to protect the little parasites from the rain! The old lady sat there serenely, quite oblivious to the fine, penetrating and soaking rain.

Pepsi drew alongside his offside kerb and wound his window down. *"Hiya Nellie, alright?"* Familiarised the sergeant who had never met her before! The cantankerous old lady continued to stare down the road at nothing in particular and grunted, *"I'm alright. Why?"*. The sergeant then asked her, *"I believe you saw a lad pushin' a child in a pushchair today, is that right love?"*. Nellie turned to the sergeant with an icy stare, *"Dunno, fuckin' might 'ave. Can't fuckin' remember"*, she replied. *"How are you fixed? D'yer want a couple of bob?"*, asked Pepsi, hoping to endear himself to the old girl. Even if she couldn't help him now, she may well be useful in the future. A couple of pound coins wouldn't break the sergeant's piggy bank. Having resumed her empty stare down the street, Nellie again turned to Pepsi and said, *"Fuckin' right! I'll always take a couple o' fuckin' quid"*. The benevolent sergeant alighted from his vehicle and went to the wet old lady and deposited two one pound coins into her grubby outstretched hand, then, as he was only in shirt sleeves, he quickly retreated back into the warm dry confines of his vehicle, out of the rain. Nellie never even uttered a word of thanks as she checked that the coins were genuine before secreting them inside her many coats. *"C'mon Nellie. What about this kid with the pushchair?"*, asked Pepsi.

"S'not fuckin' right, I'd kick 'is mother's fuckin' arse I would. Shouldn't allow fuckin' kids out with fuckin' toddlers, s'not fuckin' right", opined the old girl vehemently. *"So you did see 'em then? Where were they Nellie? Come on, 'elp me will you, I'm tryin' to find them"*, continued the frustrated but persistent sergeant. *"Jer mean the fuckin' lad with the fuckin' kid?"*, asked the eloquent graduate from Roedean. *"Yes! Yes! The lad with the baby. Where did you see them an' what did the lad look like?"*, went on Pepsi impatiently. *"What d'yer fuckin' think' 'e looked like? All fuckin' lads is all the fuckin' same aren't they? A fuckin' lad an' a fuckin' baby, that's what they fuckin' looked like"*, said Nellie getting bored with the conversation. She then stood up and said, *"I'm fuckin' off now!"*, as she brushed imaginary specks and bits from her grubby wet coat. *"Ang on Nellie, just tell me what the lad was wearin' will you, anything you can remember that will help me find 'em"*, asked the frustrated sergeant, hoping to detain her further to assist his enquiry, but 'Effin' Nellie just shuffled off into the evening's drizzle, 'interview' concluded!

It was well past midnight when the Gay Marine and Policewoman Perry dragged the very reluctant young Casey into the cold confines of Angel Street police station. Their shift had gone home long ago. The search for baby Stacey would continue with a vengeance from first light, in a few hours time. Some officers were working late, having stayed on to assist the Stacey enquiry which so far had proved negative. The station sergeant, the welfare orientated, born again Christian, Sergeant Corson, the 'balloon' (now don't let me down now will yer?), stood behind the station counter and greeted his colleagues' arrival.

"Hello John", he said, then eyeing the tired form of young Casey and being fully aware of his and his family's sordid, anti-social and anti-police attitude, he still greeted the youth with the kind words, *"Hello Danny, you must be cold and tired. Never mind son, we'll sit you in the interview room with a nice hot cup of tea*

and a blanket while you wait for your mum!" The Gay Marine really appreciated Sergeant Corson's benevolence towards the trash that was brought into the station by him and his officers, especially after some of those same officers had been subject to violence by the same trash. *"'Ang on a minute Mike, I'll go an' look for an all night store so I can get the little bastard some sweets and a bottle of pop eh?"*, said the Gay Marine to emphasise his utter disdain at Sergeant Corson's welfare. *"Oh come on John, he's only a kid"*, said the Christian sergeant. *"If it was up t' me I'd chain 'im to a post in the yard outside, the little bastard"*, was the Gay Marine's retort, adding, *"You'd better get the social services out here as well, 'cos this little bugger's goin' nowhere yet!"*

Unmoved, the 'Balloon' came from behind the counter and, taking Casey's arm said, *"C'mon son, let's get you into the interview room, it's nice an' warm there an' I'll bring you a mug of tea"*. The ungrateful and resentful young Casey was then ushered into the interview room, away from the Gay Marine's unsympathetic clutches, and locked in to await the arrival of his parents, the social worker, and - his tea.

Eventually Casey's dishevelled, unwashed mother arrived, well after Penny Cockgrave the social worker, to greet her son, demanding an explanation for his detention. Casey's father was conspicuous by his absence, *"Probably out screwin'"*, commented one officer wryly. Eventually, all entered into a welfare orientated discussion concerning Dawn's evil little offspring, as to when he would be interviewed with regard to his day's activities terminating with his 'outing' and subsequent apprehension in Leighton.

Sergeant Corson had no qualms about his granting of bail to Casey and he was eventually bailed into the care of his charming parent to re-appear at Angel Street thirteen hours later at three o'clock in the afternoon. As usual, on the little party leaving the police station, Sergeant Corson's immortal words were heard, *"Now don't let me down now will yer Danny?"*.

At 2.45pm prompt later that same afternoon, a refreshed, bright eyed and bushy tailed Sergeant Royle joined his co-sergeant, 'Pepsi' Coaler to take the afternoon parade. Of the Inspector Platt (the prat!) there was no sign. After standing the parade at ease and distributing the various files and instructions to his officers, the Gay Marine proudly announced his and Policewoman Perry's previous day's 'litter' collection from out in the sticks at Leighton.

At the same time as the Gay Marine was taking the parade, old Arnie Pearson was wandering along the winding path across the 'Moors' with his little brown and white mongrel Tess. Tess was yapping excitedly after she had found a short length of stick which she placed at Arnie's feet, willing her master to pick it up and throw for her. As usual at this time of the day, especially as the kids were all at school, plus the fact that the weather was not all that enticing, the 'Moors' were deserted except for the duo on their daily walk. Arnie duly obliged his impatient pet and picked up the stick then threw it for the energetic little Tess to retrieve it for him to repeat the ritual.

Their little game went on for a while as the two meandered along the path until eventually old Arnie, not being as young and energetic as he once was began to tire of their game. Arnie's geriatric old arm began to ache with its continual, energetic gyrations. Arnie saw the pond beyond the grass bank and decided to sling the stick out into the muddy waters as he knew little Tess wasn't struck on water polo and would abandon the game once she realised that the only way to retrieve her stick would be to swim for it!. The stick landed with a 'splosh!', causing a couple of Mallard ducks to rapidly vacate the area, quacking their dissent at the unwelcome intrusion of the wooden missile into their peaceful foraging. Tess scuttled after the stick but skidded to an abrupt halt at the water's edge. Tess looked up at Arnie, her eyes willing him to go in and get it for her.

"C'mon Tess, let's get 'ome an' I'll give you yer tin o' Chum before I put me feet up", said Arnie to his devoted little mate and co-habitee at his terraced house in Celt Street. As he made to resume his homeward journey Arnie noticed the little pink bonnet by the reeds. Wondering what it was Arnie ventured closer and with the help of a twig which he snapped from a nearby willow tree the little woollen garment was retrieved. "Mmmm!, looks new", muttered Arnie to himself as he twisted it tightly to squeeze the water from it. Arnie tucked the item into his pocket, for no other reason that it was there, looked new, – and was free! Little Tess renewed her yapping as she jumped up and down, wagging her tail, wondering if Arnie had found something else to throw for her. "*No, not for you Tess, c'mon, let's go 'ome*", repeated Arnie and resumed his trek back home, completely oblivious to the paramount importance of his find.

Meanwhile, at this very time, the notorious little Danny Casey was just arriving back at Angel Street as per his bail conditions. However, on this occasion he was accompanied by his equally objectionable and unco-operative father, Vinny. They were ushered through to the interview room and detective 'Randy' Walker was summoned from the CID office upstairs, having been made completely aware and fully up to date with Casey's and the Gay Marine's subsequent action concerning the dinner money and Leighton saga the day before.

Across town, old Arnie was almost home when he passed a group of children as they played a game of skipping with a length of rope tied across the pavement to a lamp post. The kids knew Arnie and little Tess, Arnie often gave them sweets as he chatted to them while the kids would throw a stick or their ball for his equally popular little dog. As Arnie had to step off the pavement and into the cobbled street to evade being strangled by their rope, the boys and girls shouted, almost in unison, "*Hiya Mister Pearson!*". "*Hiya kids*", replied Arnie to the little throng. One of the little girls, four year old Collette Slee left the others and cheekily asked Arnie, "*'Ave yer gorreny 'sweeties' Mister Pearson?*". Arnie stopped and patted Collette's head while little Tess jumped up at her excitedly vying for her attention. "*No, I haven't got any today*", he replied, then suddenly remembering his recent find on the 'Moors', and knowing Collette had a six month old sister Donna, Arnie retrieved the little pink bonnet from his pocket. "*Here, give this to yer mum for yer sister, it only wants washin'*", offered Arnie.

Little Collette snatched the bonnet and ran off to her nearby house shouting, "*Thank you Mister Pearson*". Collette burst into the house and excitedly deposited the little 'gift' from Mr Pearson onto the table as her mother, Teresa, sat bottle feeding little Donna, her six month old sister. "*There's an 'at for Donna*", announced Collette before dashing out to resume her game of skipping in the street with her playmates. Mrs Slee continued with the important matters in hand, that of feeding little Donna, and didn't take much notice of Collette's offering, as the energetic little girl was always rushing in with, or for, something!

Back at Angel Street CID office the sound of chairs scraping and banging about the floor echoed around the room as Detective Constable 'Randy' Walker drew up a chair and joined Mr Vinny Casey, his lovely young son Danny, the Gay Marine and last but not least, the little throng was also joined by the member from the Social Services, Mrs Penny Cockgrove. Papers were shuffled, there were coughs as one or two cleared their throats, then proceedings began with Detective Walker introducing himself to young Danny. Danny's father Vinny needed no such introduction. He was only too well aware of who Randy was, he had been dealt with by him often enough, (and the Gay Marine also!). Randy began, "*Right Danny, do you know why you're here today?*".

Casey sat and shuffled his feet uncomfortably and stared fixedly at the floor, not moving his head or his gaze. He wiped his sleeve across his nose causing the cuff of his anorak to glisten with its deposit of mucus then grunted, "*Aven't a clue!*". "*Oh I think you have*", replied the detective. "*E's told yer 'e doesn't know 'asn't 'e? So fuckin' tell the lad*", snapped his articulate father. Randy looked at the Gay Marine, then to Mrs Cockgrave, before replying, "*Very well, I'll tell you then. Yesterday morning, ten year old Michael Evans was on his way to school with Ronald Tucker, also ten, when he was threatened with violence, then robbed of his dinner money, by you Casey!......*" "*Woz fuck me! I wasn't in Park Road yisterdie!*", interrupted the cocky little thief. "*Who said anything about Park Road Danny? Nobody mentioned anything about Park Road!*" emphasised a delighted Randy. The boy's street wise father however, instantly noted his son's crucial faux pas and quickly and eloquently instructed his offspring, "*.........Say fuck all lad, we'll gerra fuckin' brief*", then for added effect he went on, "*If yer gonna charge 'im with anythin', charge 'im otherwise we're goin'!*".

It was pointed out to the father and son that statements had been taken from the two complainant boys and their parents, plus, the knife found in Danny's possession, having been retrieved from him by PC Rothwell up in Leighton, had been formally identified by young Michael Evans and, more importantly, Michael's father (also Michael), whose knife it was, having been removed from his fishing tackle box that very morning by young Micky. It was obvious, even to Casey's obnoxious father, that the only sensible thing to do now, was – enlist the services of a very able lawyer! Casey senior was asked if he had any particular solicitor in mind and subsequently the notorious defender of the town's felonious low life, Mr Fraser Warburton, was requested by the Caseys and duly sent for.

Casey was interviewed at length and questioned about his whereabouts after he left the two boys. He continued his vehement denials of having any knowledge whatsoever of the boys but eventually the futility of his denials was pointed out by Warburton, as the evidence of the boy's robbery was overwhelming. Casey was encouraged to see the futility of his idiotic behaviour and he eventually did admit only to having taken money from Evans. Casey completely denied any knowledge of other criminal behaviour, other than playing truant and jumping a train up to Leighton Halt.

Casey was eventually cautioned and charged with stealing (not robbery?) from Micky Evans. The errant young hard knock was bailed into the custody of his father to appear before Warbreckside Juvenile Court at a later date. Again, the prophesied little 'gem' from Sergeant Corson prior to Danny's departure, *"Now don't let me down now, will yer son?"*

Two hours after the hapless Casey and his father left Angel Street for their salubrious residence, Barry Tectar and his pal Eric Andrews, two 15 year old soccer fanatics were making their way through the 'Moors' en route to Sleeper Street to call for a third mate, Brian Wiley. The trio were then going to play football in Greenacres Park. Barry kicked their football over to his mate then Eric hooked a return pass for Barry to head back. And so it went on, each youth passing the ball to and fro to the other as they made their way along.

As they were passing the pond at the back of the Hudson Lane Animal Clinic Barry performed some fancy footwork and head manoeuvres with the ball before propelling a powerful volley in the direction of Brian. *"Bet yer won't stop that Bry!"*, shouted Barry as the spherical missile headed towards his mate. The full sized ball shot past Brian and hit the lower branches of one of the trees bordering the pond. The branches stopped the powerful shot, then deposited the ball into the murky waters with a plop! The ball was six feet away from the grassy bank, "*Fuckin' 'ell Barry, you get that, I'm not gettin' me fuckin' feet wet!*", said Brian. "*Bloody 'ell, it's only by the edge!*", said Barry and added protestingly, "*I can't gerrit, me trainers le' rin!*". The two went to the water's edge and realised that their prized ball was just out of their reach. Barry then noticed the protrusions of two red handles, just breaking the surface further along the bank. "*E'yar, we'll get it with this shoppin' trolley*", he said enthusiastically and confident that his· initiative would soon enable them to resume their game, and their journey.

The two youths ran along the bank and Brian held on to Barry as he leaned out and took hold of the nearest handle. "*Okay Bry, pull us back will yer, I've gorrit!*". Brian gently took Barry's weight as Barry pulled at the handle. "*Bloody 'ell, don't say it's full o' shoppin'?, it's a bit 'eavy. Keep tight 'old of me will yer Bry?*", instructed Barry to ensure that he didn't take an unscheduled dip. The red handle of the submerged 'trolley' was pulled backwards .... "*Fuckin' 'ell!*", shouted the startled Barry as he let go of the handle with shock at his gruesome discovery that it was not a shopping trolley at all, but a child's buggy, with a baby in it! Brian, equally shocked, had the presence of mind to splash into the water and retrieve the buggy with its lifeless little corpse. Without saying another word the two youths abandoned the buggy and their ball and ran out into Hudson Lane, making for the animal clinic. The breathless two arrived and banged in panic on the locked doors of the premises. The door was eventually opened by a very apprehensive assistant Martin Telford.

On seeing the breathless and excited duo, Martin asked what on earth the problem was. After hearing their story with scepticism the assistant then rang the police and informed them of the boy's gruesome find at the nearby pond.

During the time that the boys were relating their tale to the assistant at the animal clinic, a woman walking her dog became hysterical when she too came upon the child's body, left for anyone passing to see by the two shocked youths. In no time the scene of the find was cordoned off and an 'incident' room was set up nearby in the force's mobile caravan. The news of the horrendous discovery spread throughout the area like wildfire, even before the press, radio and television had released the details of the find. Witnesses were sought and those who reported their 'sightings' of the couple on the morning of Stacey's disappearance were traced and interviewed. Unfortunately no person could positively identify the boy pushing the buggy as being Danny Casey.

The horrendous details of little Stacey's abduction and subsequent finding on the 'Moors' dominated the radio and television news bulletins as well as consuming reams of space in the newspapers. Mrs Teresa Slee was later watching the 9 o'clock news on her television after getting her two little offsprings Donna and Collette finally off to bed, and was enjoying a little peace and quiet before her common law husband Wally, (not the childrens' father!) returned from playing darts down at the unsavoury 'Frightened Soldier' pub in Frodsham Street. Wally would return, half sloshed, with their pie and chips supper at 11 o'clock after which they would go to bed. Suddenly Teresa was attracted to an item on the television during its coverage of the Stacey McKenzie affair. Detective Chief Inspector Alec Davenport of Angel Street CID appeared holding a child's little pink woollen bonnet, stating that police were looking for a similar bonnet to the one he was holding which Stacey was wearing at the time she was abducted from outside Nessie's hairdressing shop in the Grange Precinct.

Teresa was transfixed, she suddenly remembered the damp, pink little bonnet that Collette had dropped onto the table earlier that day thinking she was doing her mother a favour. Teresa however, not knowing from where her daughter had obtained the garment, threw the little hat into the bin. It could have come from anywhere. Not for one moment did Teresa consider that the bonnet now residing in the bin, among the potato peelings and residue from the family's dinner and other rubbish, here in her back yard could surely be the very item displayed on the screen, could be the same item that the police were appealing for. Nevertheless, her curiosity got the better of her and she went out into the yard to forage among the smelly contents of her bin to retrieve and inspect the discarded garment again. "*Of course! It would be underneath everything!*", cursed Teresa.

Eventually she retrieved the woollen garment and took it back inside to look at it more closely under the bright florescent light in the kitchen. *"M-m-m-m!, I just wonder, ...nah!, it can't be surely?"*, mused Teresa to herself. However, she couldn't stop wondering. Again, the bonnet was shown on the ten o'clock news and Teresa was really frightened now as she conceded that the garment portrayed on her screen undoubtedly bore a very striking resemblance to the now-soiled and smelly item she was holding in her hands. At first she was reluctant to report her daughter's acquisition as, first she never even asked where she had got it from, and second, she didn't fancy making a fool of herself if the bonnet she had was not the item that the police were looking for, - but was it? The more Teresa pondered, the more uncertain and worried she became! Finally she made her decision, she would have to report her daughter's find. Anyway, she certainly did not want the police at the house now, especially if an inebriated Wally arrived home, knowing he was not exactly over fond of the police! Teresa wouldn't mention anything to Wally on his return, she would however, call in at Angel Street tomorrow and hand the bonnet in as found property.

Next morning Mrs Slee called into Angel Street with her two little children. Placing the pink bonnet, (washed since its retrieval from the bin) onto the enquiry desk, she informed Constable Garvey, *"Me little girl found this yisterdie!"*. Paul's eyes popped. *"Just bear with me love"*, he instructed, *"I'll get the CID. This could be what they're looking for"*, then picked up the telephone on the desk. *"Urry up then, I can't stay 'ere all day"*, replied Mrs Slee, she didn't like being inside a police station, 'it was bad luck'!

A short time later Detective Sergeant Foster and Chief Inspector Davenport appeared. *"Morning Madam, I'm Detective Chief Inspector Davenport and this is Detective Sergeant Foster"*, said Alec as he introduced him and Frank. *"Oh yeah, I know yer now, I saw yer on the tele last night"*, replied Teresa. Teresa was politely asked to accompany the two detectives upstairs to the CID office as Frank held aloft the counter hatch to enable Teresa and her two infants through into the inner sanctum of the building before entering the lift to take them up to the second floor. Teresa hurriedly explained, *"I didn't find the 'at, Collette 'ere brought it in didn't yer love?"*. Little Collette pressed herself into the corner of the lift trying to secrete herself behind her mother's skirt, pretending to be shy. *"I don't know where she gorrit from"*, went on Teresa and instructed her little mite, *"Go on 'Collie, tell the man where yer got the 'at from yisterdie"*. Collette, still maintaining her 'coyness, chewed at her sleeve and pressed her face into her mother's leg. *"Never mind, we'll 'ave a little talk in the nice warm office eh?"*, said the Chief Inspector in an attempt to endear himself to the little girl.

Once upstairs in the busy CID office, the two detectives put their potential star witnesses at ease and made them comfortable, furnishing Mrs Slee with a cup of tea and a calming cigarette and making little Collette happy with a chocolate Crunchie bar and a bottle of pop from the canteen along the corridor. The staccato of noise, as typewriters clattered almost in unison and radio traffic cackled every now and again added to the mayhem.

By now, little Collette had made herself at home and happily coated her face with chocolate (as well as the front of her little coat) and swigged at her pop. Without any prompting, she now started to be a little chatterbox, realising that she was the centre of attention. Detective Policewoman Bienne knelt down and wiped the little girl's face with a tissue. 'Les' managed to clean Collette's face, but not her coat. As the two detectives were talking to Teresa, Collette suddenly piped up, *"Mister Pearson give me the 'at!"*. The detectives and Teresa looked at Collette, then, in horror at her little sister Donna who was by now 'wearing' chocolate all over her face, and in her hair. *"Oh friggin' 'ell Collette, look at the baby! Yer've covered 'er in bloody chocolate!"*. The two children were now covered in the sticky mess. The Chief Inspector, anxious to maintain his good relationship with Teresa, quickly dispatched policewoman Bienne to fetch a cloth and towel to clean up the two children and (hopefully) pacify the by now irate Mrs Slee who ranted, *"Look at them, wot jer give em friggin chocolate for?"*.

Eventually, peace was restored after Detective Bienne performed a miracle of ablutive surgery and the two youngsters looked brand new once again. Collette at first became unco-operative at having been deprived of the meagre remains of her chocolate Crunchie, however, this was soon rectified, with the permission of Mrs Slee, when a bag of dolly mixtures mysteriously appeared in Collette's hand!

"*Let's begin again*", suggested Alec Davenport, "*Tell me about the pink bonnet again Teresa*". Teresa asked for another cup of tea then again said, "*I told yer, I never found it, our Collette gorrit off someone*", and turning to her now clean and once again happy little girl said, "*Tell the man where yer got the 'at*". Collette duly obliged and said, "*Mister Pearson give it us yisterdie*". "*Where was this?*", gently coaxed Sergeant Foster.

Collette was showing off now and spoke with a mouth crammed full of dolly mixtures, sharing some with Frank as she spoke, by showering the front of his suit with various bits of mix! "*When we wuz skip*"..... bits everywhere!.. "*ping in our street*". Teresa assisted, "*They were all outside our 'ouse in the street. They were skippin' over a rope on the lamp post*". "*Can you remember when?*", asked Davenport to either of the two. Teresa replied, "*She brought it in when I was feedin' Donna in the afternoon, so it would be about three I suppose*". Frank asked little Collette, "*Why did he give you a hat? 'Cos it's much too small for a big girl like you isn't it?*". Collette replied instantly, "*Coz 'e always gives us sweeties but 'e didn't 'ave any so 'e give me the 'at for me baby sister!*".

Frank was busy noting all that was said, his pen permanently poised over a ream of A4 sheets and statement forms. "*Exactly who is this Mister Pearson?*", asked Frank turning to Teresa. "*Oh he's harmless enough. He lives in Celt Street. He's always out with his dog*"........"*Her name's Tess!*", butted in Collett, "*Shurrup when I'm talkin' will yer*", snapped Teresa then continued to Frank, "*He gives the kids sweets and they play ball with his dog, he seems okay. Everyone knows 'im an' the kids love 'im an' is dog*", concluded Teresa.

The lengthy chat and interview was eventually concluded and after Teresa and Collette were thanked profusely for their valuable help, Policewoman Bienne escorted them downstairs to the door (after Teresa refused Frank's offer of police transport to take them home). Teresa informed them that she intended to so some shopping before calling to see her mother in Acrefield Gardens. Teresa was informed that she may have to be seen again during their enquiries in due course and she was again thanked for her assistance so far. The pink bonnet would have to have its owner traced if possible and formally identified. In the meantime it would be minutely examined forensically. In no time at all the little pink bonnet was formally identified and positively established as being that which had adorned the head of little Stacey McKenzie.

Old Arnie Pearson was soon traced and quickly taken in to Angel Street, protesting in vain at being unceremoniously dragged from his bed at three in the morning. Officers remained at his home to carry out a meticulous forensic search of the premises. It seemed to Chief Inspector Davenport that things looked promising for an early result in this tragic and callous affair.

Arnie was (not too gently) taken up to the CID office where he was made to remove all his clothes after he stated that they were the same clothes that he was wearing during his walk over the 'Moors' when he said he found the bonnet. He even had to remove his shoes and his two pair of holed socks. *"What the fuck's goin' on fer Christ sake?"*, protested Arnie, alarmed at his rough treatment and lack of compassion for such an old man. He was furnished with a white, one piece suit of paper overalls to don, and a pair of slippers, even though the overalls covered his feet also. *"Wot's all this fuckin' carry on?"*, he still protested vehemently, and innocently. The frightened pensioner was terrified. *"We're makin' enquiries into the abduction and subsequent murder of two year old Stacey McKenzie on Monday"*, boomed the harsh voice of Chief Inspector Davenport, his own lack of sleep now showing by his none existent sympathy for the old man's predicament!

"Murder? ME? Be'ave yerself, yer must be fuckin' crackers!", wailed Arnie and continued, *"I LOVE kids. you lot are off yer fuckin' trolley!"*. Arnie wondered if this was all a bad dream, was he having a nightmare? The stark reality of his cold and hostile surroundings indicated to old Arnie that this was not so, he was not going to wake up from his terrifying ordeal, this was the real thing! *"How in God's name jer come ter think I'd kill a child fer fuck sake?"*, he bleated to the unfriendly gathering. *"Give 'im a cup of tea"*, ordered Sergeant Foster to no one in particular. *"Stuff yer bloody tea, I wanna go 'ome, worrabout me dog?"*, snapped the irate old man. *"Dog? DOG?"* snapped Alex Davenport, *"We're concerned about the killing of a CHILD, not a bloody flea-ridden mutt!"*. Arnie quickly replied, *"Well you've got the wrong one 'ere, that's fer sure!"*. Davenport

looked at the old man and spat out, *"Have we now? We shall see"*.

Then, the Chief Inspector flashed the little pink bonnet under Arnie's nose and, hardly able to control his anger and contempt asked, *"Where the hell did you get this from eh?"*. *"I told yer, I found it in the pond on the Moors"*, protested Arnie once again. *"Yeah! The same pond as Stacey was drowned in, particles from the pond water found in this bonnet matched some found in her little lungs you lyin' bastard"*, said Davenport, his voice raised in frustration and anger. Sergeant Foster sat and laboriously itemised every piece of Arnie's clothing and meticulously went through every pocket with his surgical gloved hands. Every item was separated, noted, lettered and numbered before being placed individually into its own plastic bag. Each bag was then labelled prior to being dispatched to the forensic science laboratory for meticulous microscopic examination.

"I'm tellin' yer, you've got the wrong man!", continued the protesting Arnie. *"Quiet fer Christ sake, just speak when yer spoken to!"*, instructed the Chief Inspector. On the face of it things looked almost 'cut and dried' with regard to the outcome of this enquiry. Arnie was at the scene of little Stacey's untimely demise, and he had been in possession of her little bonnet which, on his own admission, he had recovered from the very pond where it was established that Stacey lay submerged at the time! Arnie was ruthlessly questioned at length as to where he goes, what he does, why does he give sweets to the kids, and then again, the pink bonnet. Where did he get it from? Arnie would not be shaken.

He continued protesting his innocence, insisting he had found the bonnet and later gave it away as a gift. *"What pond? Where? When?"*, the relentless questioning went on....and on....and on! *"What were you doin' at the pond Arnie?"*. *"Nuthin, I was just with me dog throwin' sticks an' that"*. *"Where's the sticks?"*. *"Oh, I dunno, they were just sticks I found an' threw away when we'd finished with 'em"*. *"Why didn't you buy a fuckin' ball to throw like most people do?"*. *"Dunno, can't afford one I suppose"*. Frank then asked, *"D'yer like kids Arnie?"*. *"Course I do, yeah. I love 'em"*, was Arnie's genuine reply. *"Do yer now? D'yer like playin' with kids? You know, playin', messin'!"*, cut in Davenport cynically. *"Course I like playin' with em, I love 'em, they all love Tess as well"*.

Arnie then changed his tone, *"I don't know what yer mean, messin'. What d'yer mean messin'?"*, asked Arnie in all innocence.*"C'mon, stop pissin' us about Arnie, you know yer did it, we know yer did it, so why carry on tellin' lies, we've got the 'at the kid was wearin' when you threw her in the pond!"*, persisted Davenport. Arnie again insisted, *"I never took no kid, I found the fuckin' 'at in the pond I tell yer. I never saw no kid. I'm sorry I took the fuckin' 'at now!". "It's lookin' bad for yer Arnie!"*, said the calm voice of Frank Foster.

"Fuck this!", retorted the affronted old man, *"I wanna see a solicitor or someone, yer can't pin this on me!". "Oh you'll 'ave a solicitor alright Mister Pearson don't worry about that, 'cos you'll fuckin' well need one"*, concluded the Chief Inspector, confident that they had the person responsible for the heinous crime they were investigating. Arnie was eventually placed into a cell pending further enquiries and a solicitor was summoned by Sergeant Corson, the ever benevolent 'balloon'.

Mud on Arnie's shoes matched the mud on the wheels of Stacey's buggy, both established as being from the bank of the pond where little Stacey was found. The cause of the toddler's death was confirmed as drowning. There were no marks of violence on the body. The poor child had simply drowned through being submerged in the murky waters of the 'Moors' pond.

A scrutinous and minute examination of the child's buggy failed to reveal any marks of value on its handles. Other than the pink bonnet and Arnie's own admission of placing himself at the scene of Stacey's demise and subsequently retrieving her bonnet from the very same pond, there was no further incriminating evidence (although this would appear to be sufficient) to confirm Arnie's responsibility for the crime. Things however, certainly did look very sinister and serious for the hapless Arnie, but not once did Arnie's tale falter or change in any way whatsoever.

Due to Arnie's detention and the overwhelming evidence against him, the matter was shifted and deemed unconnected to young Casey and subsequently the youth appeared to be off the hook. He would be dealt with for stealing Michael Evans's dinner money, for which he would be only too pleased to plead 'Guilty'.

As time went on, although Chief Inspector Davenport was by now convinced of old Arnie's responsibility for Stacey's death, Arnie's constant denials in the face of almost concrete evidence to the contrary, troubled Detective Sergeant Foster. Frank was starting to have doubts, and indeed, started to believe Arnie. If Arnie was lying, why would he so readily admit to being at the very spot where the child was later found? And why didn't he dispose of the very incriminating piece of evidence that would 'sew' matters up, the bonnet, instead of hanging on to it and drawing attention to himself by giving it away. No, thought Frank, it just didn't add up. Frank was becoming more uneasy as he turned everything over in his mind. Finally, he decided to voice his concern to his Chief Inspector.

"*What are you suggesting Frank?*", asked Davenport as they sat in his office and chatted over coffee. "*Bottom line is, I don't think old Pearson did it sir*", said Frank forcefully as he lit his pipe and waved away a pall of blue smoke before depositing his spent match in the boss's ashtray. The boss then decided to copy Frank and lit a cheroot to add to the room's pollution before replying to his sergeant, "*I do Frank, I do. Everything points to the old bastard as far as I'm concerned, the evidence is overwhelming*". Frank would not be shaken from his views, "*No, with respect sir, I think we should go right back to the beginning and start again*", he said, by now convinced that Arnie really was telling the truth. Frank went on, "*It's just too obvious, we've missed the boat somewhere sir*".

Davenport took a deep drag of his obnoxious, foul-smelling cheroot and held the smoke in his mouth before finally releasing it across the room above Frank's head with a hiss, "*Mmmmmm!, what the hell makes you think that Pearson didn't do it Frank?*", he asked, still convinced of the old man's guilt, then before Frank could reply, continued, "*He was found to have, as he readily admits, Stacey's bonnet before she was found, and he admits to being at the pond, at the very spot where she was found fer fuck sake...........!*", Frank nevertheless interrupted his boss, "*That's the very point sir! Why would anyone put themselves at the scene of such a despicable act voluntarily and unnecessarily, it doesn't make sense. He wasn't trapped or coerced into putting himself where the kid was found, an' 'e's not the epitome of intelligence is 'e? Anyone wishing to convince us of their innocence would surely make sure that they distanced themselves from that pond. Lets's not forget, we never 'ad a clue that he was anywhere near the pond until he told us himself, an' anyway, no one would be daft enough to keep such an incriminating item as Stacey's bonnet, let alone willingly give it away........, surely, the best thing to have done with that would have been to hide it, or burn it? If e'd done it!".*

There was a long, quiet pause as Davenport sat and digested the logic of Frank's careful, considered analysis. Finally the boss gave a long sigh as he examined the ash that was about to break off from the end of his weed to contaminate his meticulously tidy desk top. Frank sat and remained deeply pensive, wondering what the boss would think of his subordinate's logic?

"What do you suggest Frank?", asked the boss. *"I think............!",* "Yes?", cut in Davenport. *"Well sir, I think we're barking up the wrong tree 'ere. I must admit, I myself thought we'd cracked it when we pulled Pearson in, but his house is 'clean'! Regarding clues I mean! Plus, I think his tale is too original to be a load of lies. After a lot of thought, I think we should 'ave that little bastard Casey back in. If we can crack that little shit's story, I think we'll clear the matter up, that's my opinion sir",* concluded the deep thinking detective sergeant. *"I wish Pearson's dog could talk",* said Davenport with a frustrating sigh.

Leaning back in his chair, assuming he'd won the boss over to his train of thought, Frank said, *"The more I think of things sir, the more I'm convinced young Casey's the bastard we want for this".* Arnold Pearson was subsequently released on police bail to reappear at a later date, during which time police would continue their enquiries. Poor Arnie returned to his house to find it trashed by the local populace in their premature finding of his guilt. Hostile threats and warnings of dire consequences should Arnie dare to remain in the area were daubed in obscene graffiti on his walls, and most of his windows had been smashed. Of Arnie's faithful live in friend Tess there was no trace.

Arnie returned to Angel Street in tears, he was a broken man. He related his tale of 'wrongful' detention and his being blamed for killing a little girl, into the sympathetic ear of the Gay Marine. From the outset, Sergeant Royle was convinced Casey was behind little Stacey's disappearance and was shocked when he learned of the old man's detention. The Gay Marine had known old Arnie for a long time, but, as the evidence was so overwhelming he conceded that Arnie appeared more likely to be responsible for the child's murder. Now, Arnie having been released without charge, indicating that there wasn't enough evidence to substantiate his appearing before the court, the Gay Marine's opinion vindicated the old man, causing him once again to be convinced that Casey was the guilty one! "If you aren't to blame Arnie, I promise you I'll do what I can to catch the bastards who have already tried you and found you guilty, then wrecked your 'ouse. When I do get 'em, they'll pay dearly for what they've done. We'll let you know if we find yer dog", promised the Gay Marine.

Sergeant Royle and 'Mule Train then transported Arnie back home and helped repair some of the damage as they awaited the arrival of the Council glaziers, having been summoned by the Gay Marine himself. Sergeant Royle again colluded with Detective Sergeant Foster, reiterating his previous, unshaken belief in Casey's involvement in the saga of little Stacey, "Certainly in her abduction at least!", insisted Sergeant Royle. "I take all you've said on board", said the detective sergeant, adding, "I've been uneasy myself about the old man having done it, I must admit".

Old Arnie was kept under close observation by the police, especially the Gay Marine and his 'troops', ensuring the old man's security and welfare. Sergeant Royle made it known amongst the local 'low life' that anyone bothering the old man from now on would invoke the personal wrath of the Gay Marine, and most knew what could mean!

Casey was again interviewed at length and eventually admitted having wheeled little Stacey away from the shops that fateful morning "Just for a laff!". He strongly denied however any involvement in the child's subsequent drowning, insisting that he only took it for a couple of minutes then left her outside "Some 'ouse, a couple of streets away but I forget whereabouts now!".

It wasn't long before Casey succumbed to the skilful and lengthy questioning of the CID team who relentlessly pursued Casey's every word. Suddenly Casey turned to his father sitting next to him and blurted, "Dad, I didn't kill 'er, the pushchair rolled *down the bank, it was an accident"*. Casey broke down into uncontrollable sobbing, continually bleating, *"I didn't kill the baby honest, it was an accident an' I got frightened and ran away"*.

Eventually the full circumstances of Casey's bullying saga of that Monday morning were outlined in full by Casey in the presence of his parents and solicitor Fraser Warburton. The little tyrant was later charged with the unlawful killing of Stacey Mckenzie and kept in the care of the local authority's secure unit until his subsequent appearance before the Crown Court. Casey was sentenced to be detained for a period of two years for his wicked and horrific crime. The judge described him as *"An apprentice of the Devil himself!"*.

It was then the turn of the Casey family to receive their long overdue 'comuppence' (in the eyes of all at Angel Street at least!) when their own 'hovel' in Seldom Street was to receive the undivided attention of the hostile residents of the Meadowfield Estate, who were not known for 'taking prisoners'. The difference being this time, the Casey family's pleas to the officers of Angel Street, for help and protection were officially received, but unfortunately the Gay Marine and his sections' euphoria at the plight of the Caseys, had brought on acute deafness and lethargy to them all! Even though 'passing attention' was promised, a 'blind eye' was turned by most.

Eventually Arnie was accepted back into the community for what he was, and had always been, nothing more than a kindly and benevolent old man. Tess was never found but the Gay Marine later presented old Arnie with a pup he had obtained from his friend Martin Mear down at the Hudson Lane Animal Clinic. The grateful and forgiving old Mr Pearson accepted the little pup bitch which would hopefully ease the heartache of Tess's loss. In honour, and gratitude to the officers of the Gay Marine's section at Angel Street, Arnie named his new little pet, 'Angel'!

The risks, and the penalties !

It was almost 11-30 on a wet and windy Saturday night as Derek Wilkie and his son 'Neddie' made their way home after an evening's alcoholic imbibement down at their local pub, the Frightened Soldier in Frodsham Street. 'Big Degsy' was a retired docker and although his son Neddie was one of the country's unemployed statistics, he regularly worked, unofficially, as a doorman at various clubs in and around Warbreckside. Neddie was a keen body builder and martial arts enthusiast. Both men had enjoyed a good 'session' and a game of darts and were looking forward to getting home and in out of the rain to their supper before making to their beds.

As the two made their way up Dalton Avenue Derek suddenly stiffened, he grabbed his son's beefy arm and said, *"Am I pissed or is that my van bein' driven away from outside our 'ouse?"*. The Wilkies' van was always parked outside their terraced house under the street lamp. Degsy's tools and other bits and bobs were in the van as he carried out odd jobs now and again to substantiate his beer money.

Neddie squinted as he tried to focus his eyes before cursing and confirming his father's comments, it was indeed their van that was being surreptitiously driven off into the night. Both men broke into as much of a run as their evening's alcoholic consumption would allow. They both watched helplessly as they saw their vehicle turn left into Liverhead Road before disappearing out of sight.

At the same time as the van's unauthorised driver, Albie

Mitchel, a well known car-thief and petty crook, turned into Liverhead Road with the Wilkies' van, the Gay Marine was driving his patrol car in the opposite direction. At his side sat Constable Paul Garvey, having been picked up from his beat by the sergeant for a spell in the car out of the rain. As the two officers passed the top of Dalton Avenue, young Garvey suddenly exclaimed, – *"Hey!, 'ang on Sarje, I'm sure that was Albie Mitchel drivin' that van out of Dalton Avenue"*. Mitchel had been dealt with by most of Angel Street's officers for his persistent stealing of or from motor vehicles and was also well known to the Gay Marine. *"Mitchel 'asn't got a fuckin' van"*, lisped the sergeant. *––"And e's a disqualified driver!"*, added Garvey. *"Are you sure it was Mitchel?"*, asked the Gay Marine. *"Well no, I'm not certain, but it certainly looked like 'im Sarje"*, replied his constable enthusiastically, his adrenalin rising. Ensuring all was clear in front and behind, the Gay Marine impressed his young colleague by executing a perfect 'handbrake turn' before speeding off in pursuit of the rapidly disappearing van in the distance. In no time the powerful patrol car managed to draw alongside its 'prey' and the Gay Marine said, *"Right!, let's see if it is Albie Mitchel"*.

The two officers instantly recognised Angel Street's persistent thorn in its side! Sergeant Royle activated the blue strobe light and sounded his klaxon horns. The startled Mitchel looked in horror at the patrol car alongside him and considered trying to escape by increasing his speed, however, he then spotted who was behind the wheel of the police vehicle and all such thoughts instantly evaporated. Mitchel knew it was futile to do anything but pull over! He would try and bluff things out! The by now very frightened Albie stopped the van as requested and the two officers pulled in behind him. Constable Garvey and the Gay Marine were at Mitchel's door in an instant. Sergeant Royle opened the driver's door of the van then reached in and retrieved the keys from the ignition. He snapped at Mitchel, *"C'mon you, OUT!"*. Although the hapless thief was only too willing to comply with the sergeant's request, nevertheless the Gay Marine assisted Mitchel from the van by grabbing him by the scruff of his neck and propelling him out into the roadway. Mitchel was then held by the sergeant in a vice-like grip against the side of the van.

The rain continued to pour incessantly as Mitchel was asked by the sergeant to account for his use of the vehicle. *"I, I borrowed it off a mate to get 'ome 'cos it was rainin'!"*, Albie lied. *"What's yer mate's name?"*, lisped the Gay Marine. *"I only know 'im as Danny, I drink with 'im in the Broken Spear"*, bluffed the hopeful Albie. *"Well that's an indictable offence for a start, drinkin' in that bloody den of iniquity"*, said the Gay Marine. Paul threw in his two pennyworth, *"You're a disqualified driver, so 'ow come you're behind a wheel anyway?"*, he asked. *"Me ban's finished"*, lied Mitchel, but Garvey and his sergeant knew differently. *"Finished me' arse!"*, snapped the angry sergeant at Mitchel's audacious and feeble attempt to undermine his intelligence, before adding, *"You were disqualified for two years an' that was only eight months ago, so try again yer lyin' bastard"*.

Paul sought the sanctuary of the police vehicle and closed the door before requesting an 'owners check' regarding the van, out of earshot of Mitchel.

However, proceedings were interrupted by the arrival of a breathless Derek Wilkie and his son, having continued a hopeful pursuit of their vehicle, each wondering if they would ever see it in one piece again.

"What the fuck's goin' on?", gasped an out of condition Derek. His big powerful son Neddie had hardly broken sweat, even though, like his father, he also had consumed a fair amount of beer during the evening. *"Why?, What's it got to do with you?"*, asked Sergeant Royle, with Mitchel still in his grasp. *"What's it got to do with me?"*, Wilkie senior retorted and continued, *"It's MY fuckin' van, that's what it's got to do with me!"*. The Gay Marine was just about to place Mitchel into the patrol car before getting in himself out of the rain, but the arrival of the Wilkies and their subsequent comments concerning the ownership of the van had made the sergeant change his mind!

Constable Garvey confirmed Mister Wilkie's ownership as he alighted from the police vehicle. *"The van belongs to a Derek John Wilkie of one three one Dalton Avenue, Warbreckside, the very road we saw 'im coming out of Sarje"*, said Paul. Mr Wilkie snapped, *"See, I told yer, that's my name!, Derek John Wilkie, an'*

133

that's my van. It's just bin taken from outside my 'ouse five minutes ago, phew! I'm bloody knackered!". By now most signs of his inebriation, apart from breathlessness had left him due to his impromptu 'nocturnal and rain sodden marathon' along Liverhead Road. *"You didn't lend this prick yer van then?",* asked the sergeant knowing full well what the angry Wilkie's answer would be. Before Wilkie could reply however, his son cut in, *"Yer must be fuckin' jokin''Sarje! 'E won't even lend it to me, never mind anyone else!".*

"Well, well, well", said the Gay Marine, *"Someone's telling the most esteemed and illustrious sergeant porky pies aren't they Mister Mitchel?".* Mitchel stood there, soaked and terrified, but having looked at the size of Wilkie's powerhouse of a son, Mitchel was thankful, for the only time in his life, that he was at least in the hands of the police!

Sergeant Royle sighed then said, *"Well there seems to be some sort of a mix up 'ere, so I'll leave to you three to sort it out, byeee!".* The Gay Marine then nodded to his constable indicating for him to join him back in the patrol car out of the rain. The two officers then drove off into the wet night and resumed their patrol. Constable Garvey turned to his sergeant, *"Mitchel's disqualified Sarje, why didn't we lock 'im up?"* he asked in all innocence and disappointment. The Gay Marine turned to his subordinate and grinned, *"You know who the owner's son, big fella is don't you?",* he asked mischievously. Garvey looked puzzled, *"No why? Who is he?",* he replied. The Gay Marine went on to enlighten his young officer, *"That's the Neddie Wilkie the bouncer. I'm surprised you 'aven't 'eard of 'im, he's one hard lad, an' I mean 'ard! I thought 'e might like a 'word' with Mitchel for pinchin' 'is dad's van, an' causin' the two of em to get soaked as then ran round 'alf the bloody town!".* The sergeant grinned at the thought of the notorious young Mitchel being chastised properly for once! Constable Garvey then received his sergeant's drift but made no comment!

The two officers drove around town as they 'diligently sleuthed'!, but the rain, being the best policeman ever, kept most of the town's criminal fraternity indoors during such inclement weather. Forty minutes after the duo had left the wet trio and the van in Liverhead Road their radios burst into life as they drove along. *"Could a mobile attend Liverhead Road near to Burton Road, ambulance in attendance, man, possibly drunk, found lying with injuries!"*, announced the dulcet tone of the female radio operator at headquarters. Sergeant Royle picked up his microphone and acknowledged, *"Golf Sierra one six, I'm handy for that, cancel any other mobile an' I'll make to the scene".* *"Roger Golf Sierra one six, thank you, out"*, acknowledged headquarters. The Gay Marine headed in the direction of the 'incident' and said to his colleague, *"Oh dear, I wonder what this could be?"*. Garvey however, sat quietly in apprehensive anticipation as to what they might find on their arrival, – he was saying nothing! The sergeant and his constable arrived at the venue of the 'incident' within minutes of their radio call but of the ambulance or man lying in the road there was no trace. The area was deserted except for occasional vehicular traffic travelling to and fro. The Gay Marine reported his arrival at the deserted venue and was informed that the ambulance had cleared the scene with a casualty and was making for Warbreckside Infirmary. The sergeant was instructed to attend the hospital also. Constable Garvey still made no comment, but his hard-hearted sergeant, as usual getting his priorities right, muttered enthusiastically, *"We'll get a nice hot cup of tea while we're in casualty eh?".*

The two duly arrived at the casualty unit and witnessed yet another Saturday night's mayhem as the busy nurses and doctors rushed about repairing the town's abusive, violent and ungrateful drunks and gang fight casualties or the poor victims of traffic accidents.

Eventually a tired Sister Morley approached Garvey and his sergeant, it was obvious by her expression that her patience had been sorely tested yet again and again!. *"Thank goodness you're here Sarje"*, she said, and continued, *"There's a right yob in that cubicle over there harassing one of our young housemen who is trying to stitch up someone the yob's beaten up, he wants to continue the fight in here!"*. *"Leave it to me sister"*, said the Gay Marine and strode over to the the cubicle indicated. A crew-cut youth, obviously the worse for drink was challenging a prone patient, lying on a bunk. A young and obviously very intimidated doctor was being prevented from inserting stitches into the patient's head wound. *"Come on, me an' you outside, now!"*, snarled the threatening youth. Before he could say another word, the Gay Marine threw aside the plastic curtain and grabbed the offensive youth. *"Nah, leave 'im, come outside with me instead"*, said the lisping sergeant who then unceremoniously dragged the snarling yob out into the wet night by the collar of his tartan shirt. Once outside the sergeant tossed his patrol car keys to Paul and said, *"Here y'ar Paul, one D and D (drunk and disorderly) for yer. Take the bastard into Sergeant Corson for some ministering!"*. The drunken bully was handcuffed before being not too gently secured into the back of the car. *"Get this crap out of my sight, I'll wait 'ere for yer,"* were the sergeant's final comments as he returned inside, leaving his very able constable to incarcerate the offender into the care of the ever benevolent 'Balloon' at Angel Street.

After leaving his originally threatening, drunk and disorderly, but now considerably subdued prisoner at Angel Street, and completing the paperwork required for his forthcoming court appearance on Monday morning, Constable Garvey returned to the hospital to join his sergeant as instructed.

"That was quick Paul", complimented the Gay Marine. Paul then asked apprehensively, *"What about the casualty from Liverhead Road, Sarje?"*. *"Dunno, 'e's still in with the doctor"*, replied the sergeant. Sister Morely, although she was continually busy treating the night's casualties, found time to furnish the two officers with a hot brew of tea as they sat in her office. The sister and her overworked colleagues were grateful for the two officers' timely arrival and subsequent ejection of the violent and intimidating drunk as he threateningly hampered their efforts. Finally, young Doctor Woolfall entered the office and said, *"You can go and have a word with Mister Mitchel now sergeant. He's bruised and a bit concussed and we'll keep him in overnight, but I'm sure he will be okay tomorrow, just a bit sore perhaps. He say's he can't remember what happened to him"*, concluded the doctor as he poured himself the almost cold remnants of what was left in the tea pot before returning once again to the town's wounded revellers.

"Cubicle 3A", informed Doctor Woolfall. *"Thank you sir"*, acknowledged the sergeant as he and Garvey made for Mitchel, lying there on a bloodstained bed behind closed plastic curtains. The Gay Marine looked down at the bruised, battered and heavily bandaged head of the Angel Street 'tea leaf'! *"Good heavens, why if it's not my ol' friend Mister Mitchel, what on earth happened to you?"* asked the sergeant in mock concern. Although badly hurt, Mitchel nevertheless managed to utter, *"I walked into a fuckin' lamp post!"*. *"Is that right Albie? Is that really how you came by your injuries?"*, persisted the sergeant. *"I told yer didn' I? I was pissed an' walked into a fuckin' lamp post"*, repeated the apprehensive Mitchel, knowing only too well that to say anything else would ensure his incarceration for theft and driving while disqualified the instant he walked out through the hospital doors, he knew the Gay Marine only too well! *"That'll do me"*, said Sergeant Royle as he entered Mitchel's verbal account of his misfortune into his official note book, instructing Constable Garvey to do likewise.

Sergeant Royle, on completing the very important pocket book entry, then said, *"Right Albie, we'll leave yer to it then. Get well soon won't yer? Take it easy when yer on the ale an' keep away from 'lamp posts', goodnight"*.

The sergeant took the car keys from his subordinate then drove Paul around his beat, allowing him the luxury of riding instead of walking. Paul turned to his sergeant and said, *"Bloody 'ell sarje, you're an' animal, you really are!"*. The Gay Marine grinned and replied, *"Aye, but I bet Mitchel will think twice before pinchin' another van though!"*

A week later, the weather having improved considerably, and a warm bright sunny Sunday morning caused sergeant Nigel 'Pespi' Coaler to decide to accompany policewoman Perry, the 'Red Onion' as she resumed her beat after her mid shift break during morning duty. The two officers left the station after a hearty bacon and egg breakfast. Each looked forward to the conclusion of their day's duty at three o'clock, Pepsi was thinking of taking his wife Dawn and two young children, seven year old Martin and his five year old sister Jennifer, for a trip out into the country, perhaps for a picnic, as it was such a fine warm day. Vera was contemplating a barbie and a few drinks in her back garden with a couple of friends. Even today, warm as it was, Vera lived up to the cause of her nickname 'onion' as she wore a jersey and a cardigan under her tunic! Pepsi had considered walking about in his shirtsleeves, but his vanity preferred wearing his tunic so he could proudly display the three broad silk chevrons on each sleeve!

The smart, uniformed couple meandered around the various streets before they decided to take a short cut across the now notorious area of waste land known as the 'Moors', their notoriety due to the recent Stacey Mckenzie tragedy. Eventually the two reached Rayburn Road where they stopped for a chat when they saw wheelchair bound Maggie Tolan, who, although suffering from the dreaded and incapacitating MS, always had a cheerful and friendly word with everyone she encountered. Old Maggie loved the bobbies, 'her bobbies' as she always referred to them. The old girl could be seen out and about on most days, providing the weather, and her condition, allowed.

After ten minutes or so of idle chit-chat, Pepsi and Vera bade the friendly lady farewell and continued their walkabout. *"Isn't it always the way sarje? There's a person with the world's worries on her shoulders and she's as cheerful and friendly as they come"*, remarked an impressed and sympathetic Vera. Pepsi agreed with her sentiments entirely and added, *"And always the low-life thrives and reaches healthy old age, it just isn't fair!"*. The two strolled on through the streets, nodding occasionally to the many Sunday morning car-washers or privet hedge-trimmers, or those just sitting sunning themselves on their front doorstep as they read the Sunday papers. Eventually they turned into Slumberland Hill and started the long climb up to Liverhead Road just over a mile away.

In the distance, ahead of them, could be heard the noise of a powerful motorcycle, obviously being driven at speed. The sound grew louder indicating the vehicle's approach to the two officers. *"Bloody 'ell, sounds as though ee's movin"*, said Vera. Suddenly, some distance away the machine appeared from round a bend plummeting down Slumberland Hill towards them. Sergeant Coaler gasped and said, *"Jeeesus!, we'll 'ave this bloody maniac before 'e kills 'imself, or some other bugger".*

Pepsi strode over to the centre of the road and raised his right hand, signalling the approaching rider to pull over and stop. The machine's engine tone indicated that the rider was decelerating and appeared to be conforming to the sergeant's request. The machine's nearside indicator started to flash as the big, powerful machine slowed down. Pepsi stood as the big machine approached. It looked sinister and foreboding in its all matt black finish, its large cylinder pots and chrome crash bars protruding from each side. The big, powerfully built rider looked equally sinister in his all-black leathers, emphasising his broad shoulders. His helmet, also matt black, with its dark tinted visor down, totally concealed the rider's face. For some unknown reason, perhaps it was the menacing look of the big machine and its big 'mean' looking rider, whatever it was, all of a sudden Pepsi felt a chilling fear at the machine's approach, he suddenly felt vulnerable and defenceless. The sergeant stood his ground and prepared to go and speak to the rider. He intended to give him an almighty admonishment and record his details so that he could pass them on to his colleagues for future reference. Pepsi would give this idiot a bloody good roasting for attempting to substitute Slumberland Hill as a replacement for the Isle of Man T.T. circuit. Even though it was a reasonably quiet Sunday morning and Pepsi conceded there was very little traffic about, nevertheless, it was a thirty mile per hour area. Pepsi would check the rider's documents and if all correct, would send him on his way with a flea in his ear!

However, the rider decided differently! After pretending he was stopping for the sergeant, the rider suddenly revved the machine's engine into a deafening roar, engaged a lower gear to facilitate a rapid 'take off', then accelerated his powerful machine, driving it straight at the stranded sergeant. Such was the velocity of the three-quarter of a ton missile's acceleration, its front wheel lifted over twelve inches from the ground. The equally helpless WPC Perry stood traumatised, not daring to believe what she was witnessing. In a flash the heavy motor cycle struck the sergeant with a sickening thud that could be clearly heard by all in the vicinity. The impact threw the officer into the air and propelled him nearly twenty feet before he landed in a stunned and crumpled heap in the centre of the road, his right leg contorted hideously into a broken, torn and unnatural shape under his body, making the poor injured sergeant look grotesque. Policewoman Perry ran to her colleague, subconsciously shouting into her radio for an ambulance and assistance. As she did so the rider, somehow, skilfully having managed to remain on his machine, continued on, mounting his nearside pavement and scattering a number of people at a nearby bus stop as he did so, then driving back into the roadway and tearing on through a set of traffic lights showing red against him. The machine then turned left into Gilbey Road and vanished out of sight making good his escape.

Passers-by rushed to help the badly injured sergeant and his deeply shocked colleague. Pepsi lay there moaning as the acute pain from his shattered right knee, and his damaged right arm and shoulder brought him round from the comfort of his brief spell of unconsciousness. His right knee had taken the full impact of the engine's protruding cylinder head and crash bar of the speeding machine.

Pepsi's eyes were glazed as he tried to focus them and comprehend what had happened. He tried to move! *"AAAAAGH!, my leg, my leg!"*, he yelled and then he remembered his colleague, *"Vee, Vee, what's happened? My leg, my leg......!"*. The gentle voice of the red onion, fighting hard to retain her composure and hold back her tears, reassured her sergeant as she gently placed a blanket over him which had suddenly materialised, in an attempt to keep him warm, *"Lie still Sarje, you're gonna be okay, ambulance's on its way"*, she said, her voice faltering. 'Christ, I hope I sound convincing' she thought to herself! In no time, the welcome sound of blaring klaxon horns emanating from her colleagues' vehicles could be heard as they sped impatiently through the streets to the aid of their injured colleague.

Three cars arrived within minutes and although it was obvious that the badly injured 'Pepsi' needed to be hospitalised urgently, it was decided to await the arrival of the ambulance to convey him as it was apparent that only the skill of the paramedics could be used to move him, even though each driver was keen to get him to hospital as soon as possible.

A short time later the shrill wail of the ambulance could be heard in the distance as it too sped through the streets. A large crowd had gathered by now, some of whom were morbidly vying for the best view of the blanket covered casualty. Tea was kindly offered by one of the throng but this was discreetly and tactfully refused by the misty eyed WPC Perry who had visions of her popular sergeant's demise there in front of her very eyes, before the ambulance could get him to the sanctuary of Warbreckside Infirmary.

Her self control nearly gave way and tears almost came when the reassuring hand of a colleague gently squeezed her shoulder as he muttered, *"Alright Vee, c'mon love, the ambulance is here now, they'll look after him"*. It was all Vera could do to prevent herself bursting into tears as she watched her sergeant lying there groaning in agony as one of the medics flicked a hypodermic with his finger a couple of times before administering the relaxing and peace inducing morphine into Pepsi's left arm while the medic's colleague held up the sergeant's sleeve. Such was the state of Pepsi's badly injured leg that it took the ambulance crew many minutes gently tending the sergeant before they could finally manage to place his shattered leg into the metal splints. After almost ten minutes, the skill of the ambulance crew enabled them to raise and gently manoeuvre the partly anaesthetised Pepsi into the ambulance as the morphine took hold. The ambulance then lost no time in conveying the injured sergeant off to hospital for urgently needed surgery, together with his traumatised policewoman colleague.

The scene was then rapidly cleared of bystanders as the studio and CID arrived. The area was measured and photographed in detail, witnesses sought and microscopic examination of the scene carried out by the 'scenes of crime' officers (SOCOs). To cater for any possible inclement weather, a tent was erected to protect the scene and any clues. Traffic diversions were then instigated. No effort would be spared to bring about the apprehension of the cold blooded perpetrator of such a heinous crime. *"Bloody typical, he couldn't 'ave come off the bloody bike an' killed 'imself, oh no, those bastards never injure or kill themselves!"*, said one bitter officer. His angry sentiments were echoed by all who heard them!

On Pepsi's arrival at hospital, his uniform was quickly, efficiently and unceremoniously cut from him to facilitate a speedy assessment of his injuries before he was then taken with equal speed down to theatre. The by now delirious sergeant was rapidly put out of his pain when a general anaesthetic was administered. Then the long and laborious efforts were commenced to repair the horrific injuries to Pepsi's shattered right leg.

Back up in the casualty department, Sister Morely decided that policewoman Perry was in obvious need of sedation due to her state of shock. The officer was ordered into a cubicle where she too was seen by a doctor. The Red Onion lay quietly in a side room cubicle still fearful of the outcome of poor Pepsi's operation down in theatre.

Suddenly her black thoughts were disturbed by the welcome lisp of the Gay Marine, her 'senior' section sergeant. Sergeant Royle had already been primed by the Sister as to Vera's condition and as he sat down at the side of her bed, he took her hand in his then quietly, tactfully and (hopefully) reassuringly said, *"Sergeant Coaler's a strong bugger Vee, you mark my words, he'll be alright, you'll see!"*. The Gay Marine's kind words and the squeezing of her hand was finally too much for the woman officer to bear. She burst into uncontrollable tears and snuggled her face into her big sergeant's shoulder. Sister Morely and a doctor entered the small room and sister Morely politely gesticulated to the sergeant to vacate the cubicle while the doctor administered a sedative to the emotional and shocked policewoman. The Gay Marine had previously collected Sergeant Coaler's wife Dawn, leaving one of his officers to look after her two children. He rejoined a very pale faced Dawn as she sat in sister's office with a consolatory cup of tea, impatiently awaiting news of her husband's fate, inwardly terrified as to what the outcome would be.

Eventually Sergeant Royle was allowed to take his policewoman home after she eventually insisted that she was okay. The Gay Marine conveyed Vera to her home and on leaving her with her partner, he promised that he would ensure that she would be kept informed with regard to any developments as to sergeant Coaler's condition. Sergeant Royle advised Vera to take a few days off duty sick but she would not hear of it, insisting that she would be back on duty the following day. *"Okay, but give us a ring in the morning if you change your mind"*, instructed the sergeant. Vera promised that she would.

Sergeant Royle later went off duty at the conclusion of his day's shift. At this time, there was still no news relating to Pespi and as the Gay Marine was about to leave the station he spotted his colleague the station sergeant, the benevolent 'Balloon'! *"Any news of Pepsi John?"* asked the genuinely concerned sergeant. *"Fraid not Mike"*, replied the Gay Marine, adding sarcastically, *"I 'ope the bastard who ran 'im down gets some 'elp and counsellin' before we get hold of 'im, 'cos there's no doubt 'e'll bloody need it!"*. The Gay Marine's cynicism however, passed completely over the Balloon's head unnoticed.

Pepsi's operation lasted a number of hours before he was at last taken up and settled into ward M3. Things looked a lot worse than they were when poor Dawn was finally allowed to go in and sit at her still unconscious husband's bedside. The sight of all the drips and transfusion tubes and drains into and from Nigel's arms and leg, and the oxygen mask covering his face was more than the distraught young wife could endure and she finally broke down and sobbed uncontrollably. Sister Carter instantly appeared and provided Dawn with a hot sweet cup of tea which Dawn sipped gratefully. The sister was quick to assure her that things were not as bad as they appeared and her husband's injuries were not now 'life threatening'. He would be a more 'presentable' sight in a few days' time! Dawn was then left alone with her husband.

A short time later the sister reappeared and asked Dawn if it would be alright for a lady Detective, WDC Bienne to join her at her husband's bedside. The sister explained that her visit was first to see her colleague and secondly to note anything of importance that Pepsi may recollect when he regained consciousness. Dawn unhesitatingly gave her permission and was joined by a very concerned 'Les' Bienne.

Pepsi didn't start to stir from his anaesthetised slumbers until many hours later after his visitors, and the day staff, had all gone home. However, even then he would remain heavily sedated and would be continually monitored by the night staff. At first Pepsi didn't have a clue as to where he was, he wondered deliriously what in hell's name had happened to him, but very soon the excruciating pain in his right leg, especially his knee, and his arm and shoulder brought him almost back to reality. A special 'bracelet' was on his left wrist from which a tube led into a plastic cylinder containing morphine. This was in turn connected to a needle which had been inserted into a vein in the back of his hand. The bracelet resembled a wrist watch but instead of a 'clock' face, it had a small button. The patient could depress the button and a shot of morphine would be sent into the patient's vein to relieve his pain, a small non-return valve eliminated any possibility of overdosing. This was slowly and patiently explained to him by a softly spoken angel in the guise of nurse Pat Waddington until his numbed brain finally managed to take on board her simple instructions and he would be able to operate the contraption himself, as and when Pepsi's pain threshold forced him to do so.

Finally Pat, having satisfied herself that her poorly policeman had grasped the gist of what she had been telling him, left to continue her other chores in the ward saying soothingly, "*You're going to be okay Mister Coaler, I'll be hovering about so just call when you want anything!*". WDC Bienne had left some time earlier when it had been decided that he should be left alone to try and get some rest. Pepsi dozed intermittently and was roused again when another young nurse appeared at his bedside and gently took his left arm and wrapped the the inflatable blood pressure pad around his upper arm, placed the stethoscope to her ears and began squeezing the rubber ball to send the mercury up the registering tube. This task completed, she replaced the apparatus into its metal box.

She then tore a paper wrapper open from which she retrieved a plastic thermometer before placing it under Pepsi's tongue. Next, she held his left wrist with her right hand and tilted up her inverted fob watch at her breast with her other, enabling her to check his pulse. Even in his acute pain and delirium, Pepsi found the gentle, physical contact and attention by the young nurse to be soothing and somewhat therapeutic. The nurse then took up the pad at the foot of Pepsi's bed and wrote her findings before jesting, *"Everything's okay, you'll live to fight another day!"*. The young nurse concluded her tasks by fussing about his pillows and blankets and gave final checks to his tubes and drain before moving on to her other patients who would equally receive her undivided attention. Pepsi feebly nodded his head in gratitude and slowly sank back into a blissful, morphine induced sleep. Although he only dozed in fits and starts, he was slowly to become aware of his surroundings.

Again the wounded sergeant's sleep was interrupted when he felt the painful and acute necessity to empty his swollen bladder. Pepsi lay there but his brain wouldn't function enough to tell him to hold on to his water until he could summon the services of a bottle! Although he dreamed he was standing at the toilet in his own bathroom at home he somehow knew he shouldn't just wee there and then. However, he nevertheless just lay there and relieved himself. Ah! Utter relief he thought, but he was soon aware that he had in fact, peed the bed! He could not stop the flow once he had started and he seemed to be peeing forever. It slowly dawned on him that his bottom, back and legs were feeling a nice warm sensation, but this soon turned to real discomfort when he started to feel cold and wet and realised what he had done, and where he was!

Even in the condition he was in, Pepsi felt reluctance and embarrassment at first, choosing to ignore things in the hope that the waterlogged bed would eventually dry and no one would notice, (he was temporarily in superintendent land!). He even feared chastisement from the lovely young nurse for not asking for a bottle!

On Pat's next routine visit to monitor her charge, Pepsi managed to inform her of his embarrassing 'misdemeanour' beneath the sheets. Pat quickly put her miscreant at ease when she lifted the sheets and said, *"Don't worry pet, it's no problem, we'll have things back to normal in no time, I'll just go an' get my wellies!"*. This had the desired effect in eliminating Pepsi's acute blushes! She gave Pepsi a reassuring pat and was quickly joined by her colleague, staff nurse Edie Logan and in what appeared to be no time whatsoever Pepsi's sheets were changed and he was dried and talced and once again restored to his previous 'comfort'. Even in his painful and restricted confines, Pepsi was amazed at how efficiently nurses could change and transform a soaking bed (and its immobile patient) back into a warm and dry nest, without removing or hurting its occupant.

Even there, in the dead of night, Pepsi managed to sincerely thank and profusely apologise for causing the nurses 'unnecessary' work! The two nurses wouldn't hear of it. Staff Nurse Logan went and made a fresh cup of tea for the three to quietly consume at Pepsi's bed while things were quiet, except for the regular nocturnal chorus of coughing, snoring and farting from various parts of the ward as the patients tossed and turned in their beds. *"Christ, what wonderful girls you nurses are"*, whispered the grateful, and very impressed, even though drugged, sergeant with sincerity. As they sat and whispered in the semi darkness, the ward's only illumination being from the solitary, dimmed night-light near the door, Pepsi again succumbed to his morphine and sleeping pills and once again dozed off into a fitful sleep.

Although he slept, he was regularly brought back to reality when the powerful pain broke through the morphine barrier. There seemed to be no respite to his discomfort. Eventually the tinkling of tea cups and the rattle of the tea trolley heralded the arrival of the new day as the day staff came on duty enabling their night duty colleagues to make their way home to commence their day's hibernation. The change of staff brought new smiling faces to his bed after they had been updated by the off going staff nurse Logan as to Pepsi's overnight progress. Again the girls made sure that Pepsi was as comfortable as possible as they once again logged his various functions and attended his needs.

A short time later the friendly, smiling face of Molly the ward orderly came to ask Pepsi if he would like a cup of tea to start the day. Pepsi nodded his head in the affirmative. Molly poured out the sustaining nectar and asked, *"Milk and sugar?"*, again the affirmative nod. Molly charged the cup and placed it on the bed tray and instructed, *"Let it cool an' I'll be back in a minute to help you!"*. She then continued on around the ward supplying all those who required the morning's pre-breakfast beverage.

When breakfast did arrive later, Pepsi couldn't look at any food, the taste and sickly effects of the previous day's general anaesthetic still prevailed, maintaining a general feeling of nausea. The nurses tried to persuade the sergeant to eat something, if only a piece of toast, but Pepsi adamantly refused, to the dismay and concern of the staff. The pain was again giving Pepsi a lot of 'jip' and he once again pressed the button on his wrist 'watch', administering another shot of morphine to himself as he sought the solace and sanctuary of drug induced oblivion.

The days came and went with monotonous and painful regularity, but slowly Nigel's condition improved. The officers from Angel Street came to visit their injured sergeant at every opportunity when they were either on, or off, duty. Dawn never missed a visit to her beloved, and took the children to see their daddy as soon as the tubes and other equally frightening paraphernalia had been disconnected and removed and some semblance of normality had returned to Pepsi's complexion and he was deemed cosmetically acceptable to the two youngsters. Even then little Jenny kept enquiring tearfully why her daddy was bandaged and had 'black and yellow marks' on his face. However, it wasn't long before the little duo accepted Pepsi's 'colourful' appearance and looked forward to their visits to Warbreckside Infirmary. Pepsi would jest with them about 'stealing' his grapes as soon as Dawn brought them in and placed them onto his bedside locker.

Meanwhile, back at Angel Street, no stone was being left unturned as Sergeant Coaler's colleagues continued their endeavours to trace and apprehend the person responsible for inflicting such horrendous and disabling injuries to one of their fellow officers as he carried out his duties. Unfortunately, as yet, all enquiries had so far proved negative. The local villains however, were enduring a bad time as they were constantly being harassed, especially by the Gay Marine as he tirelessly attempted to glean any information which could lead to the individual concerned.

The Gay Marine was not impressed by some senior officers who had originally advocated that the matter be dealt with as a traffic accident! Efforts would continue with a vengeance in an effort to bring the matter to a successful conclusion. In the meantime, the Gay Marine was first to accept the fact that what had sadly befallen his colleague, Sergeant Coaler, lying there in Warbreckside Infirmary, was part of the risks and penalties of being a front line police officer, out there at the sharp end among the angry men!

Broken Bobbies

Eventually after many weeks incarerated in his hospital sick bed, Pepsi gradually grew stronger, and with the continual devoted and undivided nursing and attention by those ever persistent and thorough doctors, nurses and physiotherapists, the wounded sergeant was eventually able to hobble about the immediate area of his bed with the aid of a zimmer, closely monitored by Tracy, the ever vigilant physio, who Pepsi had christened, 'The Fuehrer', much to Tracy's intense disapproval! However, Pepsi would never forget the utter dedication shown to him by all those in whose care he was, he would also never forget his colleagues in the force who had continually shown their concern both for him and his family during the recent trying and traumatic times after his horrific ordeal.

As the days went by, Pepsi was eventually allowed out of bed, and his 'wanderings' took him further afield. Sometimes he received admonishment from Sister for 'pushing himself too far'! in his attempts to regain his fitness and mobility, and also for not enlisting the aid of the nurses when things became too much for him. However, Pepsi thought that no matter how hard he tried, he could never satisfy Tracy, the ever demanding physio who always expected that little bit more!

Pepsi was regularly visited by the Gay Marine, as his trusty co sergeant never missed an opportunity to call at the hospital to see his injured mate. It mattered not whether the Gay Marine was on, or off, duty, the big tough sergeant always found time for a visit.

As Pepsi lay relaxing and dozing on his bed one

quiet weekday afternoon, he was suddenly startled by the unexpected arrival of his Inspector, none other than Platt the Prat, as the Inspector tapped Pepsi's bedside locker with his stick. *"Afternoon Sergeant Coaler, I just thought I'd pop in to see you and assess the situation!"*, uttered the tactless officer to his drowsy subordinate. *"Oh!, hello sir, you startled me! Anyway, thanks for calling in"*, acknowledged Pepsi politely. *"Yes"*, went on the pompous Inspector as he removed his silver braided peaked cap and plopped into Pepsi's bedside chair, his cap seated in his lap, *"You're better off in here Sergeant I can tell you, it's all go back at the station. What with trying to sort out the divisional snooker fixtures and at the same time trying to unravel the overtime figures, I haven't half got my work cut out"*.

The egotistic Inspector Platt went on and on as to how, due to Pepsi's absence, his work load had suddenly increased dramatically. Pepsi couldn't believe what he was hearing. What a vane bastard he is, thought the injured sergeant. Platt genuinely believed the utter importance of the mundane tasks he was subjecting himself to instead of involving himself in the sole purpose of his (unpopular) existence at Angel Street, that of being out on the streets with his men!

Platt was completely oblivious to the dissent he was causing amongst his subordinates, especially the injured sergeant. Christ, if only the Gay Marine could hear what Platt was uttering, here at my bedside, thought Pepsi, Sergeant Royle would blow a fuse at listening to such pure, unadulterated drivel!

Platt babbled on as to how everything was just left to him to sort out, then he uttered another tactless gem, *"D'you know Pepsi, my leg is giving me some jip as well, I must have knocked it, I think I should be in here instead of you"*, he said seriously and completely ignorant at such a futile and inconsiderate comment to one so badly injured as his colleague, no doubt he even expects some bloody sympathy from me thought Pepsi.

"How long before you'll be back on duty do they reckon Sarje?", asked Platt, adding, *"You see, with you off duty sick, I'm down to just one sergeant"*. Pepsi's heart bled for the poor Inspector, perhaps I'd better get my zimmer and call in at the

station for a few hours in case there's any rowdy pubs that need sorting out, he thought cynically. *"I've no idea sir, my knee is shattered and my right elbow and shoulder are damaged as well"*, informed Pepsi in as pleasant of terms as possible. Platt still rambled on as to how various matters were being dealt with back at Angel Street, boring the bedsocks off poor old Pepsi.

Finally, as there was no sign of Platt making a move, Pepsi pretended to drop off to sleep now and again, explaining that, due to his powerful drug intake, he was having extreme difficulty keeping his eyes open. Eventually Pepsi's efforts bore fruit and finally Platt rose to his feet with a sigh as he realised that he was talking to himself! Platt donned his cap and left the ward. It was only when he heard his boss's voice in the distance bidding the sister goodbye that Pepsi breathed a sigh of relief and rose from his bed. He grabbed his trusty zimmer to help him painfully and laboriously to crawl along to the toilet for a much needed discharge of his lower colon, no doubt brought about by the laxative of Platt's visit!

On the Gay Marine's next visit to Pepsi a couple of days later, old Barney, the ward bed-wetter opposite to Pepsi, grunted, *"Friggin' 'ell, it's like a frigging cop shop in 'ere! The other day the 'Police chief' was 'ere as well!"*. Pepsi couldn't wait to inform his colleague of Platt's visit and his boring and tactless verbal tirade. *"What a bloody tosspot"*, lisped the big sergeant angrily, and continued, *"Why the hell didn't yer tell 'im to fuck off Pepsi?"*. *"What's the use John? Anyway, don't say anything though, just leave it and put it down to the fact that he's an idiot"*, asked Pepsi. Sergeant Royle retorted, *"It's just as well you've told me not to say anything 'cos I certainly would 'ave that's fer sure"*. The Gay Marine went on with venom, *"He places more priority on ensuring there's an adequate supply of bloody soap an' arse paper in the officers' toilets than gettin' out an' findin' the bastard who put you in 'ere"*. In the end the subject of Platt's visit was exhausted and Sergeant Royle reluctantly left his colleague after his visit which eventually was obviously beginning to tire Pepsi. *"No speedin' with that bloody zimmer"*, instructed the Gay Marine in banter to the amusement of those nearby as he made his exit.

The constant visits (and relentless jibes) by Pepsi's colleagues did wonders for his morale. Finally the big day came when he was allowed to go home. After nearly six weeks in hospital the wounded Angel Street warrior was discharged and taken home to recover in the comfortable confines of his home surroundings. Pepsi still had considerable difficulty getting about however, crutches had now replaced and made redundant his zimmer. Unfortunately, the excruciating pain still remained unabated in his shattered right knee. To make matters worse, the young sergeant was now suffering acute stress and deep depression due to frustration and apprehension as to his future.

As the days and weeks drew on, Pepsi became more and more morose. The constant, severe pain in his right leg never ceased. Although he became a little better regarding his mobility, he just could not manage without his crutches. Pepsi started to make excuses to avoid sitting out in the garden, throwing and catching the ball with young Jenny and Martin. Eventually the kids began to exclude their father from their activities and even though Pepsi detected this, his depression and constant mood changes prevented him from rectifying the situation which alienated him even more from his beloved children. The whole scenario was becoming one, seemingly endless and uncontrollable downward spiralling vicious circle.

Things were also becoming intolerable for poor Dawn, Pepsi's loyal and up to now tolerant and patient wife. Alas however, even Dawn's patience threshold was now starting to wear thin.

After a particularly hectic shopping trip on an equally hectic Saturday morning when the children seemed to have been at their most boisterous and mischievous, not to mention unco-operative, Dawn and the two children arrived home. Dawn was looking forward to nothing more than a nice hot cup of tea and a welcome sit down in her easy chair. After dumping her grossly overloaded and heavy shopping bags on the floor, Dawn's face dropped at the sight of her husband Nigel. He was still sat in his chair where she had left him three hours earlier, he was still sitting in the same position, just staring vacantly at the television screen, which was switched off! Pepsi gave no sign of a greeting, he didn't even turn to face them. "*Hi Dad!*", greeted Jenny — no response! Dawn walked through to the kitchen. The dishes still remained unwashed where she had left them after asking her husband to wash them for her after breakfast while she was out shopping.

Dawn put her hands to her face, the tears ran down her frustrated cheeks. She returned to the silent figure of her husband. "*Nigel, we just can't go on like this!*", she sobbed and added, "*Why don't you go to the doctor about your depression?*". No response, just a vacant stare ahead at the lifeless television screen. The two children, seeing their distressed mother, vanished out of sight up to their room. Dawn decided she'd ring the doctor herself and see if he could help. Fortunately, the Coaler family were blessed with having a very caring and understanding GP, Doctor Maurice Goldbourne. Dawn sneaked away and managed to get the doctor on the 'phone. Out of earshot of her still comatose husband Dawn poured her heart out to the doctor, apologising for taking up his valuable time. Doctor Goldbourne promised to attend as soon as he could and would 'have a word' with her and her husband. Dawn tearfully and gratefully replaced the receiver then began to worry about how her distraught husband would react on finding out about her concerned subterfuge in her desperate quest for help.

Doctor Goldbourne later attended as promised and was most concerned at his patient's demeanour. So concerned was he that he immediately placed Pepsi on a course of strong anti-depressants as well as his pain killing medication.

The weeks went by and eventually these turned into months. Pepsi's right leg showed no signs of improvement. Officers from Angel Street still maintained their constant calls to see their wounded colleague and his family and to make sure that they wanted for nothing. Finally, unable to stand the excruciating pain in his leg any longer, Pepsi again went along to see his untiring and sympathetic doctor. Doctor Goldbourne decided to refer Nigel to a prominent orthopaedic surgeon at Bayside's St Dominics Hospital in the neighbouring town of Troylands.

On his subsequent visit, after lengthy examination by the consultant surgeon, Mr Astley-Sloan, it was decided that an arthroscopy would have to be carried out to determine the amount of damage done and what the persistent problem might be. Consequently, four weeks later Pepsi attended the day ward at St Dominics. Although the pain continued unabated, Pepsi was lovingly tended and prepared for his exploratory operation by the nursing staff. As he lay there on the bed after having his leg shaved and coated in a liberal amount of cold, stinging iodine, his right leg was wrapped in green surgical paper and securely taped. He was issued with paper 'knickers' which he then put on, as well as a white gown and a hair net, prior to being wheeled down to theatre where a general anaesthetic would be administered.

Pepsi stared up at the passing ceiling lights as he was wheeled along the corridors. He could hear dinner plates being rattled nearby. His stomach rumbled as he smelled food cooking. As he lay there being propelled along as he stared, fascinated, looking up the nose of the porter as he wheeled his patient along. Even though Pepsi's leg was painful, he was hungry and he was feeling apprehensive, Pepsi couldn't help thinking to himself what a lot of hairs the porter had inside his nose!

Eventually his trolley was brought to a standstill inside a small room. The powerful smell of drugs and antiseptics was very strong. Pepsi could hear the rattle of instruments being placed on their metal trays. He could see two doors as he looked along the trolley and over his white woollen bedsocked feet, each door had a round 'porthole', through which he could see green gowned figures moving about beyond the doors. His hand was gently held by a nurse in similar attire wearing a surgical mask and cap. She squeezed Pepsi's hand before opening a large folder containing Pepsi's case notes. She perused the file then asked, *"You are?"*, *"Nigel Coaler"* answered Pepsi. *"What are you having done today Mister Coaler?"* She then asked. As Pepsi answered the latest question Doctor Jason Carruthers, the anaesthetist, appeared at Pepsi's side. The anaesthetist then flicked a hypodermic needle with his finger and thumb then tapped the veins on the back of Nigel's right hand. After this action had raised a vein sufficiently, the needle was expertly and painlessly inserted into the vein. Both the nurse and Doctor Carruthers talked to each other and the nurse verified items contained in Pepsi's file. Nigel was then asked to sign a consent form and as he did so the gowned duo were joined by the surgeon, Mr Astley-Sloan. *"So! Let's see what all the trouble is eh?"*, said the surgeon. The anaesthetist then connected a large syringe to the needle in Pepsi's hand. *"You'll feel a little drowsy, just breath into this mask and we'll pop you off to sleep"*, said Doctor Carruthers, as he gently and slowly pressed home the plunger, sending the anaesthetising drug into Pepsi's arm. *"How long were you in the force?"*, asked the doctor. Pepsi stared up at him and his eyelids started to feel very heavy. He tried to focus his eyes and answer but his speech was becoming slurred as he tried to keep his heavy, closing eyelids open. Voices were now becoming incoherent echoes fading into the distance. *"About fifteeeeee......"* - oblivion! Total darkness!.

The next thing Nigel Coaler knew was feeling a searing pain slowly manifesting itself in his right leg. It seemed to multiply as he started to come round from his deep anaesthetised slumbers. Pepsi tried to move. His leg was heavily bandaged and a sharp stab of pain shot up the inside of his right thigh from his knee. *"A a a a gh !"*, Pepsi let out a howl. *"It's alright Mister Coaler, 'all over now,"* came the dulcet female tones of a nurse as he felt her adjusting the sheet which covered him. He tried to open his eyes and lift his head but as yet he couldn't perform either task. Pepsi started to choke, then whatever was causing this was removed from his mouth. His throat was sore where it had been lodging. Of course, Pepsi now realised it was the airway being removed. Pepsi drifted back into a relieved sleep. He woke again as he was being transferred from the trolley onto his bed. He was shivering violently with cold. After another check by the nurse as he he was made comfortable in his bed and allowed to sleep off the effects of the anaesthetic.

Later, once Pepsi had regained consciousness sufficient enough to sit up, a pleasant young nurse brought him a cup of tea and some toast and marmalade. Pepsi thanked the young Florence Nightingale profusely and set about devouring the toast ravenously. Finally, after then consuming his tea, Pepsi allowed himself the comfort of another doze. Later, he was visited by Mr

Astley-Sloan the surgeon. *"How are you feeling now Mister Coaler?"*, he asked. *"Very sore sir"*, answered Pepsi politely. Mr Astley-Sloan looked serious and went on to inform his patient, *"Well, I've had a good look inside you knee. I'm afraid there's an awful lot of damage there ol' chap!"*. Pepsi asked, *"How bad is it?"*. The surgeon stood there, the sister now at his side. He folded his arms and cradled his chin in his hand and went on, *"Mmmm, we'ell, you're going to be out of action for some time I'm afraid, only time will tell if the damage is permanent"*, adding, *"and I must tell you that this could be a distinct possibility!"* Pepsi thanked the surgeon as they concluded their bedside visit. As he lay there the pain was unrelenting and Pepsi cursed the individual responsible for the predicament he was now in.

Once back home, the same routine continued. Pepsi just sat and vegetated. Even when he had to visit the bathroom it took an almighty effort to get himself up the stairs. Visits by his section and his pal the 'Gay Marine' were unable to raise Pepsi from the doldrums of acute despair. His morale was at rock-bottom. He remained constantly morose and could not be lifted out from his utter lethargy. Even the children seemed to sense there was resentment emanating from their usually doting father. Visits by the force welfare officers Eileen Henderson and Nigel Whittaker didn't help remove the dark clouds of depression. However, Eileen called again and suggested Pepsi spend a therapeutic couple of weeks down at the Police seaside convalescent home on the South Coast at Dansford.

Due to Pepsi's injuries, it was agreed that he would be transported down to the home by police car rather than attempt what would undoubtedly be an arduous, uncomfortable and physically demanding trip by train. On his subsequent arrival, again the Matron Miss Shuttleworth was there to greet the new arrival from Warbreckside.

Matron helped her charge up the steps and ushered him and his driver, Constable Donald Chalkley from his force's Traffic department, into her office for a welcoming cup of tea before Don made the long return journey back to Warbreckside. Matron instructed another Donald, the home's porter cum minibus driver and general dogsbody, to convey Pepsi's cases up to his room on the fifth floor. After their cuppa, and the completion of the administrative formalities of Pepsi's admittance, Don bade all goodbye and set off on his long return journey home. Matron helped Pepsi to the nearby lift and took him up to show him his room as she explained the rules and all the dos and don'ts, concluding her little 'lecture' with a veiled warning by saying, *"We had a bobby from the Met a short while ago who insisted on flouting most of our rules, so we sent him back to his force".* *"Oh dear, Serves him right!",* grovelled Pepsi in reply. Matron went on *"We had a bobby down here from Warbreckside a few weeks ago, Phillip Clayton, do you know him?",* she asked. *" 'Know 'im well Matron, he's one of my flock",* replied Pepsi hoping that Phil had behaved himself while he was down here!

Pepsi soon settled into the routine of the home. He liked Dansford and although he made new friends and enjoyed relaxing in the warm sun down there, his apprehension as to his future would not diminish. At the conclusion of his stay Pepsi once again returned home where he again resumed his position in his easy chair, sitting staring into space or at the television, whether it was switched on or not! He rationed his movements to minimise the constant, nagging pain, and the effort required as he was totally dependant on his crutches for mobility.

Eventually, Pepsi was summoned to Headquarters where he was to be medically examined and assessed by the force doctor, Doctor Smotte. Pepsi pleaded with Doctor Smotte not to cast him from his beloved career in the force, to which he was totally devoted. Pepsi 'promised' the doctor that it wouldn't be long before he was fit again, hoping against hope that he would be able to justify these promises! The sympathetic medic consulted his file notes at the conclusion of his examination. Finally, after a long pause which seemed unending, Doctor Smotte gave a long sigh before picking his words. *"We e e ll !, I'll leave things for a while longer and see how things develop, but I must tell you young man, your injuries are very severe and the job is very demanding, I don't need to tell you that, however, I'll see you in about six months or so before we make a decision eh?".* Pepsi thanked the doctor profusely, hoping for a miracle, as the sergeant knew only too well that the damage was permanent and his career was on the line. However, he was going to do his damndest to get back on duty if he could.

Alas, time went on and Nigel's leg not only showed no signs of improvement, but in actual fact, the leg's condition was definitely deteriorating. He could still only get about with the aid of his crutches and the pain would just not let up.

Pepsi underwent a further two operations in as many months to attempt to rectify what was now obviously a hopeless situation. Valuable time was running out. To make matters worse, his depression was now causing him, his family and his GP such concern that he was given counselling after which, as there were no signs of improvement he commenced psychiatric treatment at St Dominics Hospital Psychiatric wing, under Doctor Ahmed Rashid, the same hospital where he had seen the surgeon prior to his second operation!

Lengthy counselling and ruthless physiotherapy during the ensuing weeks did nothing to ease Pepsi's incessant pain and frustrating immobility in the sergeant's almost useless right leg. His specialists, both orthopaedic and psychiatric, were treating the unfortunate sergeant alongside each other. Pepsi received regular visits from the force welfare department and his Inspector, Platt the Prat! The latter doing precisely nothing to boost Pepsi's morale. Nigel spent another period down at Dansford in the hope that this would prove beneficial in enhancing his deplorable mental and physical condition, unfortunately, it did not! By now Pepsi's consumption of painkilling and anti-depressant tablets almost caused him to rattle as he moved about painfully on his crutches.

After another desperate consultation with Mr Astley-Sloan, it was decided that Pepsi would need to undergo yet another very painful operation, this time it was to be a total knee replacement, a major surgical operation indeed. Pepsi's hopes were again dashed when, after the op, he still remained just the same with regard to mobility but, the bloody pain was worse! Matters were not made any better when Pepsi was once again summoned to attend Headquarters to be examined by Doctor Smotte. This time there was no reprieve and, as a totally dejected Pepsi reluctantly expected, the axe fell! Sergeant Nigel Coaler's promising career was brought to a premature halt. Pepsi sat dumbfounded and tried to come to terms with the situation. He, a young sergeant on the ladder of promotion, even now he was still under the anaesthetic of promotional enchantment, then, all of a sudden, whilst doing his duty to the best of his ability, the job he loved so much had been devastatingly taken away from him by an unscrupulous piece of low life.

Slowly Pepsi gathered his wits and bade doctor Smotte goodbye. The doctor shook Nigel's hand. Tears filled Pepsi's eyes as the doctor said, "*I'm really sorry son*", the caring and sympathetic doctor really meant what he said. Pepsi hobbled out to his next door neighbour Rob. Rob had kindly transported Nigel to his medical appointment. Pepsi could not even think of driving as things were at the moment!

Once inside the car it was plain for Rob to see by the expression on Pepsi's face that all was not well. Rob said nothing and just drove the sergeant, (but unknown to him, now an ex-sergeant), back home to his equally worried and long-suffering wife Dawn who was anxiously awaiting his arrival with the latest news of his career prospects.

The worst day of Nigel Coaler's life had arrived. Now he was at Angel Street sitting opposite Inspector Platt's desk as he acknowledged the termination of the career he so lovingly cherished and served with utmost dedication. Sitting opposite him was the now, 'acting' Chief Inspector. The 'Prat' had been elevated whilst Chief Inspector Franks was away on a pre-retirement course. There, with books and forms laid out neatly before him sat Mr Efficiency himself, as usual, full of his own importance. Inspector Platt certainly relished his role as 'Chief Inspector', he was almost drunk with his new (temporary) power! Pepsi could see how much Platt enjoyed his momentary elevation as he sat there ticking off each of Pepsi's 'appointments' which the ex-sergeant would now have to surrender, increasing Pepsi's feeling of indignity. Pepsi laid out what was required by Platt, warrant card, keys, whistle, baton, notebook and other ancillary bits and bobs of his 'office'. Once formalities had been painfully completed, during which time Platt showed no signs of compassion or sorrow at the demise of Pepsi's time with force, Pepsi made his forlorn way out of Angel Street, declining an invitation by one of his ex-subordinates to venture along to the canteen for a cuppa. Nigel hobbled out into the street, now an 'ex-copper', a civvie, a pensioner!

As time went on it became increasingly obvious that Nigel's 'new' knee was anything but satisfactory. He had been warned that there were no guarantees and he was a young man to have such surgery, as usually this operation applied to older people who suffered acute arthritis. Further visits to hospital and another consultation with Astley-Sloan resulted in yet another operation. Mr Astley-Sloan advised that, contrary to the norm, he considered that his right knee replacement would again have to be replaced! Pepsi remembered only too well the severe, excruciating and crippling pain of the first replacement operation. The surgeon stated that it was not usual for second replacements to be performed but he, Astley-Sloan, considered it worthwhile to try and sort things out once and for all. Pepsi was so frustrated and in so much pain that he felt he had no alternative but to give the green light for the operation to take place and subsequently the second, right knee replacement, or 'referral' as it was known, would go ahead.

Again, the slow, painful recuperation and frenzied physio activity, endless periods of dejection and moroseness. Due to Pepsi's mental state, again his devoted but undoubtedly hard pressed family life suffered immensely. There were occasions where the totally frustrated Dawn's patience neared breaking point. She had even considered taking the children and leaving Nigel due to his many periods of unpredictable and sometimes abusive and almost violent.mood swings.

A visit to Angel Street was 'clandestinely' arranged, with Dawn's collusion, when Pepsi was asked to attend to complete 'one or two pension formalities'. Dawn attended with him on the afternoon arranged and on arrival at the station they were both greeted warmly by Sergeant Royle, the 'Gay Marine'. "*Be with you in a minute*", he lisped and suggested that Nigel and Dawn make their way up to the club bar while Sergeant Royle 'sorted things out'!

After what seemed an age, Dawn and Pepsi finally negotiated the stairs and entered the small clubroom situate at the top of the building. "*Hiya Sarje!*", greeted a young recruit politely as he held open the door for them to enter. As Pepsi followed his wife into the room a loud chorus of, "*For he's a jolly good fe-e-e-llow, for he's a jolly good fe-e-ellow......*" was struck up by all present. Pepsi had been duped, even the local press were there, cameraman and all, to record the little 'event' thrown by those at Angel Street 'nick' on his behalf. Pepsi felt humbled at the sight of his colleagues, typists, the station janitor, all there to wish him well, all there just for him! Even the Super was there. It was he who presented a large impressive and expensive bouquet of flowers to Dawn before presenting an appropriately inscribed silver salver to mark the occasion, together with other gifts from all at Angel Street, to a stunned ex-sergeant Nigel Coaler.

Photographs were taken to record the event and Pepsi was plied with drinks by his many colleagues, some of whom had tears in their eyes at losing their very popular sergeant. For Pepsi and his wife, it was certainly a most moving experience. Pepsi leaned over and kissed Dawn, and whispered, "*You bugger, you knew about this all along didn't you?*". Dawn looked up at her husband and grinned, there were tears in her eyes also. Although very emotional and sad for Pepsi, he was grateful to all who had arranged such a treat for him. Eventually, all good things come to an end and at the conclusion of the little 'party' everyone made their way home.

Regular visits to Pepsi's home continued by the officers from Angel Street when all the latest gossip and tittle tattle from the 'serious rumour squad' would be furnished with relish. At least Pepsi did not feel neglected by those who hadn't forgotten him. However, as time went on Pepsi's leg gave him constant pain and discomfort. Again he visited his sympathetic GP. Again he was sent to see Mr Astley-Sloan. "*I'm afraid there seems to be little more we can do for you now as we seem to have exhausted everything*", said the eminent surgeon. Pepsi pleaded for some

161

remedial treatment to bring about the demise of his constant body wracking pain that continually and incessantly emanated from his right leg. As he seemed to be getting nowhere, Pepsi made other appointments with other equally prominent surgeons, but all spoke the same language, - *"There's nothing we can do!"*.

One Sunday afternoon in late summer saw Pepsi in his usual position, sitting 'vegetating' in the easy chair just staring at nothing in particular. Dawn came into the room and said, *"Seeing as it's so nice, we'll have a barbie in the garden eh?, the kids will love that"*. *"No, maybe tomorrow"*, grunted an expressionless Pepsi without even turning to his wife. *"But, tomorrow never comes, you always say we'll do things tomorrow!"*, snapped an exasperated Dawn, tears welling up in her eyes. Pepsi looked up at his faithful and patient wife, mindful as to how his attitude was affecting all in the house. Suddenly Pepsi buried his head in his hands and broke down completely. This had been bottled up for a long time. *"Oh sweetheart!"*, gasped Dawn, instantly rushing to his side and placing a comforting arm around her troubled husband's shoulders. Pepsi's tears flowed uncontrollably. *"I'm finished, Finished!"*, he cried repeatedly. *"No, no, You're not!"*, reassured Dawn, hoping she believed what she was saying. She couldn't bear to see her once proud and family caring husband's lethargy and total despair continually dragging him down like this.

Once again Dawn made a decision. She contacted Doctor Goldbourne and asked if he could come out and see her troubled husband. Later that day Dawn answered the ring of her front door bell. There stood a pleasant lady who introduced herself as Doctor Emily Steele, the new partner in Doctor Goldbourne's practice. *"Oh, please do come in and thank you for coming"*, said the appreciative Dawn. *"What exactly is the trouble? I have briefly read your husband's notes but I'm not totally familiar with his problem at the moment"*, whispered the doctor as she was admitted. Dawn sighed and whispered, *"Oh gosh, where do I start?"*, anxious not to alert her husband until she had briefed doctor Steele on all of the salient circumstances leading to his unenviable condition, both physically and mentally, the latter being why she had called the doctor today. At the conclusion of Dawn's woeful rendition of her husband's late pedigree Doctor Steele said, *"Right, lead on! Let's see what we can do"*.

Dawn led the way through to the lounge, informing the still seated and pensive Nigel, *"This is Doctor Steele love, she's just popped in to see how you are!"*. Pepsi looked up at the lady, then stared hard at his wife, making her shift uncomfortably. *"A-hem! Er, I'll go and make a cup of tea while you two are talking"*, said Dawn, adding, *"D'you take milk and sugar doctor?"*. Doctor Steele replied, *"Er, do you mind if I have coffee please, milk but no sugar"*. *"Certainly, no problem"*, said Dawn and made her way to the kitchen to carry out her task. The doctor placed her medical bag on the floor and placed a dining chair next to Pepsi's easy chair then said, *"Now then, let's see what we can sort out for you eh? What exactly is the trouble?"*. Pepsi's eyes became moist again as he fought hard to prevent a lump manifesting itself in his throat. He turned to the doctor and gave a long, drawn out sigh. *"Have you got a couple of hours to spare?"*, asked Pepsi sarcastically. *"Oh come on, perhaps I can help you sort things out, at least we can have a go?"*, said the doctor. Pepsi's eyes filled more now and a tear overflowed and ran down his cheek, more in frustration than anything else. He looked the doctor straight in the eye, *"Doctor, please, can we do something with this bloody leg? The pain is absolutely unbearable"*, he pleaded. Nigel and the new doctor discussed everything at length. Their detailed conversation was interrupted by Dawn as she arrived to the sound of rattling tea cups. The new doctor was indeed privileged! Dawn had aired her best tea set for the occasion.

After their refreshing and sustaining beverages had been consumed over a very lengthy and detailed conversation during which nothing had been missed, Doctor Steele concluded her stay after prescribing (yet more) tablets in the form of sleeping pills hoping to enable Pepsi to get some rest from his continual nightmare. The doctor promised that she would drop in again in a week or so to see how Nigel was progressing. This pacified the previously cross Pepsi at his wife's initiative in calling the doctor and he now awaited the doctor's efforts with a possible feeling of hope.

Nearly a fortnight went by during which time Pepsi received visits by some of the Angel Street patrols, (and Doctor Steele), including his regular 'audience' with the ever-informative and updating Gay Marine. Pepsi was also surprised, and pleased, to receive an unexpected visit from two of Angel Street's traffic wardens, Billy 'Staybright' Button and his colleague, the infamous Dolly Keffer (Keffer the Heifer).

There was yet another visit from Dr Steele who, when Pepsi answered the door asked in banter, "*Well! Aren't you going to ask me in?*". "*Oh, I'm so sorry doctor, yes, yes of course, please do come in, I was miles away!*", apologised an embarrassed Nigel. "*I can't stop*", said the as always overworked GP, and went on, "*I would like you to to see a surgeon at Layforth. He's good! Would you be prepared to travel the forty miles to see him?*". Pepsi ushered the doctor into the lounge. "*Yes of course I would if you think it will do any good*", said Pepsi, grateful at his doctor's effort on his behalf, but with an acute lack of enthusiasm, which did not go unnoticed by the concerned GP! "*Well*", said the doctor, "*I can't promise anything but, I've outlined your circumstances to him and I personally think he's a very good, wise and experienced orthopaedic surgeon. He is very highly regarded in the profession*". Doctor Steele went on, "*I really think you should at least go and see him and let him have a look at you*". Pepsi was more than grateful for his doctor's efforts and promptly engaged himself into 'enthusiasm' mode. Doctor Steele gave Pepsi the telephone number of the surgeon's secretary to be contacted at Beetmore Hospital in Layforth. Pepsi had heard of Beetmore Hospital and knew it was supposed to have a good reputation with regard to orthopaedic successes.

An appointment was made and Dawn drove her husband along to Layforth after depositing the children with her mother for the day. Pepsi and Dawn entered the large hospital after parking as close to the impressive ornate entrance as possible for Pepsi's comfort. Dawn displayed her husband's orange badge prominently inside the windscreen just in case there were any over-zealous security officers about who might clamp the wheels of their car. On entering the building, the apprehensive couple were politely directed along a highly polished, block floored corridor. Pepsi's rubber ferrules on the end of his crutches squeaked as they made contact with the shiny floor. The two made their way along to the clinic of the highly reputable orthopaedic surgeon, Mr Adrian Christian. Pepsi had refused the services of a porter and wheelchair but now the corridor began to seem endless as he hobbled along, Pepsi wished he had accepted the facility offered.

Eventually Dawn drew Pepsi's attention to a small sign on a door which read, 'Mr Adrian Christian FRCS, Consultant in Orthopaedics'. *"Here we are love, it looks as though we've arrived"*, said Dawn and knocked on the door. Whilst awaiting a reply the two had to squeeze themselves into the recess of the doorway to allow a trolley bearing a patient for theatre to be wheeled past them. There was no response to Dawn's knock from within so she knocked again. This time there was a shuffling sound from within then the door was opened by a smartly uniformed sister who greeted them with, *"Hello, how may I help you?"*. Dawn introduced themselves and informed the sister of the purpose of their visit to Layforth. *"Oh yes, Mister Coaler. You're the injured policeman to see Mister Christian aren't you?"*, asked the sister before answering her own question with, *"Do come in, You will have to excuse me as I'll have to leave you for a moment, but please make yourselves comfortable"*.Sister introduced herself, *"I'm Sister Ogilvy"*, she said, *"Mister Christian will be along shortly. You are a little early"*. The sister kindly furnished Dawn and Pepsi with a cup of tea while they waited for the doctor, before vanishing into an ante room to carry out other chores, closing the door behind her. The only thing to break the 'deafening' silence was the slow, deep methodical ticking of a large wall clock nearby and the occasional click clack of a female's shoes as they walked by along the corridor outside.

The two sat there and spoke in whispers as they sipped their tea. Pepsi suddenly realised what they were doing and said loudly, *"What the hell are we whispering for?"*. Dawn giggled and replied with amusement, *"I don't know love, why are we whispering?"*. Sister returned a short time later, apologising for leaving the couple on their own, *"Sorry about that, I had to deliver a blood* sample to the Path Lab along the corridor", she said. After what seemed an eternity but was in fact only a quarter of an hour sister again went into the ante-room and could be heard speaking to someone. A deeper tone of a man's voice was then heard before both the sister and a white coated gentleman wearing gold rimmed, 'half moon' spectacles and a smart burgundy coloured bow tie appeared, his head was almost devoid of follicle life. The gentleman extended his outstretched hand to Dawn and Pepsi and said, "*Hello, I'm Adrian Christian and you are the wounded policeman Mister Coaler – ' that right?*", he asked Nigel. "*Yes sir, Nigel Coaler*", confirmed Pepsi. Mr Christian then sat at his large desk and opened the standard, buff coloured folder containing notes and x-ray plates. The doctor leaned sideways and slotted the plates into illuminated panels on the wall nearby. Nigel and Dawn could see the damaged femur, tibia and fibula with vivid white screws and pins situated at various locations in and around the knee area. The top of the femur and tibia were highlighted by the steel and plastic knee joint itself for all to see. "*As you can see*", said Mr Christian to his little audience, "*the pictures display a very badly damaged leg indeed*". The surgeon rubbed his chin with the thumb and forefinger of his right hand before carrying on. "*Hmmm!*", he muttered to himself. Finally he turned to Nigel and said, "*Right, could you take your pants off and pop up onto the couch and I'll have a look at this leg of yours*". Dawn shifted in her seat and asked, "*Ahem! Would you like me to leave the room doctor?*". "*Not at all*", replied Mr Christian in his usual friendly manner, adding, "*God bless us, you're his wife aren't you? I'm sure you've seen it all many times before!*", hoping his banter would defuse what was a serious occasion as he examined his patient and put Dawn at ease at what the surgeon knew was to come! Mister Christian poked and prodded, felt and probed as well as attempting gentle manipulations which drew gasps of pain from Nigel. The surgeon's thorough examination could not be carried out however, without such pain and discomfort being incurred.

Eventually, at very long last the very meticulous examination was (thankfully thought Pepsi) concluded. Mr Christian went to the nearby wash basin and washed his hands before returning to his patient and his very worried wife. "*Okay, you can get dressed now*

Mister Coaler", instructed the surgeon as he sat himself behind his desk and made copious notes into Pepsi's already thick file which lay before him. Finally he put down his gold nibbed fountain pen as Pepsi put himself back together and sat back in his chair alongside Dawn. Pepsi could see one or two letters still glistening as the ink had not yet dried on the surgeon's paper. Mr Christian leaned forward and cradled his chin in both of his hands as his elbows rested on his desk top. Choosing his words carefully mister Christian spoke slowly, looking at both Pepsi and Dawn as he spoke.

"*I'm afraid the news isn't good"*, said the surgeon. After allowing his dramatic words to sink in he went on, "*I am of the opinion that the only solution to this problem will be an above knee amputation. You will have occasional phantom pain, but nothing like you are enduring at the moment"*, concluded Mr Christian. Again time was allowed for the dramatic news to be digested by both Pepsi and his disbelieving wife who both sat silently traumatised by what had been said.

Dawn looked at her husband's wan complexion and had to steel herself and grit her teeth to prevent tears from flowing down her cheeks. Pepsi sat tight lipped, unable to believe what he had just been told. "*W-when will this be done?"* asked Pepsi, his voice trembling with emotion, not knowing what else, if anything, to ask! "*Well"*, said Mr Christian, "*I'd like you to go away and think about what I have said. You may like to talk it over with your lovely wife (No response from Dawn!) and I also suggest that you discuss the obvious implications with your GP as well,"* Pepsi was advised.

Mr Christian informed Pepsi that a letter confirming the examination, its result and conclusion would be sent to Doctor Goldbourne right away. Finally the surgeon advised, "*You may like to discuss my findings with Doctor Rashid at St Dominics Hospital. I shall be writing to him also"*, concluded Mr Christian. Mr Christian also suggested that he may find counselling to be of benefit regarding such a traumatic and life-altering decision, although he conceded that this would no doubt be mentioned during his forthcoming consultation with the eminent Psychiatrist.

Mr Christian ended the emotional and heartbreaking

examining consultation over another cup of tea provided by Sister Ogilvy while all present absorbed and considered what had been said. *"Come back and see me in three weeks and we will take matters from there"*, said Mr Christian.

Finally Dawn took her husband's arm and assisted him on the long hobbling trek back along the polished floors of what seemed to be an even longer return journey to the sanctuary of their car. Once inside the car Dawn could control her sympathetic emotions no longer. After inserting the key into the ignition she leaned over and buried her head into her distraught husband's right shoulder. *"Oh my poor sweetheart - I'm so, so sorry. Please forgive me crying, I just can't help it. It's so bloody unfair!"*. Pepsi sat there numb. *"Don't cry love, it's not the end of the world"*, and, trying to put on a brave face in view of the adversity ahead, and hoping to bring about the demise of Dawn's tears, added, *"I'll just 'ave to buy a bloody parrot won't I?"*. His attempt failed miserably and Dawn sobbed for some time before she was able to compose herself sufficiently enough to make the long drive back home. The whole journey was made in silence as the two could hardly believe the inevitable predicament that the popular Pepsi found himself in. It was due entirely to a hazard of his previous, dangerous occupation.

The ultimate chop, and worse!

As Pepsi and his family were preparing for the forthcoming operation, life went on as usual at Angel Street. However all there, as throughout the whole force were devastated at the outcome of ex-sergeant Coaler's injuries, sustained while he patrolled the streets of Warbreckside.The Gay Marine as usual maintained visits to his wounded colleague and his charming wife and family and continued keeping them up to date with all the news and 'scandal' from the ever interesting 'Serious Rumour Squad'!

One wet Monday morning Sergeant Royle was being driven around the division by Policewoman Perry, the 'Red Onion', Pepsi's 'colleague in arms' at the time he was run down. Vera had kept a constant rapport with her injured sergeant and was now accepted by Pepsi and Dawn as almost one of the family. As they roamed the wet streets Vera turned to her 'other' sergeant and asked, "*Any chance of us sneaking off to Pepsi's for a cuppa Sarje?*". Although Nigel lived 'off the patch' the Gay Marine didn't hesitate with his lisped reply, " *'Course we can! Just keep your ears to the radio Vee*". In a short time the two alighted from their patrol car and knocked on the door of Pepsi's home. The door was answered by Dawn, the two children were at school. "*Oh Hi, come in, come in*", invited the smiling Dawn, always appreciative of visits by her husband's concerned colleagues. In no time at all, all four were sitting in the lounge enjoying tea and toast. Pepsi sat in his usual armchair, the morning papers at his feet.

The Gay Marine enthusiastically commenced to update Pepsi as to the latest 'scandal' emanating from the ranks of Warbreckside Police. "*'Ave yer 'eard about Andy Moreover from Tyler Street nick?*" asked Sergeant Royle. Pepsi looked puzzled for a moment then asked, "*Is that the newly promoted Inspector Moreover who transferred up 'ere from Brighton last year?*". "*That's 'im, they call 'im the Brighton Belle*", confirmed the Gay Marine. "*Yeah!, I know 'im by sight*", said Pepsi, "*Why? What's 'e done John?*". "*Well*", informed the Gay Marine, "*I don't know about 'is name bein' Moreover, it should be Andy bloody Legover! 'E was caught in the toilets in Saltworth playground messin' with another bloke, an' 'e was wearing womens' knickers, stockin's an' suspenders when they frisked 'im*", lisped the Gay Marine with amusement and relish. "*Bloody 'ell!*", gasped Pepsi, "*When was this?*". "*A couple of days ago, last week sometime I think*", said the Gay Marine. "*Last Friday afternoon, with a sales rep*", confirmed and corrected the Red Onion, adding, "*The lads were keeping 'obsees' on the bogs in Saltworth playground after complaints of queers frequenting the place an' they caught the two of 'em bang at it!*". The Gay Marine then cut in, "*An' when they got 'em in to Angel Street an' searched 'em all was revealed, literally!*", and concluded his juicy bulletin with, "*The bloody 'phones are red 'ot an' buzzin' all over the place. Wait 'til the press get 'old of this little gem, the Chief Con will 'ave a bloody duck egg!*"

Eventually the novelty of this little saga was exhausted and the idle chit chat came to a close. Dawn had sat throughout John and Vera's visit and hardly said a word, but she never ceased to be amused and fascinated by the way bobbies sat and gossiped about one of their own when the opportunity arose.

The Gay Marine rose to his feet, donned his cap and gloves and turned to Vera saying, "*Come on Vee, let's get some more diligent sleuthin' done*". Pepsi started to rise from his chair but the Gay Marine placed his big hand on his pal's shoulder and said, "*Stay where you are Nige, we'll let ourselves out*". "*It's alright, I'll see you to the door*", interjected the ever pleasant Dawn. As she stood at the front door and bade the two goodbye, she squeezed Sergeant Royle's arm and said, "*Thank you very much for calling John, he loves visits from the gang at Angel Street, they mean so much to him*". The big sergeant replied, "*We love comin', it's the least we can do, an' anyway we like yer tea an' toast!*". The uniformed duo then left the Coalers in peace and returned to patrol their division.

Eventually, after attending Beetmore Hospital for final checks,

X-rays and an ECG, the day came for Pepsi to enter hospital for the 'big chop'. Dawn drove her husband to Beetmore and for most of the trip neither said a word as each was worried sick as to what the future now held for the Coalers! On arrival Pepsi was shown to his bed in Ward 5 and Dawn carefully placed his shaving items and soap, flannel etc into the drawer of his bedside locker, as all wives do! Of course, Pepsi was very apprehensive but he managed to maintain an air of 'normality' on seeing the worried expression on his poor wife's face. He knew she was having a difficult job hiding her deep concern and preventing tears from flowing. Each hoped to God that the decision to go ahead with this operation wouldn't be regretted, there was no turning back now. Dawn sat in a bedside chair and a nurse came to obtain Pepsi's details which she meticulously entered onto a large yellow form clipped to a pad on her lap as she sat on Pepsi's bed.

Pepsi was a little annoyed as the ward fell totally silent at this juncture, thus enabling the rest of the previously talking or reading patients to hear all. When all was completed, Dawn rose and gently kissed her husband and squeezed his hand and said reassuringly, "*Bye for now love, I'll be back after tea with the kids for an hour, see you later*", then made her way out and vanished from view.

During the next hour Pepsi was visited by Maud the physiotherapist who explained at great length what she would be doing once Pepsi was able to respond after his traumatic operation. Maud was a pleasant, middle aged lady who was obviously very experienced in her job although she did look a little thin and frail for such a physically demanding role as hers. Next a lady came from the pathology department to take a blood sample from Pepsi's arm. "*Hi*", "*I'm Dracula's assistant*", she bantered as she wrapped a restricting band around his upper arm to ensure that a good supply entered her large syringe! Having obtained her sample she then emptied the contents of the syringe into a little glass phial and endorsed its lable with the appropriate details. No sooner had the lady left when Sister Baxter arrived at Pepsi's bed accompanied by the great man himself, Mr Christian, together with some junior medics at his side. The screens were drawn around Pepsi's bed to ensure privacy from prying eyes, although no doubt everything could be heard by those interested enough up and down the ward who wished to listen! Mr Christian greeted his patient and asked if he minded his juniors, Doctor Bentley his registrar, and a young male and female medical student being in attendance. *"Not at all sir"*, replied Pepsi. The surgeon then then addressed his colleagues. *"This is Mister Nigel Coaler. Mister Coaler was a Police Sergeant and he was run down by a high powered motor cycle"*. At this point Mr Christian took a large folder from sister and removed some X-ray plates from within. *"We'll try not to be too long"*, said the surgeon politely.

Mr Christian perused the plates, holding them aloft against the fluorescent ceiling lights above to enable him and his colleagues to see, and began, *"You will see the repairs to the shattered tib and damaged femur, and note also the damaged patella lying slightly out of alignment"*. The surgeon indicated various items of interest for his colleagues to note with the point of his ball pen and went on, *"Mister Coaler has undergone numerous arthroscopies on this knee since the original repairs to the shattered leg were carried out and he underwent a total knee replacement. Unfortunately, he had to then undergo a referral twelve months later. This was done eight months ago. As you can see here (pointing to a spot on the plate) fusion has been impaired and here (pointing elsewhere) recovery has been hampered by this.....".* The little group talked and laboured over the X-rays and notes, using phraseology and medical terms which were completely alien to Pepsi.

Finally Mr Christian instructed Sister Baxter to remove the sheets to enable a scrutiny of the damaged leg to take place followed by yet more proverbial and painful prodding, squeezing and probing of the damaged limb. At times this drew gasps of pain from Pepsi, followed immediately by the doctor's apologies. Pepsi tried his best to assist the medics by being as co-operative as he could but such was the pain and discomfort that eventually he had to voice his sentiments and bring about the demise of the little gatherings' exploratory exploits. The understanding and sympathetic surgeon and his colleagues then finally left a very sore Pepsi to await the arrival of the teatime meal, after which he could look forward to the arrival of Dawn and the childrens' evening visit before his 'big day' tomorrow!

As Pepsi lay there deep in thought, one of his fellow patients from the bed opposite came across and introduced himself.

"*Awright mate? My name's Andy Stocker, I'm avin' me appendix out tomorrer. Worra you in for?*" asked the nosey ward mate. Pepsi sighed, he knew the man was only trying to be friendly but he felt like telling him to fuck off and mind his own business! However, Pepsi replied, "*They're amputating my right leg in the morning*". Even as he said the word 'amputating' tears filled Pepsi's eyes and a lump came to his throat causing his voice to falter. "*Fuckin' 'ell mate, I'm sorry, I wouldn't 'ave asked if ----*". "*It's okay*" interrupted Pepsi putting the embarrassed man at ease. Andy realising that his new ward mate appeared to be distressed, mumbled his sorrow and sincere best wishes as he retreated over to his own bed to resume reading his daily paper. Pepsi raised his arm and acknowledged Andy's kind sentiments then lay back staring at the ceiling, deep in thought as to what tomorrow's ultimate 'saga' would bring, and how it would effect his and his family's future destiny. Understandably to Dawn, but not the children, their visit found Nigel to be very subdued and morose during their stay and many questions were asked of Dawn on their way home, such as "*Why is Daddy cross Mummy?*".

Eventually the big day arrived. Pepsi, although in pain, had lain in his bed and watched through the window after 'lights out' and saw the moon creep laboriously and ever so slowly across the cold, cloudless sky until eventually, the grey light of dawn arrived. Pepsi lay and witnessed it all! He was also hungry now, not having been allowed any food or drink since last night. As Pepsi lay there listening to the tinkling of tea cups as the early morning tea trolley was wheeled round the wards. At the same time, Staff Nurse Underwood was consulting her drug list inside the lid of her 'mobile pharmacy' as she issued various pills and potions to those requiring them. The friendly tea lady, Julie, noticing the 'Nil by mouth' sign on the headboard behind Pepsi's head, said sympathetically while she poured tea for the patient in the next bed, "*Sorry love, you're not allowed anything I'm afraid*". Pepsi managed a friendly smile in acknowledgement. Staff Nurse Underwood gave Pepsi a tablet in a small plastic pot and said, "*Here, you can have this though, it will help calm you down. You can help it down with just a sip of water*". Pepsi did as he was told and popped the pill into his mouth and swallowed it unaided. Just then somebody farted loudly in the ward and someone else caused Julie to giggle when he acknowledged the sound by remarking , *"Good arse!"*. Even Pepsi with his pain, discomfort and apprehension managed a smile. *"Who on earth was that?"*, asked the staff nurse pretending to be shocked. A surly old man further down the ward near to the person responsible replied sarcastically, *"It's 'im 'ere, Gary the gale, e's always doin' it, I'm gonna buy 'im a bloody kite!"*. This brought laughter from all including Julie and the staff nurse. *"It bloody smells, I'll tell you that"*, said the old geriatric in the end bed as he peed into his bottle, oblivious to the presence of Julie and the nurse as he sat on the edge of his bed revealing all!

Later, Pepsi sat up reading the morning papers as those around him not going to theatre consumed their breakfasts of cereal followed by bacon, egg and beans, Pepsi's favourite! Shortly after the breakfast dishes were collected a young nurse arrived and drew the screens round Pepsi's bed. She carried an instrument tray covered by a towel. *"Okay Mister Coaler, I'm just going to shave you and prepare you for your op"*, informed the sprightly young nurse who looked young enough to still be at school! Pepsi nodded and was instructed to remove what clothing he was wearing. *"Just pop this gown on then I'll shave you and do the prep then you can put these paper knickers on!"*, instructed little nurse efficiency. Pepsi lay there more than a little embarrassed as the nurse proceeded to shave him from below the knee right up to his groin area, even the area around his 'dangly bits' was not spared and laid bare! Pepsi's lower abdomen looked and felt like a chicken prepared for Christmas. Then the nurse sploshed iodine onto the shaved area in lavish quantities. At first it felt really cold and boy, did it sting! His right testicle felt as though it was on fire! It stung so much he felt like dipping it into a bucket of water. The nurse finally finished her delicate and embarrassing pre op' chores by wrapping as much of Pepsi's right leg in green paper as she could, which she then secured with tape before issuing him with his paper 'knickers'. Eventually, when all was concluded the nurse took her bowl and towel and the little bundle of Pepsi's shorn foliage, opened the screens and disappeared. *"Yer okay mate?"*, asked Andy Stocker opposite. *"As good as I'll ever be"*, replied Pepsi. *"She'll be cummin' to me next I suppose, 'cos I'm gettin' done this mornin' as well"*, went on Andy. He was right! The young nurse reappeared a short time later and repeated her performance to prepare Andy for theatre.

Pepsi was hoping to go to theatre and get things over with as soon as possible, but it was not to be. He lay there for what seemed an eternity as the cleaner arrived and washed and polished the floor and fussed about tidying everybody's locker. Another young lady came to Pepsi. She wore a long white coat that seemed far too big for her. She was small and of Chinese appearance. A stethoscope protruded from the top of one of her pockets, causing her coat to hang lower on one side. She wore wire rimmed specs and her jet black hair framed the beautiful olive coloured skin of her face. She also had the proverbial buff coloured file in her hand!

"*Good morning, you are Mister Nigel Coaler, yes?*", she greeted. "*That's right*", confirmed Pepsi. The oriental lady introduced herself by saying, "*I'm Doctor Yue. I'm your anaesthetist. I'll be looking after you during your op and I've just come to check one or two things with you*". The pleasant young doctor put Pepsi at ease as she went through her list of questions and instructions. She explained briefly what would happen down in theatre prior to his operation. "*I'll give you a little injection and you'll pop off to sleep and when you wake up it will be all over, okay?*". Pepsi nodded his acknowledgement. The doctor asked a few more questions, noted some of his replies and ticked off others. Name, date of birth, next of kin, any allergies, etc, etc. Finally, after giving Pepsi an injection, she concluded her 'interview' then moved over to mister Stocker opposite to repeat the same task with him. After she had completed her little chat with him she then left the ward, waving to both on her departure.

An hour or so later a green gowned porter appeared with a trolley and Pepsi's heart missed a beat. No! It wasn't for him, it was for a patient in an adjacent ward. The next time the porter and trolley appeared Pepsi's heart again fluttered and he prepared to vacate his bed. No, again it wasn't for him! This time Mister Stocker was assisted from his bed and on to the trolley before being whisked away down to theatre. Although Pepsi had been given an injection to 'calm' him, he was nevertheless trembling a little at the thought of what was to befall him soon. After what seemed an age, the trolley bearing the prone form of Andy Stocker appeared and he was transferred to his bed to sleep off the anaesthetic after his operation.

Now it was Pepsi's turn! "*Mister Coaler?*" asked the porter nodding to Pepsi, "*Yes this is our injured bobby*", confirmed the accompanying nurse. As Pepsi moved from his bed on to the trolley, which was a little higher that his bed, Pepsi was assisted by the porter and the nurse, the one who had earlier prepared him for theatre. This time she was almost totally hidden behind her green theatre cap, face mask and gown. The nurse informed Pepsi, "*Your wife rang before to wish you all the best*". Pepsi thanked her as she and the porter wheeled him along the endless corridors to the theatre down in the basement of the hospital.

Eventually, he was wheeled into a small room with cabinets and shelves stocked with a variety of drugs, dressings and instruments. Although heavily gowned Pepsi instantly recognised the little form of the Chinese anaesthetist who attended him earlier on the ward. "*Hiya again, orkeh?*" she said as she greeted him and squeezed his hand. His big buff file had been placed upon Pepsi as he lay there looking at the ceiling. He was also attended by two other equally friendly nurses one of whom held his hand and comforted him. As the anaesthetist was once again confirming her earlier answers, the imposing figure of the surgeon, Mr Christian in his pale blue cap and gown appeared, his mask hanging down below his chin. During subsequent conversation, a needle was inserted into a vein on the back of Pepsi's hand which was then taped in place before the large syringe containing the anaesthetic was connected. The pretty little anaesthetist slowly depressed the plunger of the syringe as she asked Pepsi about his time in the force. The nurse still had hold of Pepsi's other hand as he tried to answer the anaesthetist, but he needed to take occasional very deep breaths as the anaesthetic gradually started to take effect. His eyes were becoming difficult to focus and their lids felt very heavy. He tried to see those around him but darkness overcame him and he sank into oblivion as the voices faded into the distance.

"*MISTER COALER!*", Pepsi could hear his name being called from somewhere in the distance! He felt strange, he seemed to be in another world. As his senses slowly returned his mouth felt thick with the nauseating taste of the anaesthetic, the sore throat caused by the removal of the airway, he couldn't open his eyes or lift his head but he could hear again his name being called and felt his hand being held, "*MISTER COALER, wake up, it's all over now*", said the dulcet tones of a female somewhere in the distance. Then the pain struck with a vengeance, - bang! Pepsi thought he was back in the roadway after being struck down, "*Fuckin' ell*", he cried out, and tried to move. This only magnified the pain, "*JESUS CHRIST, my leg, it's on fire*", gasped Pepsi. Again the comforting female's voice filtered through his pain racked body and into his brain, "*It's alright Mister Coaler, it's all over now, try to lie still. You'll be alright when we get you back to your bed*". Pepsi then drifted off again into a thankful sleep.

It was some time later that he awoke to the sound of someone sniffing or sobbing. This time he managed to open his eyes and saw the wonderful sight of his wife Dawn sitting in his bedside chair. She held his hand with one hand while she dabbed tears from her eyes with the other. Pepsi groaned, Dawn leaned forward at the sound of her husband coming round and gently kissed him on his forehead. Pepsi could see he was connected to various drips and at first wondered what was impairing his vision before realising he was wearing an oxygen mask. The pain in his leg was agonising. Pepsi wondered why he still had his leg as his foot was painful and his toes were cold! Pepsi moved his left foot over to rub against his right but there was nothing there? He tried again, wondering where his foot was. Then he moved his right hand under the sheet and felt a big clump of dressings where his thigh had once been. So they had taken it off! Pepsi was hoping that they hadn't now! Once again tears welled up in his eyes as he realised that he no longer had a right leg! "*Christ, they've taken it off almost up to my arse!*", muttered Pepsi in utter despair to no one in particular. His distressing comment was however heard by the vigilant Dawn who said, "*Oh sweetheart, you'll be alright, we'll fight this together!*". Although the pain and the mental anguish were making themselves felt to Pepsi already, his wife's love and support meant all to him. He loved his wife so dearly, he would be totally lost without her he thought as he gently squeezed her hand, even though he had tubes in both arms! Dawn reciprocated affection by pulling his mask away and pecking him on his lips. Nigel turned to his wife and feebly uttered, "*I don't half love you*

Dawn!". Dawn smiled and squeezed his hand again and replied, *"I love to too sweetheart"*. Pepsi slowly came back into the world of reality. Although he could turn his head from side to side he still couldn't lift it up from the pillow when he tried. *"It's okay, I'm not going anywhere, just try and get some sleep and you'll feel better"*, instructed Dawn, the 'boss' as she still maintained her grip on his hand. A nurse came and checked all was well and tucked in his blankets as Pepsi sank back into a deep sleep.

He woke again later and saw the face of one of the nurses close to his. She was holding his arm checking his pulse and when she saw he was awake again she once more uttered her assurances that all was now well. Pepsi opened his eyes fully and saw that Dawn was also sitting alongside his bed. Nurse Potts then checked his blood pressure, again all was well. *"I still feel my foot's hurting but it can't be can it nurse?"*, asked Pepsi. Nurse replied, *"That's quite natural after an amputation, it's called phantom pain, you'll get that for a while but don't worry, everything's okay!"*. When Dawn left Pepsi lay thinking of what the future held. Although he was heavily sedated, the pain was really bad.

For the next few days Pepsi just lay there and slowly recovered from his major operation. He received visits from colleagues and relatives and the nurses ensured that all his needs were attended to. After a few days had elapsed Maud Langley the physio appeared. *"Do you mind if I have a peep?"* asked Maud as she lifted the blanket. The very short stump was covered in dressings but Maud only wanted to see how much of the leg had been removed. Pepsi was naked and Maud could see that the wounded warrior was blushing! *"Please, don't be embarrassed Mister Coaler, I've seen it all before"*, said Maud clinically, and added, *"I just want to see how things are"*. Maud replaced the blanket and said, *"My assistant Moira and myself will pop back later and help you with one or two exercises"*. *"Oh, how nice, aren't I the lucky one?"*, replied Pepsi relishing the thought of being 'manhandled' by the physios. However, when Maud returned later and introduced her young junior it wasn't as bad as Pepsi thought it would be, for now at least. *"This is Moira"*, said Maud as she introduced her attractive assistant, *"We've come to get you gently started with a few basic exercises"*. Pepsi was encouraged to try and pull himself up with the aid of the wooden handle above his head. After being assisted a couple of times Pepsi persevered and eventually (and painfully) managed to pull himself up the bed unaided, which impressed and pleased the two ladies considerably. After ten minutes Maud said, "*Enough for today!*", and informed Pepsi that they would get him to sit on the edge of the bed on their next visit the following day.

As promised, the two returned the following day and as yet Pepsi still couldn't manage to put on his pants, the screens were drawn and Pepsi was assisted to sit up and swing round so that he could sit on the edge of the bed. What Pepsi thought would be an easy manoeuvre very nearly ended in disaster! He pulled himself up to a sitting position as the two physios stood by. "*Very good*" remarked Maud encouragingly, "*Now try and put your left leg out and over the side of the bed*". Revealing all, he painfully gyrated himself round to try and sit on his bedside. However, it was just not that easy as there was no counterbalancing weight on his right side and he nearly made a very undignified exit from the bed altogether but for the timely rescue by the two physios, who were well prepared for this, having experienced this many times before after such an operation. "*Take your time, take your time, it's not as easy as you think*", said Maud as they restrained a very bewildered Pepsi who was amazed at how physically unbalanced his body now was. "*Christ, I'll never get used to this!*", muttered Pepsi dejectedly. "*Oh you will, you'll see*", said Maud reassuringly and instructed Pepsi to try the move again. The manoeuvre was repeated a number of times before Pepsi finally managed to perform the move himself unaided, it wasn't easy at all but the physios were pleased with him, so that is encouraging thought the very frustrated ex-sergeant. He was asked to repeat his exercises but only if and when there was someone present just in case there might be a repeat performance of today's earlier fiasco! Tomorrow they would bring a wheelchair for Pepsi to get into.

The following day the act of getting from his bed to the wheelchair proved extremely difficult and once again Pepsi didn't cater for the loss of weight on his right side and he fell headlong into the arms of the two physios who had earlier assisted him into a pair of loosely fitting shorts, which left nothing to the imagination! The frustrated amputee couldn't believe how difficult it was to try and get himself upright without falling to his right. The feeling was horrendous and he just could not keep control. As ever the encouraging Maud genuinely promised, *"Don't worry, you'll soon be able to keep your balance"*, after seeing alarm and frustration in her patient's face, as well as the tear rolling down his cheek. Pepsi sure hoped she was right! Maud and Moira attended Pepsi every day and slowly he regained his confidence. After a short time he became very independent and insisted on getting into the wheelchair himself. Pepsi then started to wheel himself around the ward then eventually he ventured out and along the corridors, 'patrolling' the adjacent wards and finally he started started helping the tea lady on her rounds! He was constantly scolded by Sister Baxter for 'overdoing' things. He received chastisement from her so often that he christened her 'Tin Hat' because that's what he felt he should be wearing when she was around!

The day came when Pepsi had to attend at the limb centre which was situate some distance from his ward on the other side of the hospital complex. He would have to be transported by ambulance for the short journey. As Jerry the ambulancemen wheeled Pepsi past sister's office, out she stepped. With a face like thunder she demanded, *"And where d'you think you're going with no top on?"* (Pepsi always just wore his shorts as he flitted about the ward in his chair!). *"I've got to go over to the Limb Centre, Sister"*, replied Pepsi meekly. *"Not like that you're not, it's snowing outside"*, then turning to Jerry she snapped, *"He's not going out like that, you should know better, he'll get bloody pneumonia goin' out half naked like that, get a blanket round him"*. *"I'm okay Sister"*, said Pepsi but sister retorted, *"You might have been in charge in the police, but I'M in charge 'ere, an' what I say goes!"*. Gerry quickly went and retrieved a blanket from his vehicle and returned to cover the scolded Pepsi before the journey to the Limb Centre could be resumed. As they made their way along the corridor Pepsi apologised to Jerry, *"Sorry about that but I never wear anything much and I don't feel the cold"*. Jerry accepted Pepsi's apology and remarked, *"You don't know Sister Baxter, she can be a right cow at times!"*

The visit to the Limb Centre did not enhance Pepsi's morale at all! Jerry wheeled him into the reception area and deposited him amongst a number of wheelchair bound geriatric amputees before leaving saying, *"I'll be back to collect you in an hour!"*. Pepsi felt extremely lonely and most vulnerable as he was left amongst those who were outpatients brought in from various venues for their daily or weekly therapy. Pepsi was the only in-patient, and the youngest by far of all those present which included a couple of women. The looks of utter despair, dejection and total resignation on most of their aged faces only added to Pepsi's acute depression, especially as he had just started to climb up out of such. One old gent wheeled himself alongside the despondent Pepsi and moaned, "*I'll tell yer mate, you'll never get used to this, I lost me leg two bloody years ago an' I still can't 'andle it!*". Oh great, that's all I need thought Pepsi, angry and totally pissed off at the old bugger's unwanted intrusion.

Pepsi wheeled himself out of reception to distance himself from those ageing, morale-sapping individuals from the 'Doom and Gloom' brigade and went exploring the surrounding corridors. He was 'captured' when a lady came out of a nearby office carrying a sheaf of papers, almost colliding with the wheelchair wanderer. The quite indignant lady looked at Pepsi through her horn rimmed spectacles and asked sharply, "*Can I help you?*". Pepsi informed her who he was and why he was here. "*You're out of bounds here, you'll have to see Mavis she's in charge, follow me please!*", retorted the snooty school ma'am! Pepsi was escorted to the office of a very charming lady who introduced herself. "*Hello Mister Coaler, you're from Sister Baxter's ward aren't you? I've been expecting you*". The 'school ma'am' then left and Mavis asked, "*What on earth were you doing in Miss Pringle's neck of the woods?*" Pepsi explained all saying as to how he didn't want to be in the company of those sitting in reception, and why! "*Yes, some of them are complete defeatists I must admit, and they can by quite trying*", agreed Mavis and promised she would ensure that he wouldn't be left in such a position again. She then took him him to meet Doctor Karabak who would oversee his progress while he attended the centre.

Pepsi attended the Limb Centre daily and in no time the day came for a 'home visit'. After initial 'training' to familiarise himself with household chores, he was taken from the ward to his home by Janine, a social services health care nurse, and Moira his physio. Pepsi was asked to demonstrate his household capabilities, especially in the kitchen and bathroom, the latter having been fitted with various apparatus by the social services prior to his visit. Although a proud and delighted Dawn was present, she didn't assist her husband as he demonstrated his prowess. Pepsi passed his little 'home exam' and returned to hospital for a few more days before his final discharge, although he would still have to attend the Limb Centre twice weekly for some time yet.

On his subsequent return home Pepsi was inundated with a constant stream of visitors, not to mention the regular postal delivery of cards from well wishers. Things got so hectic that Dawn had to tone things down to ensure that her husband received adequate rest. Although having been instructed to 'take things easy' for the next twelve months or so, Pepsi wouldn't hear of it!

He was eventually fitted with a new prosthesis, but alas his stump was too short and it was far easier, and considerably less painful, to manage without and he relied on his wheelchair for his mobility. Pepsi became very efficient in his heavyweight DHS standard issue 'chariot'. Visits from the force welfare department ensued and he was invited to a number of various functions and gatherings by his colleagues.

Pepsi decided to keep fit by propelling himself in his 'tank' around the streets each day. Sometimes he would 'clock up' six or seven miles per outing. One day somebody joked, "*You should go in for a marathon or something!*". This remark stuck in Pepsi's mind and when he heard that a charity coastal 'walk' was to take place on a future date, he gave this event a lot of thought. After making enquiries he was informed that the actual event was an annual 15 mile walk that raised thousands of pounds for various charities. Those taking part donated to the charity of their individual choice and participants numbered approximately two thousand or so. Pepsi was told by the organisers that although wheelchairs had been pushed for part of the way in the past, none had ever completed the event, especially under the power of the chair's occupant. and anyway part of the route was cross country!

Pepsi delved further and was told that although he could enter, it was highly unlikely that he would be able to complete such a distance in a front castered wheelchair that was solely intended for use about the house or hospital wards, or at most, a gently push to the local shops! However, he would receive acknowledgement for whatever distance he would manage to complete. By hook or by crook, Pepsi decided he would have a damned good try to complete the whole distance in his trusty DHS, 47lb standard wheelchair! The official event was known as the Warbreckside Coastal Walk. It ran for 15 miles along part of the Warbreckside Estuary coastline starting from Easthead and eventually led inland to its final destination at Grobleton. The event received a lot of press coverage and many charities benefited from those who enthusiastically took part.

Nigel persevered with his daily treks but now he was covering greater distances and set out in the very early hours while the roads were quiet. Now it wasn't just a 'daily run', he was in serious training for the lengthy forthcoming marathon. He had flashing lights fitted on the back of the chair by the local bike shop owner Steve Tanner, together with a white light on the front. The enthusiastic Pepsi never missed a single day's energy sapping jaunt. Clad in singlet and shorts he completed lengthy mileage every morning irrespective of the weather and soon became known to all the milkmen and postmen who were out at that time of the morning!

One morning an incident occurred that was so despicable that the whole saga was blasted out via the press and local radio. It was six o'clock on a wet Wednesday morning and Pepsi was almost home after completing eleven miles. He had been on the road since four fifteen. Suddenly a car drew alongside him with three skin headed youths aboard. The rear nearside window was open and the youth sitting in the back seat was drinking from a large glass bottle. All three started laughing hysterically at the sight of a man in a wheelchair in just a singlet at that time of the morning, in the rain. The back seat yob asked, "*Ave yer gorra fuckin' licence for that Dickead?*". Pepsi tried to keep going but the car rolled along with him and the back seat youth screamed, "*Let's kick 'is fucking 'ead in!*", then added furiously, "*Ere, touch for this*" and tried to hit Pepsi in the face with the bottle he had been drinking from. The bottle missed and slipped out of the yob's hand. It hit Pepsi's chest that bounced onto the metal frame of his chair and shattered with a loud bang, covering him in what appeared to be fizzy orange juice. His hair, face and chest were covered with tiny glass fragments. The loud bang caused lights to go on in the nearby houses and one or two of the disturbed residents peered from their bedrooms to see what was going on. This panicked the driver who then accelerated away at a fast speed before vanishing down a nearby side road out of sight. The orange drenched and shocked, but otherwise unhurt wheelchair pilot made his way home and on arrival contacted Angel Street to report the incident.

Feelings were high and although enquiries were commenced by Pepsi's determined colleagues, no one was ever brought to book over the incident and the brave trio managed to escape justice, and the outraged wrath of the Gay Marine and the rest of those at Angel Street. The incident did not deter the keen adventurer from continuing with his training however, and Pepsi devoted himself to his new found venture. He was encouraged by some but also discouraged by some of those who feared for him because his of demanding and punishing routine. He was held in high esteem by his colleagues in the force who would regularly stop and chat during his nocturnal outings, or flash their blue lights as they passed him on the road.

The forthcoming Coastal Walk event received wide media publicity as the day approached. Ex-Police Sergeant Coaler's wheelchair attempt was also mentioned at great length each time the item was put out over the air. The press had called at his home to interview him and took photographs for their newspapers. He was now quite inadvertently receiving a lot of notoriety. Pepsi adopted the Cancer Gene Appeal as his paramount pet. This was organised by the Oncology unit at Warbreckside Infirmary and he deemed it worthy of his efforts to contribute to such a worthwhile and important cause. The day of the coastal walk arrived, less than six months after Nigel's amputation, he wasn't even halfway through the period he was told he would have to 'take things easy'! The only concession Pepsi asked for and was granted was a one hour start as he didn't want to get under the feet of the hordes that were expected to compete. The day started with wind and rain, but Pepsi was keen to get moving, the inclement weather didn't bother him. After 'booking in' the brave wheelchair pilot left Easthead at nine o'clock and set off on his marathon trek into the unknown! The words of the starting official rang in his ears, *"We don't expect you to do the whole distance but just do what you can, good luck!"* Do what you can my arse, thought a very determined and confident Pepsi as he pumped his arms and powered himself along the wet roads through the puddles. Meantime, the Gay Marine and his driver

Ged 'Mule' Train were sitting in their patrol car, strategically parked along the route to witness their colleague's historic endeavours. Eventually the soaking wet figure of the concentrating 'athlete' passed the front of their car, unaware of their presence as they sat secreted in the little gateway to a field on the outskirts of the town. "*Okay Mule, go an' draw alongside 'im an' we'll wish 'im well*", instructed the sergeant as the wet figure was putting distance between him and the patrol car. Ged did as he was told and the vehicle crept alongside Pepsi who was alarmed at first due to the last time a car crept up on him, but his alarm turned to delight when he saw who it was. "*Fuckin' good luck Pepsi, you'll do it*", lisped the enthusiastic sergeant through his open window, "*Best o' luck Sarje*" echoed Mule. The car rolled along with Pepsi for a few yards then roared of to resume its patrol. The sergeant's silver, silk chevrons stood out sharply as the Gay Marine's arm waved goodbye from the nearside window.

Pepsi pounded on for the first three miles before the rain eventually stopped. The wind however remained and was a nuisance to Pepsi everytime he rounded a corner and met it head on. Occasionally the opposite happened when it would get behind him and assist to propel him along. The rain returned later with a vengeance. His yellow sash and endorsed vest were soaking and sticking to him. Even in this inclement weather there were a number of kind people which included pensioners, women and even children, who approached him and placed coins into his little labelled plastic bucket hanging from the handle of his chair. Cyclists did the same and even a couple of motorists stopped and donated money to his collection, which was swelling and getting heavier as he went along.

There were refreshment stops along the route but Pepsi preferred to keep going to get as much distance completed as he could before the main body caught up with him. Eight miles into the 'walk' Pepsi was joined by two friendly ladies, one of them, Jill Thompson, was known to Pepsi from his days in the force. She was a store detective in one of the major stores in Warbreckside. Suddenly Pepsi started to find it hard going after about ten miles and this was noticed by Jill who immediately furnished him with some chocolate. After consuming this the transformation was almost unbelievable. Pepsi's energy and stamina returned and he

185

carried on without further ado. Obviously he had allowed his sugar count to drop and the chocolate intake rectified this, a point he would remember in future! Pepsi took advantage at the next refreshment stop and consumed a plastic beaker of orange juice and sucked an orange segment while he was on the move.

Things were difficult when he had to cross fields, he even negotiated a stile, all, completely unaided! The two ladies stayed with him to keep him company (and no doubt as mother hens to ensure all went well with him). Pepsi did suffer two mishaps, first he fell into a ditch and further on he lost control and fell out as he rolled down a grassy slope but each time he recovered and got back into his chair and continued, not allowing anybody to assist him, he remembered only too well what had been said by those who thought he wouldn't make it! Eventually Pepsi's heart lifted. He could hear the band playing in the marquee at the finishing line. That was indeed a tonic, he was going to make it after all! By now he was continually being passed by the front line of the mass but he didn't give a monkey's, he was almost home now. He was covered in mud and his hands were bleeding but he felt great. Even the pain in his leg did nothing to dampen his enthusiasm. The people passed him and slapped him on the back congratulating his mammoth exploit, men, women, children, they all offered their kind and friendly sentiments at Pepsi's successful feat.

As he arrived at the finishing line and entered the large tent to be 'booked in' and given his certificate, he was given tumultuous applause and cheers by competitors, spectators, and those officials who had doubted him, they all swarmed around the muddy and bleeding hero. He was then taken to a nearby first-aid tent to have his hands cleaned and dressed. There, he was interviewed and photographed by the press. Pepsi's chest swelled with pride, it was a wonderful feeling of achievement, he was indeed very proud. Then, the elated Pepsi was joined by his wife Dawn and the two children. Here we go again thought Pepsi as the tears flowed down his wife's cheeks as she hugged and kissed her hero proudly! Pepsi not only amazed those who said he couldn't do it, but he managed to raise a lot of money for the cancer gene appeal. Now, after completing this marathon, he decided to continue in his quest to raise money for his pet appeal by doing anything that he could to facilitate this.

Ex-Sergeant Nigel Coaler was to become somewhat of a celebrity due to his success on the coastal 'walk'. He was asked to give a couple of after-dinner speeches concerning his life in the force and exploits to date thereafter. Pepsi was only too pleased and his fees went straight to his gene appeal in their entirety.

Dawn was of course Pepsi's real tower of strength and undoubted cause of his success, Pepsi never thought otherwise. He idolised his wife, she and the kids were his everything, what the hell he would do without her he couldn't even imagine. She was always there to comfort and encourage him whatever his whims and fancies. There was no doubt in his mind that due to his wife's devoted love, care and support he continued to improve in leaps and bounds. They had been going together since they were kids at school. Pepsi had never been with any other female, only Dawn. *"Life isn't so bad after all"*, confided Nigel to Dawn as they sat watching television one evening after the children had gone to bed. *"You are a big softie aren't you?"* said Dawn as she kissed her husband gently.

Pepsi now devoted most of his time to raising money for his charity and also he wished to try and become, somehow, an inspiration to others in a similar predicament to himself, especially those who had 'given up the ghost' like some he had met at the Limb Centre. As with most men however, it was the love and support of his wife that would be his own inspiration and which would give him the incentive and strength to carry those intentions out. Pepsi went on various jaunts to country parks and similar venues to establish for the authorities which areas and paths etc were 'wheelchair friendly' and which were not. He was transported on most occasions by the Gay Marine but occasionally Dawn managed to accompany him on the little outings. The reason for Pepsi's endeavours were to enable the appropriate councils to print leaflets and brochures with the results of his findings at each location for the benefit of disabled or handicapped people to enable them to visit such places. At the conclusion of these 'jaunts' Pepsi was more than elated at yet another achievement and source of generated revenue for his gene appeal. However, his elation was dampened when he caught sight of Dawn as she stood in the kitchen after their last trip to Balmore Way, once a railway track but now converted into a pleasant four mile walkway.

"What on earth's the matter love?" asked Nigel most

concerned Dawn looked pale and seemed to be gasping. *"I, I'm alright, I just can't seem to get my breath"*, she replied laboriously. Pepsi looked up at his wife from his wheelchair and told her to go and sit in the lounge while he brought in the two cups of tea. The two sat and drank their tea and Pepsi noticed just how pale his wife was. *"If you're no different in the morning, YOU can take a trip to see Goldbourne"*, said Pepsi sternly. *"I think I'll have to love, I really don't feel well at all"*, replied Dawn to a very worried Nigel. Dawn never complained, and the fact that she did so now indicated that something was just not right, and this filled Pepsi with concern.

Dawn was to have driven the two of them out for lunch the next day while the children were at school but she just didn't feel up to it, yet another indication of something definitely being amiss! The next morning Dawn was feeling a little worse and had to ask Rita her next door neighbour if she would take the children to school for her, even though it was Dawn's turn to take hers and Rita's. Rita willingly obliged and Dawn went to see the doctor. Doctor Goldbourne checked her blood pressure, her pulse and listened intently to her wheezing and bubbling chest for some time. Finally, after giving Dawn a thorough examination doctor Goldbourne leaned back and said, *"Well I think it's asthma, I'll prescribe an inhaler but if things don't improve after a week or so, come back and see me straight away"*. Dawn thanked her GP and returned home after calling at the chemist's for her prescribed inhaler.

As the days went on it was Pepsi who was monitoring Dawn's condition, not the other way round as it had been for so long! Poor Dawn seemed to find things, especially the children, difficult to cope with. Two further weeks passed and on a damp Sunday morning as Dawn and Pepsi sat reading the morning papers after breakfast, which Dawn had hardly touched, the doorbell rang. *"It's okay love, I'll go"*, volunteered Pepsi and propelled his chair through to the front door. On opening the door he saw the welcome figures of Ged 'Mule' Train and the Gay Marine. *"Just thought we'd call for a cuppa"*, lisped the cheeky sergeant as Pepsi reversed down the hall to let them in. They all made their way through to the lounge and on seeing the breakfast plates on the table, the Gay Marine said, *"Oops, I'm sorry, I didn't realise you were 'avin breakfast!"*. *"It's okay, sit down the kettle's just boiled, Dawn will make you a cup of tea won't you love?"*, said

Pepsi. Normally Dawn wouldn't need to be even been asked, she would have been up from the table in an instant in her hostess role. There would have been two cups of tea furnished at the mere sound of Sergeant Royle's voice.

Dawn rose slowly from the table and made her way to the kitchen to make a fresh brew for her two guests. Pepsi and the Gay Marine however, couldn't fail to notice Dawn's lethargy as she moved slowly from the room. Pepsi turned to the big sergeant and whispered, *"I'm really worried about Dawn John, she's not well at all!"*. Dawn eventually and slowly reappeared with a tray of tea and biscuits and said, *"Will you excuse me please? I'll have to go and lie down. I don't feel too bright this morning"*. *"Certainly love, you go and get some rest"*, replied the Gay Marine. Dawn again apologised and excused herself then made her way upstairs to bed. The two children were still asleep in their beds. *"Fuckin' 'ell Nige, that's not like Dawn is it?"*, whispered sergeant Royle. Pepsi replied, *"I'm gonna call the quack out, I'm worried sick John"* The Gay Marine signalled Mule to finish his tea and said, *"We'll shoot off an' leave yer to it Nige, you ring the doctor an' get Dawn seen to"*. Pepsi saw them out and promised John he'd ring him later and tell him how Dawn was.

Doctor Goldbourne was summoned and attended shortly after. This time, after seeing Dawn the doctor was now concerned that Dawn seemed to be suffering the symptoms of pneumonia and said to her *"I'd like you to attend Warbreckside Infirmary for X-ray. I think you may have pneumonia"*. Rita next door, looked after the the Coalers' children while her husband Rob drove Pepsi and Dawn to hospital. X-rays and subsequent examination confirmed that Dawn was indeed suffering from severe lung congestion. Pepsi had been training hard for his next big marathon in a few weeks time, the Great North Run up in Newcastle, where again he would be the first to complete the famous event in his type of wheelchair. Dawn was so looking forward to her and the children accompanying Nigel at this major event which drew professional athletes as well as those just wishing to take part, from all over the world. The event was also televised nationally every year. Due to this Dawn asked the doctors if she would be okay by the time the event took place in three weeks time. The doctors' faces seemed to indicate that this may not be possible and this made Dawn frightened as she realised that she must be quite ill.

After the initial examination and X-ray scrutiny was completed, Sister Thompson went to the wheelchair bound gladiator and informed him, *"I'm afraid we're going to have to admit your wife up to the ward"*. Dawn was admitted to Ward E 9 and was to see the chest consultant, Doctor Salisbury, the following day. As Rob drove his worried neighbour home he turned to the very concerned Nigel and said, *"Don't you worry about the kids Nigel, we'll look after them until things return to normal"*. Pepsi was really upset. *"Thanks a lot Rob, would you? Just until I can arrange for her mother to take them"*. *"No trouble at all mate"*, confirmed the samaritan neighbour. That evening Pepsi visited his wife again and on her on seeing him greeted him with smiles and affection. *"How did you get here?"*. asked Dawn. *"Rob next door dropped me off, he's picking me up in an hour"*, replied the doting husband. Dawn looked a little brighter but still had difficulty with her breathing. *"How're the kids and where are they now?"* asked a concerned Dawn. *"Your mum's going to have them, but for now they're okay with Rob and Rita's kids next door, they think it's great staying with young Nicky and Andrew!"*, answered Pepsi, much to Dawn's relief. *"Your mum and dad are calling in to see you tomorrow evening"*, he added hoping to pacify her further.

Pepsi visited his wife every day. Him and his wheelchair were transported by friends, relatives and even colleagues with their Police carrier ensured that he never missed an opportunity to go and see the love of his life. Alas, poor Dawn's condition didn't warrant an early discharge from hospital and it was two weeks before she was allowed home. On the day of her discharge, Friday, Dawn was told that she must return three days later on Monday morning to enable a further investigation to be carried out in the form of a bronchioscopy, which would be carried out under a general anaesthetic. Rob conveyed Pepsi and Dawn home after her lengthy stay and little Jenny and Martin were delighted at their mother's eventual return. The children were told not to make a noise and play quietly as mummy wasn't very well. Dawn showed no signs of getting better over the weekend and on Monday morning, the ever obliging Rob conveyed Dawn and Pepsi back to the hospital for Dawn to undergo her dreaded bronchioscopy. This entailed a tube being inserted down into her lungs under a general anaesthetic to enable a meticulous examination of the inside of her lungs. During the operation a sample of tissue was taken to enable a biopsy to be carried out for analysis. Pepsi sat all day waiting for his wife and at the end of the day Dawn was again allowed to return home. She was given an appointment to attend the following week to be informed of the result of the tests. Rob then drove the duo home.

The week went by slowly with Dawn getting more worried each day as her breathing was showing no signs of improving. Pepsi's big day, the Great North Run loomed. Dawn so much wanted to go but she didn't feel up to the long journey and overnight stay and knew there was absolutely no hope of her accompanying her husband on his event of a lifetime. Dawn did however, insist that Pepsi still go and complete the prestigious event. The Gay Marine would go with him instead and Pepsi promised his wife that he would do it 'for her'! He promised that he would complete the marathon and present his medal to his wife on his return. The Gay Marine conveyed Pepsi and his heavyweight wheelchair up to Tyneside on the following Saturday prior to the event the following day. The two friends made the long journey North and on arrival settled in to their overnight digs, (furnished via their Newcastle colleagues) and after an evening meal followed by a couple of pints, the two decided to hit the sack after their tiring day. Before turning in Pepsi rang home to tell Dawn of their safe arrival.

The following morning the dynamic duo were up with the lark. Pepsi again rang home after a light breakfast then he and the Gay Marine were collected by their colleague Gareth Owen from the local force and transported to the starting point 15 miles away. Gareth, a Police motor cyclist and their Tyneside 'mentor' during their stay, deposited Pepsi among the officials and TV cameras at the starting line. When Pepsi set off on his long journey Gareth would then transport Sergeant Royle back to the finishing line to await Pepsi's subsequent and hopeful completion of the lengthy trek. At the starting line it was sheer (but pleasant) pandemonium. The weather was kind, sunny but cool, which suited the competitors admirably. There was no repetition of the foul weather endured during the coastal walk down in Warbreckside. Pepsi looked forward to getting under way, intending to savour every minute of this fantastic event as he was making his way to the distant coastline at South Shields. As he set off he was mobbed by the media who ran alongside him for the first few yards, filming his departure and wishing him well, the cheers of the many spectators was deafening, Pepsi felt elated, but also very disappointed and upset that his beloved Dawn and the kids were not up here with him to witness such a spectacle.

Although it was a fantastic, carnival-like atmosphere and Pepsi was very proud, he did however have a large lump in his throat as he thought of his wife's absence and and illness as she waited for him back home, hoping his subsequent return would be triumphant. Pepsi was confident he would do it, but if necessary, he vowed to himself, he would complete the distance, even if he had to crawl it, to make sure he took that medal home for her! Due to Pepsi's relentless and constant early morning roadwork he completed the distance without any problems. Those lining the route, again filled his plastic bucket, a much bigger one this time, with coins and even banknotes as he made his way along. Echoes of 'Away the Lad' and 'God bless you son' rang in his ears as he passed the enthusiastic supporters lining the route. Finally, as he propelled himself triumphantly over the finishing line to tumultuous cheers from the mass of well wishing spectators, he was again swamped by the press and TV. Pepsi then heard his name booming from the large Tannoy speakers on the gantry above the finishing line, "......and here, in his ordinary DHS wheelchair to complete a first, as it's never been done before, is the disabled ex Warbreckside Police Sergeant Nigel Coaler!, Well done Nigel!", this was followed by other equally complimentary accolades to others who had performed their individual tasks in the name of their chosen charities. Many were in bulky and heavy fancy dress, an achievement in itself to have made such a long journey in such heavy clothing, no doubt causing them acute discomfort as they sweated profusely.

Again Pepsi relished the utter elation when he was presented with his medal, he kissed it and held it aloft for all to see, including the TV cameras. To add to his joy he was joined by his pal the Gay Marine and their host, Gareth. Gareth's wife Tanya was also in attendance and she furnished all with a picnic which they enjoyed sitting on the grassy banks of the bay amongst all the turmoil. It was a wonderful occasion, but again, tinged with sadness as Pepsi pined for his wife and teenage sweetheart Dawn. Pepsi borrowed Gareth's mobile 'phone and rang home to speak to Dawn confirming his success. *"I know, I know! We've all seen you on the tele, the kids have got half the road in to see you!"*, said Dawn excitedly, adding enthusiastically, *"I'm so proud of you love!"*. Pepsi concluded his little chat with Dawn and returned the 'phone to Gareth. They sat among the crowds of competitors, spectators and officials, the little gang enjoying their picnic of pies, sandwiches and soft drinks together with the proverbial welcome brew of tea.

Later, as the masses were starting to disperse and make their way home to their far flung destinations, Pepsi again rang Dawn from the digs as he and the Gay Marine prepared to start their long journey back home to Warbreckside. *"Hiya sweetheart, we're just about to leave for home. How are you now?"*, asked Pepsi. *"I'm not one hundred per cent I'm afraid Nige, it's my damned breathing, there's no air"*, replied his loving spouse. *"Never mind sweetheart, I'll be home soon with your medal!"*, and concluded the call with *"love you!"*. *"I love you too Nige"*, replied Dawn as Pepsi replaced the receiver and made his way out to the car with his pal the Gay Marine. Gareth and some of his police motor cycle colleagues escorted the two pals out of the mayhem via various short cuts until they were safely deposited onto the M6 en route for home.

Dawn, even though she was unwell, nevertheless waited up until the Gay Marine deposited her husband on their doorstep late that night. *"I won't come in, it's late so I'll be in touch tomorrow. Hope you're feeling better Dawn"*, he said as he departed into the night to drive the short distance to his own home a couple of miles away. *"Thanks for taking him John"* said Dawn gratefully. She closed the door behind Nigel as he wheeled himself through to the lounge. Pepsi kissed his wife and the first thing he did was to place the Great North Run medal around his wife's slender neck then took out his camera and took a photograph of her as sat there proudly wearing her new 'gong' as it hung on its blue silk ribbon, *"That's all yours!"* said Pepsi with affection. *"Thanks my love, I'll really treasure this"*, replied a very grateful and proud Dawn as she held the medal up and kissed it. *"Right!"*, said Pepsi, *"A quick cuppa and off to bed eh love?"*. After the refreshing cup of tea was consumed, the two crept upstairs and retired for the night.

Pepsi was woken during the night by the sound of Dawn's heavy, rasping as she gulped in air to her lungs. His wife's condition continued to give rise for concern as she endured similar nights of discomfort as the days and nights went on. By the time the day arrived for her to attend hospital for the test results from her bronchioscopy Dawn was in a terrible state. She was so bad she could hardly breath. Her eyes bulged as she sucked in air. Pepsi had to dress her and when the Gay Marine arrived to collect them both to convey them to the Infirmary, Dawn had to be taken out to John's car in Pepsi's wheelchair.

On arrival at the hospital Dawn again had to be conveyed inside in a wheelchair by the Gay Marine while the anxious Pepsi followed behind in his own. John kindly wheeled Dawn in to see the consultant before beating a discretional retreat out to the waiting room. As Pepsi was also in a wheelchair there was little room for anyone to move in the small consulting room. Today they were seen by Dr Lathom the hospital's oncologist.

Doctor Latham took Dawn's hand in his and spoke slowly and deliberately. *"Mr and Mrs Coaler, I'm afraid the news isn't good!"* Dawn's rasping breath was the only sound to be heard now as she squeezed her husband's arm with her free hand, which Pepsi could feel was trembling. The po-faced but very sympathetic doctor went on, *"I'm afraid we've found a very virulent, malignant tumour in your lung Mrs Coaler. This is a particularly aggressive form of lung cancer and the only thing that we can now try is chemotherapy. This is in no way a cure, but it might prolong your life".* Dawn and her equally devastated husband sat there traumatised. Each just could not believe what they had been told. Dawn remained composed and asked bravely, *"H-h, how long long will I have to have chemotherapy for doctor?"* The doctor replied, *"I'll be able to tell you more once we start the treatment. It could be a few weeks or so".* Utter silence

All sat there not knowing what, if anything, to say. Finally Dawn broke down and wept. After all she had been through with her husband's problems! Now this added crisis, she looked at Nigel, *"Oh Nigel, what on earth are we going to do? Oh my god, this is awful",* she sobbed. The doctor tried to comfort her and said, *"Let's see how the chemo behaves shall we? I'll make an appointment for your first session"*. The two were advised that a letter would be sent informing Dawn when to attend the Oncology department for her first treatment. The doctor opened the door and the big frame of the Gay Marine appeared and gently took Dawn's chair to take her out to the car. A very distraught Pepsi hung back and with a trembling voice asked doctor Latham *"Am I going to lose her doctor?"*. The doctor looked very sad. He replied quietly, *"I'm afraid there's little if anything we can do. We are no further advanced with this particular type of lung cancer than we were at the end of the Second World War"*. Pepsi sat there, totally pole-axed. *"Can't we operate?"* he asked in vain. *"I'm afraid we can't"*, said the doctor. *"Tell me straight doc, how long do you think we've got then?"*. Again the doctor found it difficult to answer. *"Well it could be only a matter of weeks or it could be a couple of months, I just cannot be more optimistic than that I'm afraid"*, he replied as truthfully as he could.

A totally dejected Nigel Coaler wheeled his unseeing way through the outpatients' department and caught up with Dawn and the Gay Marine as John was helping the tearful Dawn into the rear seat of his car. John returned Dawn's wheelchair to reception before folding Pepsi's chair and placing it into the boot of his vehicle. Once in the car Pepsi turned round and took Dawn's hand. *"I'm frightened, I don't want to leave you and the kids"*, sobbed Dawn. Tears then fell down Pepsi's cheeks also as they were driven back to their home with their shattering problems. Big John Royle didn't need to ask, but even he was visibly moved, hard as he was, when Dawn said, *"I've got cancer and I'm going to die John!"* then sobbed pathetically, her face in her hands. The Gay Marine eyed the inconsolable Dawn in his rear view mirror and said, *"They can work wonders now with this new chemotherapy, I've read about it in the papers"*, but his words fell on the deaf ears of Pepsi and Dawn, who knew the tragic truth they had to face.

Days later Dawn's condition was such that Pepsi had to call Doctor Goldbourne out to tend her. Dawn had to be re-admitted to hospital where it was deemed necessary to drain her lungs of nearly seven pints of fluid! After this had been done Dawn seemed to improve considerably and when Pepsi visited her later and learned what had been done to cause such a pleasantly surprising improvement, Pepsi said, *"No wonder you couldn't breath, you must have been bloody well drowning!"*. His wife seemed to be quiet perky apart from a slight soreness where the incision had been made in her back for the drainage tube to be inserted. This would have to remain in-situ for a few days. Pepsi visited Dawn every day, even conveying himself through the streets on occasions when lifts were unobtainable. After a two-week stay Dawn was allowed home, having completed her first chemo session. Whilst there Nigel knew his wife's health had hardly improved except for the initial period when the fluid was removed. Unfortunately, her breathlessness returned with a vengeance. Again Dr Golbourne was sent for and yet again it was deemed necessary for Dawn to be re-admitted into hospital. On her being admitted to the ward Dawn's condition was such that she had to wear an oxygen mask to facilitate her breathing. The nurses were absolutely wonderful under the watchful and devoted eye of Sister Martindale.

Dawn, being a very popular lady, was inundated with visitors but after a week or so it was clear that her condition was worsening and she was sinking. As Pepsi sat with Dawn one day, sister fitted a syringe 'driver' to his wife's chest to enable a constant flow of drugs, including diamorphine, to be administered to ensue Dawn's comfort and to alleviate her pain. At first all seemed okay with this instrument attached but as time went on Pepsi noticed that his wife was becoming more lethargic and drowsy. She was sleeping for longer and longer periods. Pepsi had to wake her more often to give her sips of water or ice cream which he took in for her. On one occasion she woke and took ice cream from a spoon and squeezed his hand. She drew Pepsi to her, held her oxygen mask away from her face to enable her to kiss her husband. Although Pepsi doted on his beloved wife and would do anything to ensure her comforts, nevertheless, it was absolutely breaking his heart to see Dawn like this. He just couldn't believe how fate had dealt such a bloody cruel blow. Here am I, he thought, pulling my bollocks off to raise money for cancer research and it turns round and bites my own wife, while all the scum of the earth survive to a ripe old age!

Tracey the Macmillan nurse called regularly to Dawn's bedside. She would stand there looking forlorn and uttering sweet nothings. As she held Dawn's hand she would sigh and say, "*She's so peaceful now, don't wake her!*". Eventually she would 'advise'

Pepsi when she called and caught him trying to rouse his wife from her drugged sleep by instructing him, *"No!, Don't wake her, let her sleep!"*. In the end Pepsi resented her visits which he considered violated their privacy and valued time together. On one occasion his patience and tolerance of Tracey was exhausted when she again told him not to wake her. *"No bloody chance!"*, he retorted, *"she's drifting away because of this bloody driver!"*, indicating the confounded syringe that was causing his wife's almost continual slumber. He went on, *"I don't want her like this, I want to talk to her for Christ sake!"*. Pepsi now totally resented Tracey's visits. How dare she advocate and cater for his beloved wife to be in such a condition that communication was being rendered almost impossible and non existent?

The condition of Dawn continued to deteriorate and Pepsi and sometimes Dawn's parents were now her only visitors. Somehow, the staff had managed to put her into a side room on her own which a very grateful Pepsi found to be most advantageous, especially with him being in a cumbersome wheelchair. Such was the state of poor Dawn that Pepsi finally stayed at his wife's bedside. He just sat in his wheelchair alongside Dawn's bed, occasionally he would sit on the bed with Dawn in his arms when she stirred deliriously. On one occasion he was rewarded when Dawn opened her eyes, and feebly pulled her oxygen mask away from her face as she had done once before, kissed her husband's lips and whispered weakly, *"I do love you Nige, you're a good man,"* before drifting back into her deep drug-induced sleep. Pepsi was broken hearted. The nurses and staff ensured that Dawn wanted for nothing and Pepsi himself was fed and watered by those truly wonderful angels. Sister Martindale furnished a camp bed from somewhere and instructed Pepsi to get some nocturnal rest during his constant, heartbreaking and distressing vigil. Dawn's parents catered for Pepsi's constant supply of clean clothes.

Alas, all the tender, loving and devoted care could not prevent the inevitable and after seven long, vigilant and totally despairing days and nights, - as the distraught Pepsi sat holding his beloved treasure, at half past seven on a misty Sunday morning of the eighth day Dawn gave a sigh and an incoherent whisper and was gone for ever. She passed away peacefully in her lifelong lover's arms. Pepsi sat there cradling his lifeless wife in his arms, hoping she'd wake up and get better but it was not to be. He knew full well that the end had come. He continued to sit with her in his arms whispering his undying love for his treasured and loving wife. His tears now flowed uncontrollably down his face. He couldn't believe after all these happy years that the love of his life, his pillar of strength, his totally dedicated rock of support and total inspiration during his own times of need, had been finally and so cruelly, taken from him.

After what seemed an age, but was in fact only minutes, a completely broken man wheeled his way along to sister's desk and informed young nurse Taylor of his wife's demise and requested Sister Martindale be informed. A short time later sister arrived at Dawn's bed where Pepsi sat holding his lifeless wife's hand. Sister was accompanied by a colleague, the 'Practitioner', who checked if there was any sign of life before officially pronouncing life extinct. What a pitiful sight Pepsi was as he slowly wheeled his emotionally shattered form out of the ward and back home to come to terms with the unbelievable.

When news of Dawn's demise became known, Angel Street was equally devastated. Although everything that could be said and done was conveyed to a totally distraught Pepsi, the poor man was totally and absolutely inconsolable. So bad was he that he was seen by his doctors and the force welfare department who promised that whatever could be done would be done. Pepsi however remained totally distraught and could not be pacified

After losing his limb and suffering numerous injuries and setbacks in the service of the community, fate had dealt him one blow too many. Only time would tell if or how Pepsi would go on. Dawn's parents would help with the childrens' upbringing as Pepsi was already finding things difficult to cope with.

However, whatever was to be the outcome of this cruel and distressing period. One thing was certain, ..., the previously vibrant and energetic ex-Sergeant, Nigel 'Pepsi' Coaler, so badly injured whilst carrying out the job he loved so much, then almost winning his subsequent battles with adversity, was now physically, mentally, totally and completely, out on to the ..... **final leg!**